Joerg Rieger is Associate Professor of Systematic Theology at Perkins School of Theology at Southern Methodist University. He is the author of *God and the Excluded: Visions and Blindspots in Contemporary Theology* (2001) and *Remember the Poor: The Challenge to Theology in the Twenty-First Century* (1998).

Opting for the Margins

AMERICAN ACADEMY OF RELIGION

REFLECTION AND THEORY IN THE STUDY OF RELIGION SERIES
SERIES EDITOR
Mary McClintock Fulkerson, Duke University

A Publication Series of The American Academy of Religion
and Oxford University Press

Opting for the Margins

Postmodernity and Liberation in Christian Theology

EDITED BY JOERG RIEGER

OXFORD
UNIVERSITY PRESS
2003

OXFORD
UNIVERSITY PRESS

Oxford   New York
Auckland   Bangkok   Buenos Aires   Cape Town   Chennai
Dar es Salaam   Delhi   Hong Kong   Istanbul   Karachi   Kolkata
Kuala Lumpur   Madrid   Melbourne   Mexico City   Mumbai   Nairobi
Sao Paulo   Shanghai   Taipei   Tokyo   Toronto

Copyright © 2003 by The American Academy of Religion

Published by Oxford University Press, Inc.
198 Madison Avenue, New York, New York 10016

www.oup.com

Oxford is a registered trademark of Oxford University Press

Library of Congress Cataloging-in-Publication Data
Opting for the margins : postmodernity and liberation in Christian
theology / edited by Joerg Rieger.
p. cm.—(AAR reflection and theory in the study of religion)
Includes bibliographical references and index.
ISBN 0-19-516119-X
1. Liberation theology. 2. Postmodernism—Religious
aspects—Christianity. I. Rieger, Joerg. II. Reflection and theory in
the study of religion.
BT83.57 066 2003
230'.0464—dc21   2002015840

9 8 7 6 5 4 3 2 1

Printed in the United States of America
on acid-free paper

*To Rafael Marin
and Proyecto Juntos,
and to Gustavo Gutiérrez
on the occasion of his seventy-fifth birthday*

Acknowledgments

Earlier versions of a number of the essays in this volume (by Goizueta, Hopkins, Kwok, and Rieger) were presented at a Research Symposium at Southern Methodist University, Perkins School of Theology, in honor of an honorary doctorate conferred upon Gustavo Gutiérrez in May 2000. We are grateful to Perkins Dean Robin Lovin for supporting this project and the production of this volume. Due to his own interest in the topic of the book, my research assistant, David R. Brockman, has made significant contributions in bringing this book to publication. Thank you also to Mary McClintock Fulkerson, editor of the AAR Reflection and Theory in the Study of Religion Series, and Cynthia Read, editor with Oxford University Press, who have supported the publication of this project. It is people like Rafael Marin, coordinator of Proyecto Juntos, a collaborative project for Latinos and Latinas who suffer from disabilities, and who does all of his work from a wheelchair after an accident at work in 1998, who inspire us and keep us honest. The book is dedicated to him and to Gustavo Gutiérrez on the occasion of his seventy-fifth birthday.

Contents

Contributors

David N. Field, at the time of writing his essay, was senior lecturer in Christian ethics and systematic theology at Africa University, Mutare, Zimbabwe. He is a South African theologian and currently househusband and independent scholar living in Germany. He and Ernst Conradie are coauthors of *A Rainbow over the Land: A South African Guide to the Church and Environmental Justice* (2000).

Roberto S. Goizueta is professor of theology at Boston College. He is the author of *Caminemos con Jesus: Toward a Hispanic/Latino Theology of Accompaniment* (1995) and coeditor (with Maria Pilar Aquino) of *Theology: Expanding the Borders* (1998). His essays have appeared in *The Church as Counterculture* (2000), *Theology and Lived Christianity* (2000), *Beyond Borders: Writings of Virgilio Elizondo and Friends* (2000), *From the Heart of Our People* (1999), and *El Cuerpo de Cristo* (1998). He has also published articles in *Theology Today*, *Cross Currents*, *Journal of Hispanic/Latino Theology*, and *Modern Theology*.

Gustavo Gutiérrez, founder and director of the Instituto Bartolomé de Las Casas in Lima, Peru, and John Cardinal O'Hara II Chair in Theology at the University of Notre Dame, is one of the most recognized theological thinkers in the world today. Many see him as one of the most important theologians of the twentieth century. Gutiérrez is the author of numerous books and essays, among them the famous *Theology of Liberation* (1971), one of the theological classics of the twentieth century, which has appeared in numerous editions and has been translated into many different languages. To date, eight of his books have been translated into English. An anthology of his work appeared in the series The Making of Modern Theology, which introduces the works of great theologians of the last two hundred years.

M. Gail Hamner is assistant professor of religion at Syracuse University, with teaching specialties in religion and mass culture (film and advertisement), feminist theory, feminist theology, pragmatism, critical theory, and continental philosophy. She has published *American Pragmatism: A Religious Genealogy* (2002).

Dwight N. Hopkins is associate professor of theology at the University of Chicago. His works include *Heart and Head: Black Theology—Past, Present, and Future* (2002), *Introducing Black Theology of Liberation* (1999), *Down, up and over: Slave Religion and Black Theology* (1999), *Black Theology USA and South Africa: Politics, Culture, and Liberation* (1989), and *Shoes That Fit Our Feet: Sources for a Constructive Black Theology* (1993). He is editor of *Black Faith and Public Talk: Essays in Honor of James Cone's "Black Theology and Black Power"* and coeditor of *Religions/Globalizations: Theories and Cases* (2001), *Changing Conversations: Religious Reflection and Cultural Analysis* (1996), and *Liberation Theologies, Postmodernity, and the Americas* (1997).

Kwok Pui-lan is William F. Cole Professor of Christian Theology and Spirituality at Episcopal Divinity School, Cambridge, Massachusetts. She has published extensively in Asian feminist theology, biblical hermeneutics, and postcolonial criticism. Her recent books include *Discovering the Bible in the Non-Biblical World* (1995) and *Introducing Asian Feminist Theology* (2000). She coedited *Women's Sacred Scriptures* (1998) and *Postcolonialism, Feminism, and Religious Discourse* (2002) and serves as coeditor of the *Journal of Feminist Studies in Religion*.

Joerg Rieger is associate professor of systematic theology at Perkins School of Theology, Southern Methodist University, in Dallas, Texas. He is author of numerous articles in English and German and of *Remember the Poor: The Challenge to Theology in the Twenty-First Century* (1998) and *God and the Excluded: Visions and Blindspots in Contemporary Theology* (2001). He is editor of *Liberating the Future: God, Mammon, and Theology* (1998), *Theology from the Belly of the Whale: A Frederick Herzog Reader* (1999), and *Methodist and Radical: Rejuvenating a Tradition* (2003).

Mark Lewis Taylor is professor of theology and culture at Princeton Theological Seminary. Among his works are the books *Paul Tillich: Theologian of the Boundaries* (1986), *Remembering Esperanza: A Cultural-Political Theology for North American Praxis* (1990), and most recently *The Executed God: The Way of the Cross through Lockdown America* (2001). He is coordinator of Educators for Mumia Abu-Jamal (www.mumia.com).

Elina Vuola is senior research fellow of the Academy of Finland at the Institute of Development Studies, University of Helsinki, Finland. In 2002 and 2003 she is serving as a research associate at the Women's Studies in

Religion Program at the Harvard Divinity School, Cambridge, Massachusetts. Her recent publications include *La ética sexual y los límites de la praxis: Conversaciones críticas entre la teología feminista y la teología de la liberación* (2001) and *Limits of Liberation: Feminist Theology and the Ethics of Poverty and Reproduction* (2002).

Opting for the Margins

Introduction: Opting for the Margins in a Postmodern World

Joerg Rieger

The preferential option for the poor has been one of the most significant developments in theology and the church in the twentieth century, signaling a broad shift in theological sensitivities. In conjunc-
tion with other options for people at the margins, the option for the
poor has provided major new impulses for biblical studies, systematic theology, and church history; for the official documents of the
church; and for ecclesial practice. Equally important, the option for
the poor and the margins has broadened the guild of theologians to
include those whose theological voice has hardly ever been noticed.
The theological voices of women, minorities, and lower-class people
have contributed both to fresh ideas and to new opportunities for
life. Just as we can no longer overlook God's own concern for the
marginalized in both Old and New Testaments, neither must we overlook the peculiar shape of God's justice which lifts up the lowly and
pushes the powerful from their thrones (Luke 1:52; 1 Samuel 2:4),
reflected in the repressed faith traditions of the common people and
martyrs and in the existence of grassroots communities within the
institutionalized churches.

Yet options for people at the margins are more and more challenged now by a wide range of developments in theology, politics,
economics, and elsewhere. Options for the margins are replaced by
other things—liberals argue for "equal opportunity" and their conservative counterparts promote "charity"—and even established programs like Affirmative Action have either been canceled or are under severe attack from all directions. Shifts in intellectual, social,
political, and economic climates that are labeled postmodern are

putting their own spin on preferential options. Even though there is an emerging interest in pluralism and multicultural diversity, postmodern talk about otherness and difference usually refers not to the relation of oppressor and oppressed but to the free flow of differences. The postmodern observation that there are no firm foundations anywhere seems to leave us all in the same boat and ushers in the claim that we are all "other." Everybody appears to be floating in space, all are homeless wanderers through life and exist in marginal spaces; middle-class North Americans are in the same bind as their illegal and underpaid housekeepers from Latin America, and neither privilege nor oppression seem to exist any more.[1] Options for the margins are therefore (at best) reduced to the special interests of certain minorities or (at worst) rejected as antiquated and irrelevant for the twenty-first century. And where options for the margins are still acknowledged in a more positive way, they are often quickly sucked into the free flow of differences of the postmodern situation, where the margins are more or less fun places that allow for playful transactions with life and the traditions of yesterday. As a result, the matter is relayed to charitable projects (such as the faith-based initiatives of "compassionate conservatism") or to a firm belief in the free flow of differences (with all its resemblances to the free market). In this context, the challenge which the margins used to pose for theology, the church, and society as a whole has all but disappeared.

Yet while it is possible to repress the challenges of the margins—the unconscious is not only a psychological but also a social category—can it ever go away as long as people are being pushed to the breaking point both in the United States and around the globe, with thirty thousand children dying every day worldwide from preventable causes? In this volume we deal with such challenges from various points of view and develop new ways of interpreting the option for the poor in a postmodern world. The collaboration of authors writing from the (mostly hybridized perspectives) of Latinos and Latinas, Latin Americans, African Americans, Asian Americans, Euro-Americans, Euro-Africans, and Europeans, both male and female, produces a much-needed broadening of the horizon and uncovers new sources of energy in the life-and-death struggles of people all over the world today. Readers concerned about the worsening position of people on the margins will find a wealth of new visions. Readers interested in matters of postmodernity will find a fresh approach that leads the debate to a new level.

Changes in Culture and the Market

There is a general feeling that things have changed dramatically during the past few decades. Nothing escapes the winds of change: global economic structures are just as much affected as relationships within families and the shape of our communities. The term *postmodernity* is often used in a broad sense to refer to these changes.

One commonly observed change has to do with our visions of reality. What is considered real, what really matters and counts in our world, is now reshaped by virtual realities of all sorts. As computers and other electronic circuits shape much of our daily lives, the line between reality and virtual reality is becoming more and more blurred. Cyberspace, a term shaped by a science-fiction writer,[2] has become more than real as a sphere where millions of people spend much of their lives, not only their leisure time but also much of their working time. Many of the most significant business transactions are now taking place in cyberspace as well. Even things which used to have the strongest impact on reality in the modern industrial age—hardware like heavy machinery and the fuel that drives them, for instance—are now useless without the virtual reality of a computer program and the integrated circuit. How much virtual reality defines our everyday lives is reflected in the fact that computer failures or even simple power failures, including the recent blackouts in places like California, have ever more severe impacts. What really matters in this context is more and more relocated from the realm of personal encounters to a virtual realm of symbolic exchange. Even the lives of the vast groups of people who do not have immediate access to virtual reality are affected by it because they can be safely bypassed (or organized for business interests without ability to resist) due to their lack of access. In the process, phenomena like other people's suffering and the thumbscrews of oppression become less and less real.[3]

Culture is another area where things are changing. From the vantage point of the dominant cultures it looks as if uniform cultural values and norms are more and more challenged by multicultural points of view. The conventional assumption, reinforced by the heritage of imperialism and colonialism, that differing cultural points of view are to be integrated into the dominant paradigm at all cost (the proverbial image of the "melting pot") is now open to revision. And even though the dominant paradigm still exists and exerts power, alternative points of view are beginning to break through the concrete and have some impact, however small. Increased awareness of other religious traditions in the United States allows for a little more flexibility, for instance, around traditional Christian holidays such as Christmas or Easter. Changing roles of women and minorities also lead to a transformation of accepted values. Despite the fact that traditional nineteenth- and early twentieth-century images of women as less capable of leadership and rational decisions are still with us and that much of the work identified with the home and the family is still done by women, fewer women accept the narrow world and the traditional roles of the stay-at-home housewife. Furthermore, the traditions and values of minorities are becoming more represented within the mainstream. In this process, postmodern concepts like otherness and difference are more valued than ever before, and the notion of truth becomes contextualized: whether something is true depends to a large degree on circumstance and social location. In this new intellectual climate the room for tolerance is increasing. Here, postmodernism and what is now called postcolonialism share some common concerns. At the same time, however, postmodern interest in the traditions and values of minorities often does not transcend their entertainment value as measured in food, folklore, and music, and women who venture into new positions often encounter invisible glass ceilings that make sure that positions of patriarchal power are not disturbed too much. While culture seems to be opening up—supported also, of course, by economic changes such as a new awareness of the market power of minorities and the need for women to contribute to family income—the postmodern fails to connect to the less (re)presentable realities of people on the margins that exist only between the lines.

One of the key changes, and perhaps the prime engine of all the other changes, is occurring in the way that wealth is produced. Not long ago the most significant accumulations of wealth were generated by industrial production. The success story of Henry Ford and his empire represents this era. Here wealth, and the social power and prestige that goes with it, was connected to tangibles like brick and steel and built on the productive force of blue-collar labor. Now wealth is produced—and lost—more and more through the mechanisms and (virtual) realities of the stock market and the investment of capital.[4] Rather than production and products, the virtual reality of the stock market has become the focal point of the economy, and even the most powerful institutions, nations, and their leaders see no other choice than to be subservient to it. Not even the chairman of the U.S. Federal Reserve Board, Alan Greenspan, would risk displeasing the stock market. Much of Greenspan's work has, in fact, to do with keeping investors and the markets happy and in balance.

This new foundation of the market differs dramatically from other sorts of foundations, in that it appears itself to be free floating. Since the 1990s it has often seemed to be strangely disconnected from many of the usual indicators of a strong economy, such as unemployment and, to a certain degree, even its own performance. The rise of the stock of the internet companies in the late 1990s, for instance, illustrates this process. While the more recent fall of the markets throughout the year 2001, including the free fall of many of the internet companies, seems to correct this trend by relating more closely to performance indicators, the salaries of managers and CEOs still flow freely and continue to rise.[5] In fact, there seems to be an assumption that if certain key components of a happy market such as executive salaries and financial success at the very top were tied too closely to real market indicators, catastrophe would ensue. The general mood at the grassroots is determined less by the actual experience of hardship than by solid trust in the indestructibility of the free flow of money and the ability of the market to recover, boosted by the good fortune of the wealthy and the subservience of the public sectors through cuts in interest rates and taxes. Even in the immediate aftermath of the terrorist destruction of the World Trade Center in New York City and the attack on the Pentagon on September 11, 2001, hope in the market continued, and Merrill Lynch placed one-page ads in the business sections of newspapers across the country reassuring investors that "through every major crisis of the past 80 years, it is the fundamentals, not events that drive the markets long term. While equities may experience an emotional aftershock from the actions of the past week, history shows they do recover." Fredric Jameson observes that the type of capital that is now at the center of it all (finance capital, money market, investment funds), "like cyberspace[,] can live on its own internal metabolism." As a result, the "real world" does not only matter less for the movement of the markets but is also becoming more and more "suffused and colonized" by the free flow of capital.[6]

The colonizing process itself has changed dramatically. The swords of the Spanish in Latin America of the sixteenth and seventeenth centuries and the government institutions of the British in nineteenth-century India and Africa are no longer necessary. Colonization—long after its abandonment in politics—has found a new space of existence in the so-called postcolonial world in the virtual reality of economics that is not only virtually omnipresent but also much harder to detect. The new communications technologies make it possible for capital to abolish both time and space and to be present wherever it pleases.[7] As the presence of capital increases, those who have no access to capital disappear from view. In a single day, trillions of dollars change hands around the world electronically without ever being touched by human hands and without being affected by the life-and-death struggle of vast numbers of the global population.

The weakening of traditional values and foundations and less concern about tangibles does not mean that things are necessarily becoming more open and that there would be more room for radically different paradigms. Just the opposite. Once again, what is happening in the realm of the economy sets the pace and illustrates what is at stake. David Harvey notes the paradox that "capitalism is becoming ever more tightly organized *through* dispersal, geographical mobility, and flexible responses in labour markets, labour processes, and consumer markets."[8] The flexibility of money, for instance, does not lead to greater access to the economy for more people but creates an additional advantage over the slower pace of the labor market and thus secures money's hegemony. In the days of Henry Ford's industrialism, labor power was an essential part of economic progress that deserved a certain minimum of attention and care. Today, as capital is becoming more and more independent of labor, workers are becoming more and more disposable. Since they are not as flexible and movable as money, they are left behind whenever money is transferred from one labor market to another. The free flow of money across national borders stands in stark contrast to the very strict limits that are placed on the flow of workers. As a result, the workers' room for resistance is severely diminished.

The flexibility and adaptability of capital in the postmodern world safeguards therefore not the democratization of wealth and its broader dispersion, but the advantage of those who control the monetary interests.[9] This way of organizing things feeds back into all other areas of life. In the words of Harvey: "Entrepreneurialism now characterizes not only business action, but realms of life as diverse as urban governance, the growth of informal sector production, labour market organization, research and development, and it has even reached into the nether corners of academic, literary, and artistic life."[10] No wonder that notions like the preferential option for the poor are now being challenged at all levels. If there are preferential options left, they are options for the market economy and capital, as for instance the practice of the U.S. government to increase "corporate welfare" while reducing welfare to the lower classes demonstrates. Resistance seems futile.

Postmodernity and Resistance

Postmodern sentiments, developed in diverse places around the world, correspond in many ways with the changes in the market economy. Rather than belonging to the realm of esoteric disciplines, postmodern thought has close ties to the logic of late capitalism, whether it is aware of it or not. Postmodern cultural and intellectual trends gather strength through transformations in the economy, which is progressively subsuming not only the spheres of politics, civil society, and religion—all of which once seemed to possess a certain autonomy—but also the most remote spaces around the globe.[11] These economic transformations affect everything down to our personal lives, from our retirement accounts and 401(k) plans, which are now directly linked to the stock market, to the way we think about ourselves and the world.[12] The flexibility of the market is reproduced not least of all in personal relationships: shopping for partners, for communities such as churches, and for affirmation are more and more the norm.

In this situation a moralizing response does not help. Well-meaning outrage and a superficial rejection of postmodernity that fails to recognize how much we are part of it may even be counterproductive. In the words of Jameson, one of the earliest and most substantial critics of postmodernity, "This is our world and our raw material, the only kind with which we can work. Only it would be better to look at it without illusions, and get some clarity and precision about what confronts us."[13] The postmodern world in which we find ourselves is defined by a new set of assumptions about what is "natural." The fact that capitalist markets, for instance, are more and more seen as natural, corresponding to human nature and the way the world works, shows how deeply engrained the postmodern condition has become.[14] We need to understand how we—as individuals, as members of society, and even as members of the church—are all part of it.

If in postmodernity the outside has virtually disappeared, how do we address the postmodern from within? The common moralizing accusations of "materialism" and "consumerism" don't make much sense if they assume that we could somehow get out and become "less materialistic" at will. In this volume we seek to identify forms of resistance that do not come from an illusionary outside but from the underside, from places that are under great pressure within the system but that have not completely surrendered to the powers that be.[15]

The experience of "depthlessness"[16] may serve as an example of the postmodern condition. While modern minds were constantly concerned with the foundations of things (their origins, roots in reality, place in the order of the world, etc.), postmodern minds do not care much about such questions. What matters is the thing at hand. Consumers, for instance, care about the finished product rather than its origin or its "essence." Even the product itself is secondary at times: what matters more are the even more abstract worlds of labels and brand names. In the global economy, raw materials—origins and foundations—are at the very bottom of monetary value, followed by the value of labor. What matters most of all is market position. The craze about the Beanie Babies in the 1990s illustrates what is at stake. Made of "all new" material, the fact that those beanbag animals are "handmade" in China does little to determine their value. The sometimes enormous value of the Beanie Babies has to do with clever marketing and a projected shortage (which may or may not be real): they become valuable only when they are no longer produced. Resistance to this sort of thing can no longer come from the outside, by examining the Beanie Babies' "real value" or their production cost. Likewise, few people worry about the "real value" of designer clothes, and the status attached to them cannot be assessed by researching how they were produced.

A view from the underside, however, might point us into a different direction. By learning about who produces and about the lives of those people, their blood, sweat, and tears, the postmodern myth of depthlessness, which suggests that these things do not matter and therefore do not exist, appears in a new light. Such an awareness of the underside might even help us to reconsider our view of raw materials and natural resources.

Postmodern critiques of foundations are closely related to the experience of depthlessness. One such critique, developed by poststructuralism, has had tremendous influence on postmodern thought not only in France but also in the United States. Michel Foucault recalls a "point of rupture" in French thought which "came the day that Lévi-Strauss for societies and Lacan for the unconscious showed us that 'meaning' was probably a mere surface effect, a shimmering froth."[17] Even more strongly than their structuralist predecessors, French poststructuralist thinkers argue that the meaning of concepts and ideas is not so much dependent on some external foundation or referent, but on the arbitrary relation to other concepts and ideas.[18] What matters is not some deeper level of meaning inherent in a concept but its use in relation to other concepts. "Meaning is relational" has become the motto. But, contrary to a common misperception, this poststructuralist discovery of a "point of rupture" is not the idle speculation of a few avant-garde philosophers. Jacques Lacan finds traces of this condition in his psychoanalytic praxis, and postmodern thinkers base their argument that we are dealing with a new "emotional ground tone" (Jameson) on cultural analysis. If the rupture of an older way to make sense of the world is indeed one of the markers of our time, the sense that we lack solid foundations cannot easily be rejected. The mere insistence on foundations by fundamentalists and others will not be able to overcome the nagging doubt that is fostered by our experience of constant change in all areas of life.

A peek below the surface, however, not at some abstract set of foundations but at that which has been pushed underground by the dominant formation of meaning, might broaden our postmodern horizon. What if the language of the status quo is not as free floating and arbitrary as it looks at first sight? This can be explored only by those within the system who find ways to be in solidarity with what has been repressed and dare to take a fresh look at what really shores up the way things are and on whose backs our identity (and our success) is really built.

Even though there is no more "outside" in postmodernity, resistance seems to develop precisely from those places on the "inside" that we have forgotten or overlooked. In the context of the crumbling of Argentina's economy at the end of 2001, an Argentinean worker put in words in regard to the free-market economy what most economic analysts were not even able to think: "The [Argentinean free-market] economy just doesn't work the way it does in other countries. I don't know what the solution is, but it's obvious that something is very wrong."[19] Latin American theorist Nelly Richard argues that what is now seen as the poststructuralist/postmodern rupture has been part of the experience of those at the underside of history for a long time: "Ever since Spanish colonization forced the continent divisively to verbalize itself in the conqueror's language, Latin America has recognized the division between sign and referent [or between signifier and signified]."[20] From the point of view of the African American community Dwight Hopkins makes a related point when he explains that Africans and African Americans have long endured postmodernity.[21] In other words, those on the underside of history understood quite well that things are not always what they seem to those on top. A sense of the challenges of radical difference and otherness, which did of course matter little to the initial colonizers and those in charge, was born quite early on at the underside of modern history. The "melting pot," for instance, and the idea that all can be molded into one image were the ideas of those in power; those who were excluded saw right through it. Even where difference was emphasized in systems of apartheid, it was not in order to challenge the identity of those in charge but to protect it from being challenged in relation to other people. The challenges from the margins are, therefore, among the few things that might have the potential to push us beyond the status quo of postmodernism.[22]

Postmodernity, Theology, and the Church

The postmodern condition has also shaped theology and the church. Unfortunately, here the countless debates about things postmodern still often proceed as if postmodernity were simply another idea to be pondered by the theoreticians or a mood that deserves attention from the practitioners. Theologians usually wonder if we should incorporate or reject this or that insight promoted by postmodern thinkers (from questions of antifoundationalism to matters of difference and otherness). Those concerned to be "up to date" and "cutting edge" almost automatically assume that they need to develop their work in correspondence with postmodern ideas. Those who used to make up the modern camp are eager to go on to the next step and form a postmodern camp. The more traditional camps feel that, having finally been liberated from their modern nemesis, postmodern sentiments confer on them a new role as the sole gatekeepers of the traditions of the church. As a result pluralism, communitarianism, confessionalism, neotraditionalism, and a host of other "isms" are flooding the scene, and some proudly proclaim that their project is the thing "most talked about" in contemporary theology (a move that is clearly postmodern in the attempt to create its own reality).[23] While theologians try to position themselves at the forefront of the market of ideas, many leaders of the church try to adapt and cater as much as they can to what they call the "postmodern generation" or "Generation X," those middle-class North Americans born after 1964. Whatever the market asks for, needs to be done, whether this be more informal worship services at times other than Sunday morning or more professional arrangements for church activities and the exploration of what really matters in the postmodern world: cyberspace and multimedia.[24] But how is this all connected to the giant vortex that is produced where economic interests are wedded to cultural and theological images?

Theologians and churches still need to address the fact that postmodern modes of thinking are not just ideas to be promoted or rejected but are deeply rooted in the economic and cultural developments of the postmodern world. A recent statement by President George W. Bush allows for a closer look at what is at stake. In a speech to the economic and political leaders of the Western world in Quebec, Bush pointed out that "open trade reinforces the habit of liberty." Bush's dream of "an age of prosperity" is closely connected to the "hemisphere of liberty." This provides us with yet another clue that without the economic background, our concepts (such as liberty) can no longer be understood. Defined by postmodern economics, liberty now has to do with the promises of "commerce moving across our borders."[25] Under this influence, other ideas of liberty, like modernity's freedom of the individual and the personal pursuit of happiness or the religious idea of freedom from sin, take on new meaning. The same is true for many other theological concepts. The meaning of seemingly familiar traditional terms like *charity, mission,* and *salvation* also take on new meaning when connected to the increasing flow of "commerce moving across our borders." In the Southwest of the United States, for instance, the North American Free Trade Agreement (NAFTA) is paralleled by more and more mission trips to Mexico, often connected to one-sided forms of charity and a reaffirmation of our own salvation through both our service and our economic standing. While commerce is flowing back and forth across the borders, there is free flow of people from only the side that has the economic advantage (not least because anything else would put commerce at a disadvantage).

These overlaps of theology and economics are mirrored in increasing overlaps of culture and economics that have been observed by Harvey and Jameson. While economic categories are more and more integrated with cultural ideals such as freedom, diversity, and happiness, cultural ideals themselves are shaped by economic ideals.[26] American film and television, for instance, among the primary exports of the United States, can be described as both economic and cultural phenomena. Cannot churches, too, be described in this way, as both economic and cultural phenomena? While the churches in the United States understand themselves mainly as cultural phenomena,[27] they follow business rules and tend to blossom where the economic conditions are right, primarily in the suburbs and newly established developments. A good deal of the revenue of the denominations depends on this. Moreover, as cultural entities the churches are feeding back into the economic situation. When they create space for gatherings of people of common status and interests, when they prime people for the demands of their work, when they alleviate the tensions of everyday suburban life, and when they disperse charity to the needy, churches support the flourishing of economic prosperity, much in the sense that President Bush indicated in his Quebec speech. All this happens, whether accelerated by marketing or not, as part of how the postmodern system as a whole functions.[28] To be sure: becoming aware of the cultural and economic reality of the church has less to do with moralistic condemnation than with understanding where we are. This new awareness might be the first step in developing a sense that our cultural and economic involvement may take different shapes. We cannot choose whether we want to be economic and cultural entities, but we might be able to shape what our economic and cultural affiliations will be.

A new set of questions emerges when theology begins to understand its own integration into the postmodern world. Most importantly, theology as reflection on God's reality in the world is no longer locked into the narrow category of "religion." Religion can no longer be considered a separate entity that is somehow independent from other concerns. At no point in its history could Christian theology ever be captured by the religious alone: God's work in Christ relates to all of reality, including historical, cultural, and economic structures. As a result, theology is neither exhausted in philosophical speculation, cultural reflection, or historical analysis nor is it merely a resource of ethical and moral advice. All these things have been tried before. We need to engage a broader vision of reality which includes also the fundamental changes that are occurring at the level of the global economy. Theology and the church can no longer operate exclusively on any one level alone. Furthermore, since here the distinction between high culture and mass culture finally breaks down, theology is no longer the privilege of the elite and ready to transcend one more artificial distinction introduced by those in charge.

How do we avoid the perennial temptation of theology and the church simply to tag along with the mood of the times? Even the work of those who try to resist some of the consequences of the postmodern condition often only feeds back into it once again. The now-fashionable communitarian efforts to form new communities in a fragmented society, for instance, often end up merely reproducing a postmodern kind of pluralism where each group is free floating and not related to other groups, thus mirroring the model of the postmodern gated communities in our cities. Likewise, the ubiquitous critique of postmodern forms of individualism will hardly be able to overcome the problem if it overlooks that beneath the seemingly free flow of individuals lies a tight web of dependency and exploitation.

Alternatives and the Return of the Repressed

Fredric Jameson sums up the spirit of the present when he points out that "it seems to be easier for us today to imagine the thoroughgoing deterioration of the earth and of nature than the breakdown of late capitalism." He goes on to suggest that "the word *postmodern* ought to be reserved for thoughts of this kind."[29] Many of us know the sinking feeling that the postmodern situation does not really allow for alternatives any more. Since the days of British Prime Minister Margaret Thatcher and U.S. President Ronald Reagan in the 1980s, we have been told over and over again that there is no alternative to capitalism. This position seemed only to be confirmed in the late 1980s when the Berlin Wall came down and the Soviet Union collapsed mainly under its own weight. What is left, except the straightjacket of one economic system and the cultural hegemony that goes with it?

In this situation, transformation appears to be restricted to minor improvements within that system. The postmodern appetite for otherness and difference is so convenient because it does not promote a real alternative. Rather, it fits in with the needs of the system to broaden its power base. Even the most prestigious institutions and corporations are now promoting a certain level of diversity in their leadership. It is often overlooked, however, that most of these changes work for the good of the capitalist market economy and strengthen its foundations: the free circulation, the mobility, and the diversity of sources of capital.[30] Little wonder that even multiculturalism often remains within the system and serves the status quo. Multiculturalism is one of the pillars in the creation of new markets. While exotic people and places help revitalize old markets and sell old things like beer, multiculturalism in advertising also helps to explore new markets. In some parts of town even the language of the billboards shifts—from English to Spanish. On the whole, the market is no longer as monolithic as in the industrial age and grows by adjusting to the needs of various subgroups. Fordism is out, "Toyotism" is in: production is no longer "one size fits all" but pays ever closer attention to what different customers want.[31] Some of the churches are not far behind when they embrace multicultural perspectives out of the sheer recognition that their membership base is threatened due to demographic changes.

One of the paradoxes of postmodernity is that in some ways the margins are part of the picture and are recognized as never before. But those margins are also more strongly pulled into the system than ever before. In this situation, options for the margins that hope to break out of the system appear as a thing of the past. Having become part of the system, people on the margins go under in a sea of pluralism. Everything and everybody is thought to be other, suspended in a metonymic web of difference and existing on the surface only; nothing is underground. Neither privilege nor oppression seem to exist any more. No specific place is left for the repressed. The homeless, the unemployed, the undocumented workers in sweatshops, and a whole new group of people sucked into the phenomenon of a new slavery are made to blend in and thus drop from the screens of postmodern consciousness.[32] There is no alternative.

Yet while even the thirty thousand children that die of hunger and preventable diseases every day do not matter on the postmodern maps of otherness, this may be precisely the place where we can start over. The fault lines and tensions that postmodernity tries to integrate pose a challenge that is hardly recognized at present. Those of us whose social location is not restricted to the underside might start by reminding ourselves that the free flow of money, for instance, is not just a game that can be played more or less well (as those high-school programs that invite students to play the stock market and see how far they get). As my friends from El Salvador, whose currencies have recently been replaced by the U.S. dollar remind us, there is a close connection between "dollarization" and "dolor-ization,"[33] between the rule of the global economy and the infliction of severe pain for many people at the grassroots. There is a significant difference between postmodern differentiation and repression. Everything changes once we come to realize that some forms of otherness produced on the underside are clearly the result of repression and that nothing is romantic or exotic about them.[34] If otherness is not just a harmless differentiation of things that are not the same, this might be precisely the place where resistance finds new roots and new sources of energy. Daring to take a closer look at what is repressed in postmodernity—at what has been pushed underground, despite the claim that no such space exists any more—helps in devising some alternative strategies for breaking out of the system where even the more radical alternatives are easily assimilated.

In the realm of theology and the church, few have dared to take an extended look at the underside. The various liberation theologies have been at the forefront of this enterprise, but more needs to be done. This perspective is more important than ever in postmodernity, where it is commonly assumed either that the underside does not exist any more or that that underside is just another normal manifestation of the system. No matter how hard we try, the fault lines of the system—severe poverty, increasing gaps between rich and poor, misuse of power, and even massive death—cannot easily be done away with and keep haunting us.[35] One ally for a contemporary effort to take a closer look at the lives and struggles of people on the underside is subaltern studies. Subaltern studies, in the words of proponent John Beverley, "is not so much preoccupied with the articulation of multiculturalism as a value in itself as with bringing to a critical point the antagonisms created by the social relations of inequality and exploitation inherent in multicultural difference."[36] Multicultural dynamics can be integrated into the status quo only if the tensions are overlooked and the repressions remain hidden. Alternatives emerge precisely at the point when we go beyond multiculturalism as fun and diversion to the darker regions that do not make their way to public awareness. Here, a whole new process begins. Repression, exploitation, and exclusion are never the last word. In repression a "surplus"[37] is created that can never be quite controlled by the powers that be and which therefore presents us with two important new openings: on the one hand, the repressed might help develop a critique of the status quo;[38] on the other hand, the repressed might aid us in looking beyond the status quo to new alternatives.[39]

While there is no easy escape, alternatives emerge when we encounter those places in postmodernity where the pressure is greatest, a location that Christians believe is shared by God in Christ. In some African cities, there is a distinction between "high-density" and "low-density" neighborhoods. The distinction refers to wealthy and poor neighborhoods: poor people are forced to live within the boundaries of very limited space, and only the rich can afford a low-density lifestyle. But it is precisely the high-density worlds of the margins across the globe, for all the repression that they endure, that cannot easily be controlled and subvert representation.[40] For such reasons, in this book we search for new sources of energy and resistance precisely in the places of high density. There are alternatives.

A Global Perspective

The essays in this book are written from a wide range of hybridized perspectives, bringing together experiences from diverse locations. Opting for the margins shapes up differently in each location, and each essay expands the meaning of such options in new ways, creating new space by engaging the tensions of our postmodern and postcolonial worlds.

Mark Lewis Taylor addresses a question that is existential for the project as a whole and for most of the readers of this book: In opting for the margins, what is the role of those of us who are not among the most marginalized, intellectuals and academics, for instance, who enjoy certain entitlements and powers to act? The complexity of this role is illumined by a conversation with what is now called "subaltern studies." Taylor's own position as a North American intellectual and activist with various ties to Latin America is the matrix for this exploration and leads him to engage postmodernist discourse in constructive ways and to develop new modes of advocacy in terms of a "doubling" of voices, where the lines between advocates and subalterns become blurred and redefined.

David Field, writing as a Euro-African theologian from South Africa and other places in sub-Saharan Africa, notes a similar challenge. While postmodern, post-Fordist capitalism is taking over more and more of the economies of the world and the power of the North Atlantic Rim has solidified, Third World intellectuals—Field talks about a "Third World bourgeoisie"—are not off the hook. This postmodern situation presents an urgent need to develop new ways for listening to the margins. A breakdown of simplistic binaries between oppressor and oppressed, for instance, is experienced by Euro-African theologians in their own bodies, where they have internalized the conflicts between colonizer and colonized and between North and South. Field constructs his engagement with the postmodern on the basis of God's own option for a diverse set of margins, which relocates the centers of the postmodern global village and liberates the elites from their self-centeredness.

Kwok Pui-lan, an Asian-American feminist theologian who grew up in Hong Kong, broadens the option for the margins further by adding the aspects of cultural and religious diversity and the situation of women in these contexts. From the Asian perspective, where the majority of people on the margins are non-Christian, an option for the margins needs to include encounters with the non-Christian world and more specific critiques of the imperialism of both

Christian theology and Western religious studies. Kwok's essay introduces the category of postcolonialism in order to subject the concepts of modernity, postmodernity, and masculinist paradigms in liberation theology to a transcultural critique.

Readers may be surprised to learn that the encounter with the non-Christian world is also a topic of increasing importance from a Latin American perspective. Gustavo Gutiérrez, well-known liberation theologian from Peru with roots in Europe and, most recently, in the United States, notes a similar challenge. The questions of religious pluralism are closely connected with the ongoing challenge, emphasized by Gutiérrez, to deepen our understanding of the complexity of the world of the poor. Such questions arise with a new urgency from the world of the poor. Tracing the history of the preferential option for the poor (seen as the most important contribution by the Latin American church and by liberation theology to the universal church), Gutiérrez reminds us of the continued importance of this option and the need for further explorations, which include a closer look at the numerous contributions made by the poor themselves.

Elina Vuola, a Latin Americanist feminist theologian from Finland, deals with a similar challenge and develops it further. She finds support for creating new space for the role and agency of impoverished and marginalized Latin American women in the postmodern insistence on different subject positions—as developed further by feminist, postcolonialist, and Latin American thinkers. Vuola reminds us that matters like reproductive rights and health (particularly abortion and birth control) become literally matters of life and death, especially for the poorest and most marginalized women. She concludes that options for the margins need to be rethought, both in terms of a more complex understanding of who the margins are and what it means to opt for them.

Moving back closer to the option for the margins in the United States, Dwight Hopkins grounds his argument in African American traditions. Drawing on this heritage, a rereading of key biblical passages, and the work of Gustavo Gutiérrez, he demonstrates that in a postmodern world we need the preferential option for the poor more than ever. In bringing together these major perspectives, Hopkins, as an African American theologian, initiates a new transcultural and transtheological conversation that leads to the expectation that the Spirit will speak in new ways through the majority of humanity—constituted by those on the margins.

Roberto Goizueta, a Latino theologian whose work connects North and South in the Americas, deals with the question of truth that has come under attack in postmodernity, and he reshapes it in relation to the preferential option for the poor. The challenge is both theological and existential: Without opting for the margins, we will miss the reality of a God who opts for the margins, one of the most challenging and threatening claims of liberation theology.

Without opting for the margins, however, we will also miss a sense for what reality as a whole is like, an important issue for Latinos and Latinas who need to know what is true not for speculative reasons but in order to be able to survive.

Gail Hamner, writing from a North American feminist perspective, suggests a new move beyond both identity politics and a postmodern disdain for political alliances by reconsidering the notion of love. The way love is employed in the work of three prominent feminist theorists adds a new dimension to the option for the marginalized. Despite much misuse of the notion of love and despite the fact that love appears impotent to both academic and popular culture, Hamner argues that it helps us to bring together two important things that are now seen as mutually exclusive: (1) coalition politics that joins the marginalized and the privileged and (2) nonessentializing notions of subjectivity. The parallel between the uses of the notion of love by feminist theory and by theology (in a broad, interreligious sense) lies in the fact that love elicits hope in something that we cannot control.

My own essay at the end is written from a Euro-American perspective, shaped by interactions with centers and margins in both Europe and the Americas and informed by life in the Southwest of the United States as a place where many of these realities meet. It takes up key concerns of a postmodernism of resistance such as the critique of identity, the possibility of resistance, and the critique of modernity, and examines what happens when this perspective meets with more explicit options of the margins as developed by liberation theologies and others. In the process, two things develop: a deeper awareness of the tensions of the present, seen best from positions of repression, and a deeper awareness of new sources of energy that may sustain us all in the ongoing life-and-death struggle.

Among the most exciting aspects of this volume are the concerns that connect this diverse group of authors. At the core are a deepening sense both of the complexity of life at the margins and of the complex realities of those who attempt to relate to it. Here is one of the most fundamental challenges of the volume, and the various reminders that we need to dispense with our fantasies of control in order to dig deeper leads to an exciting array of new visions, strategies, challenges. These visions include life in all its dimensions, and thus even the concern for interreligious dialogue picked up explicate by Gutiérrez, Kwok, and Taylor is integrally related to all other concerns raised by encounters with the margins.

Finally, all authors in their own ways see the challenge as a theological one. Opting for the margins is not first of all a social imperative; rather, such an option is at the core of our identity as human beings before God. If Godself opts for the margins, as many of the essays argue, our options for the margins are at the very heart of our lives as people of God. According to Gutiérrez, we must overcome the idea that encountering the margins has only to do with a social problem. Hopkins leaves no doubt: "To be a Christian in any time period is to practice a preferential option for the poor." Goizueta wonders whether we can be Christians *at all* without this option. At the end of the book, I formulate this question the other way around: Without developing new respect for other people in ways that give up control and allow for a sense of complexity, can we ever hope to develop new respect for God, manifest in giving up our efforts of control and allowing a sense of divine complexity? There is a mystical dimension in the encounter with the margins that, as Taylor reminds us, continues to surprise us all.

NOTES

1. No wonder that much of postmodern literature is aimed directly at the plight of the middle class.

2. William Gibson, *Neuromancer* (New York: Ace Science Fiction Books, 1984).

3. At the same time, cyberspace can of course also be a place where resistance is organized.

4. Michael Hardt and Antonio Negri, *Empire* (Cambridge: Harvard University Press, 2000), 285, remind us that industrial production is, of course, not abandoned. Just as agriculture has been transformed and made more effective by industrialization, industrial production is reconstituted by the informational revolution.

5. Editorial, *Dallas Morning News*, September 5, 2001: Executive salaries have risen by 18% during the last year of economic slow-down. The average executive now makes 531 times the salary of the average worker, up from 419:1 in 1999 and 70:1 in the late 1980s.

6. Fredric Jameson, *The Cultural Turn: Selected Writings on the Postmodern, 1983–1998* (New York: Verso, 1998), 161.

7. Ibid., 143. Jeff Bezos, the founder of Amazon.com, recently declared in a television interview that what matters most for internet commerce is no longer the exact stage of technology but its omnipresence.

8. David Harvey, *The Condition of Postmodernity: An Enquiry into the Origins of Cultural Change* (Oxford: Blackwell, 1990), 159.

9. Hardt and Negri, *Empire*, 297: "The geographical dispersal of manufacturing has created a demand for increasingly centralized management and planning, and also for a new centralization of specialized producer services, especially financial services."

10. Harvey, *Condition of Postmodernity*, 171.

11. See the essays in *Liberating the Future: God, Mammon, and Theology*, ed. Joerg Rieger (Minneapolis: Fortress, 1998).

12. Hardt and Negri, *Empire*, 291, point out that while in modern industrialism we learned to act like machines, today we are learning to think like computers: "Interactive and cybernetic machines become a new prosthesis integrated into our bodies and minds and a lens through which to redefine our bodies and minds themselves."

13. Jameson, *Cultural Turn*, 112; idem, *Postmodernism; or, The Cultural Logic of Late Capitalism* (Durham: Duke University Press, 1991), 62: "The point is that we are

within the culture of postmodernism to the point where its facile repudiation is as impossible as any equally facile celebration of it is complacent and corrupt."

14. Hardt and Negri, *Empire*, 386: "Capital has become a world."

15. See Joerg Rieger, *Remember the Poor: The Challenge to Theology in the Twenty-First Century* (Harrisburg, Pa.: Trinity Press International, 1998), chap. 3, on the distinction between "reality" and the "real."

16. Jameson, *Postmodernism*, 12.

17. Michel Foucault, *Qinzaine littéraire* (May 15, 1966), quoted in Elisabeth Roudinesco, *Jacques Lacan & Co.: A History of Psychoanalysis in France, 1925–1985*, trans. Jeffrey Mehlmann (Chicago: University of Chicago Press, 1990), 376. Foucault refers to the transition from structuralism to poststructuralism.

18. In Lacan's appropriation of French structuralism, and this signifies his move into poststructuralism and the postmodern, the bar which separates signifier and signified becomes more important. Ferdinand de Saussure's structualist "turn to language" seeks to give an account of the arbitrarily established but apparently stable relationships of signifier and signified as it can be found in actual language. In Lacan's conception of the symbolic order, on the other hand, any stable relation between signifier and signified is questioned.

19. As reported—of all places—in the *Dallas Morning News*, January 14, 2002, p. 10A. In the same report is a reference to the fact that more than two-thirds of Mexican citizens do not believe that free-market programs such as privatization have benefited their country. Almost 60% doubt that Mexico profits from the North American Free Trade Agreement (NAFTA). In the words of a female sales clerk: "They sold us a dream, simply a dream that will never be a reality for us poor people. We don't count. We're just labor."

20. Nelly Richard, "The Latin American Problematic of Theoretical-Cultural Transference: Postmodern Appropriations and Counterappropriations," *South Atlantic Quarterly* 92.3 (Summer 1993): 454.

21. Dwight N. Hopkins, "Postmodernity, Black Theology of Liberation, and the United States: Michel Foucault and James Cone," *Journal of Hispanic/Latino Theology* 3.4 (May 1996): 22–23.

22. Cf. Teresa L. Ebert, "The 'Difference' of Postmodern Feminism," *College English* 53.8 (December 1991): 887, who identifies the postmodern status quo as "ludic postmodernism": "A theatre for the free-floating play . . . of images, disembodied signifiers and difference."

23. The Radical Orthodoxy series published by Routledge and edited by John Milbank, Catherine Pickstock, and Graham Ward describes itself at the beginning of each volume as "the most talked-about development in contemporary theology."

24. There is now an overabundance of literature on these subjects, mostly from the churches' own publishing houses.

25. In a speech to the thirty-three leaders of the Western hemisphere in Quebec, Canada, gathered for the third "Summit of the Americas," considering a Free Trade Area of the Americas, as reported in the *New York Times*, Sunday, April 22, 2001, p. 4, Bush said: "We seek freedom not only for people living within our borders, but also for commerce moving across our borders. Free and open trade creates new jobs and new income. It lifts the lives of all our people, applying the power of markets to

the needs of the poor. It spurs the process of economic and legal reform. And open trade reinforces the habit of liberty."

26. Jameson, *Cultural Turn*, 73, talks about a "dedifferentiation of field" where economics overlaps with culture, where "everything, including commodity production and high and speculative finance, has become cultural; and culture has equally become profoundly economic or commodity oriented." As a consequence, culture has now more impact on reality than ever (277).

27. Much contemporary theology is still preoccupied with this perspective, trying to achieve either harmony with contemporary culture or a countercultural stance.

28. Marketing in itself is not necessarily the problem. For this reason, the critique of the market-driven paradigms promoted by the church-growth movement easily misses the point.

29. Jameson, *Cultural Turn*, 50.

30. Hardt and Negri, *Empire*, 150: "Many of the concepts dear to postmodernists and postcolonialists find a perfect correspondence in the current ideology of corporate capital and the world market. The ideology of the world market has always been the anti-foundational and anti-essentialist discourse par excellence. Circulation, mobility, diversity, and mixture are its very conditions of possibility. Trade brings differences together and the more the merrier! Differences (of commodities, populations, cultures, and so forth) seem to multiply infinitely in the world market, which attacks nothing more violently than fixed boundaries."

31. Jameson, *Postmodernism*, 325, sums it all up, wondering: "Is not the production of the appropriate new group-specific products the truest recognition a business society can bring to its others?"

32. For the phenomenon of the new slavery—more vicious than any form of slavery in history—see Kevin Bales, *Disposable People: New Slavery in the Global Economy* (Berkeley: University of California Press, 1999). Cautious estimations say that the lives of twenty-seven million people are affected.

33. The phrase plays with the Spanish word for pain, "dolor."

34. The difference between differentiation and repression is also reflected in the difference between the postmodern concern for "metonymy" and a concern for "metaphor." See Rieger, *Remember the Poor*, 78 n. 6. Hardt and Negri, *Empire*, 156, sense a similar problem without, however, distinguishing between different forms of difference: "The only non-localizable 'common name' of pure difference in all eras is that of the poor. The poor is destitute, excluded, repressed, exploited—and yet living! . . . It is strange, but also illuminating, that postmodernist authors seldom adapt this figure in their theorizing. It is strange because the poor is in a certain respect an eternal postmodern figure: the figure of a transversal, omnipresent, different, mobile subject; the testament to the irrepressible aleatory character of existence."

35. In my *God and the Excluded: Visions and Blindspots in Contemporary Theology* (Minneapolis: Fortress, 2001), I deal with these fault lines in regard to the way theology has shaped up since Schleiermacher.

36. John Beverley, *Subalternity and Representation: Arguments in Cultural Theory* (Durham: Duke University Press, 1999), 165. Not surprisingly, Beverley considers subaltern studies as the secular manifestation of liberation theology's option for the poor (38).

37. See Rieger, *Remember the Poor*, 79, with reference to Lacan. In a similar vein, Hardt and Negri, *Empire*, 397, remind us that "the kinds of movement of individuals, groups, and populations that we find today in Empire, however, cannot be completely subjugated to the laws of capitalist accumulation."

38. Beverley, *Subalternity and Representation*, 101–2, talks about the "deconstructive function of the subaltern."

39. These two elements are combined in Rieger, *Remember the Poor*. See also Hardt and Negri, *Empire*, 157: "The poor is a subjugated, exploited figure, but nonetheless a figure of production. This is where the novelty lies."

40. We cannot expect to be able to represent the subaltern: "Subaltern studies registers . . . how the knowledge we construct and impart as academics is structured by the absence, difficulty, or impossibility of representation of the subaltern." Beverley, *Subalternity and Representation*, 40.

I

Subalternity and Advocacy as *Kairos* for Theology

Mark Lewis Taylor

I sometimes think of subaltern studies as a secular version of the "preferential option for the poor" of liberation theology, one which shares with liberation theology the essential methodology of what Gustavo Gutiérrez calls "listening to the poor."

—John Beverley, *Subalternity and Representation:*
Arguments in Cultural Theory

The subaltern cannot speak.

—Gayatri Chakravorty Spivak,
"Can the Subaltern Speak?"

With her four-word phrase, Gayatri Spivak, a feminist philosopher and literary critic from India, when commenting on the worlds of "urban sub-proletarian women" in South Asia,[1] identifies a pervasive problem for John Beverley. Beverley, as we shall see, is well aware of the problem. It is a problem, moreover, for any who presume to speak *for*, *with*, or *about* or even *to listen to* the poor, marginal, excluded, oppressed, or exploited, that is, those "subaltern" peoples who are made both subordinate and other (Latin *alter*) to more powerful systems.[2]

This is not a problem for just anyone. In the main, it is a problem for those who have access to colonizing and powerful orders, because of some cultural entitlement made possible by their access to wealth, ethnic identity, gendered being, educational opportunity, or other cultural/political regions of power. I will speak of the problem in this essay as that of "entitled advocates" of subaltern peoples.[3] Spivak herself refers to these advocates as "benevolent *Western* intellectuals."[4]

My use of the word *entitled* needs clarification. I use it in this essay simply in its basic definition, describing those who have received a title, claim, or power to do something that others not entitled cannot do or cannot do so readily. One who is entitled, in this sense, is not necessarily a better or more virtuous person, however one judges those valuations. Nor should it be assumed that those in positions to invoke some entitlement are in a better situation even for themselves, somehow happier, healthier, more fulfilled. Some assume that entitled people are necessarily more virtuous or more fulfilled, but that does not necessarily follow. It may be true, but often is not. Most certainly, it should never be assumed. The entitled ones are simply those who, usually by some group affiliation (class, ethnic identity, gender, educational experience, political position) or because of some combination of these affiliations, have an access to enabling power that others do not. Spivak makes it clear that for such entitled ones it is no simple process to hear the speech of the subaltern, those who lack certain forms of empowering entitlement.

There are many more examples of entitled advocates, and they all are challenged by the problem that Spivak explicates. These might include profeminist men seeking some common cause with their feminist women colleagues, white folk trying to fight against their own white supremacy alongside black folk, straight folk sliding along the scales of sexual orientation to find some supportive presence with their gay/bisexual/lesbian and transgendered friends. It includes high-income women seeking to work or speak on behalf of poor women, U.S. citizens in Peru or Guatemala resisting U.S. imperialism alongside Central American actors, Europeans from developed countries seeking "humane" or liberating "development" in poorer countries, liberation theologians anywhere publishing books and seeking that elusive thing called "solidarity" with communities of the poor, and poor community organizers working even with their own neighbors to "raise consciousness." Indeed, postcolonialist advocates of subaltern studies like Spivak are themselves not outside the problem in their search to construct strategic alliances and studies of the poor of India, as they have done within the radical collective of Indian scholars in the Subaltern Studies project headed by Ranajit Guha.[5] In all these instances and more, there is the problem posed by subaltern peoples to the entitled advocate who dares to enter into some shared speech and work with them.

This essay unfolds this problem, seeking to clarify its nature while also proposing various responses to it. The problem of the entitled advocate, of the "benevolent *Western* intellectual," puts theological discourse—especially liberation theology and theologies of the marginalized—into a state of crisis. Reflecting on that crisis, however, can also uncover opportunity for new steps forward. Hence, the problems emergent between subalternity and advocacy make for a *kairos* moment in theological discourse: dilemma and confusion arise (crisis), which might also provoke and enable new growth (opportunity). Let us approach the *kairos* by entering the problem and unfolding it more slowly.

An Aporia of Postmodernism's Politics: Seeking a Liberatory *a Priori*

The problem of the subaltern for entitled advocates needs to be situated in an overall problematic of postmodernism's politics. To understand this problematic we need, in turn, to offer some working definitions of key terms.

"Postmodernism," as I use it in this essay, is a set of discourses noted for theoretical and cultural emphases that celebrate difference, eschewing foundations and championing qualities of fragmentation, hybridity, the ephemeral, surfaces (more than "the depths"), flux, play, and carnival.[6] I distinguish postmodernism as a set of discourses from another term, postmodernity. This latter term refers to the complex conditions, combining economic, political, and social dynamics, which provide the matrix within which postmodernist discourse circulates. Often the conditions of postmodernity are also determinate forces that generate postmodernism and account for its widespread occurrence as a discourse, especially under "late 20th-century capitalist" conditions.[7] Just what precisely these conditions are that generate postmodernist discourse and how determinative a role they have played in producing postmodernist discourse are topics of important debate that I need not engage now.[8] The main point here is that postmodernism's concerns are largely discursive, especially elaborated forms of speech and writing that are related to and often dependent upon other factors, such as historical conditions of political, economic, and social life. This means that postmodernism, prevailing largely in the societies of the world's wealthier regions, thrives on what many would call an "ideological" level, though I here use that term not in a disparaging sense but descriptively.

The important question is what effect postmodernism has when, as a discourse or ideology, it feeds back its ideas and notions into the realm of political conditions. It is in this feedback that we encounter an "aporia," in the sense of a troubling exposure to conflicting pressures. It is this situation of conflict that characterizes postmodernism's relation to political life. Postmodernist discourse has had a profoundly ambivalent impact in the political domain, where marginalized peoples wrestle with overwhelming centrist and more powerful forces.

On the one hand, postmodernism can foment a politics of resistance. In 1983, Hal Foster wrote of a "postmodernism of resistance," in which a homogeneous and massive modernity would be unsettled and subverted. Postmodernism here could inject numerous destabilizing shocks to undo repressive regimes and systems.[9] Philosopher of religion and "*a*theologian" Mark C. Taylor hoped for a celebration of difference that would dissolve "the economies of domination," so that the entire foundation of domination "crumbles."[10]

These are clearly high hopes. Indeed, there is some truth in trusting to some fruitful destabilizing action, in society, politics, and academic institutions, which testifies to the ways postmodernist discourse can unsettle retrenched powers. Postmodernist discourse has often nourished greater openness to multicultural studies in universities and has shaken the confidences that in previous times were used to keep the different out of centers of power. Feminists in North American academies and elsewhere, for example, used postmodernist criticisms of modernity and of foundations to critique the "cults of objectivity" and to give voice, place, and location to a reconstructed female difference,[11] so that sex and gender, themselves unstable categories, became "epistemologically relevant"[12] in new scholarly paradigms of intersubjectivity. Elsewhere, postmodernist subversions and a destabilizing of metanarratives, as John Beverley and Marc Zimmerman note about the revolutionary periods in Central America, helped to prepare a terrain for various forms of cultural resistance.[13]

On the other hand, some of these same sources, supplemented by other critics, have called attention to the way that postmodernist qualities actually reinforce the economies and ideologies of domination. Manuel Castells notes in *The Rise of the Network Society*, for example, that at the same time that postmodernism may give place and location to previously excluded people and territories, "what most postmodernism does is to express, in almost direct terms, the new dominant ideology: the end of history and the supersession of places in the space of flows."[14] In the recent book, *Empire*, by Michael Hardt and Antonio Negri, postmodernism's discursive qualities are analyzed as postmodernizing forces that reinforce the new imperialist spaces occupied by networks of transnational corporate power, which are anchored in the U.S. hegemony over global use of military force.[15]

Among feminists, criticism of the politically unfriendly side of postmodernism was memorably articulated in Susan Bordo's lament about the timing of postmodernist critiques of "female reality": "It is no accident, I believe, that feminists are questioning the integrity of the notion of 'female reality' just as we begin to get a foothold in those professions which could be most radically transformed by our (historically developed) Otherness and which have been historically most shielded from it."[16] Similar laments, by other long-subordinated groups claiming a new subjecthood, have also arisen when postmodernist critiques dismiss newly won identities (e.g., Mayan, Native American, womanist) as mere "essentializing."[17]

Is there a pervasive trait of postmodernist discourse that we can identify which most explains postmodernism's penchant for reinforcing ideologies and structures of domination, whether these be patriarchal, neoliberal, or some other type? I believe that the basic trait is postmodernism's tendency to fetish-ize its distinctive qualities, especially those of play, flux, volatility, even com-plexity. These, of course, are not problematic in themselves; indeed, they are necessary whenever forms of domination reassert ever-new repressions and orders that devise hierarchies and reinforce stasis. Postmodernist celebrations of flux and difference remain politically fruitful for challenging such forces of domination.

The fetishization of play in postmodernism, what some have called "ludic postmodernism," entails the neglect of what I will call in this essay a liberatory *a priori*, albeit in a somewhat eccentric philosophical sense. The term here is similar to what is usually called an *a priori*, because I use it here to signal a persistent concern to value freedom that is deeply etched into, and assumed in, human thought and action. Yet, and here is the eccentricity, this *a priori* is encountered in shifting and always new, perhaps surprising, modes. I do not make it a transcendental universal, even though many thinkers and actors often find it necessary to invoke it.

I use the word *liberatory* for this persistent tendency to value freedom, because "liberation" and its related terms (liberate, liberatory, liberative) more usually connote the crucial political, social, and economic dimensions of free-dom. I cannot here offer a fully complex theory of freedom, but I presuppose that it is these structural freedoms (political, economic, social, cultural) that provide the enabling matrix for the more personal, or internal, freedoms ("lib-erties"). A liberatory *a priori* is a pervasive tendency to assume, desire, and imagine these kinds of structured freedoms.

Celebrations of difference and play which do not attend to that liberatory *a priori* are fetishizing, in the sense of giving excessive attention and reverence to difference and play, in a way that masks and shifts attention away from the liberatory *a priori*, which, in fact, is necessary to guard the positive functioning of difference and play.[18] This fetishization often results not just in making a fetish of play, but also in estheticizing oppression and repression. Chilean economist Martin Hopenhayn says it well in the present period:

> The social contradictions of capitalism, accentuated on the Latin American periphery, disappear behind the exaltation of forms and languages. The economic crisis—the worst we have experienced in this century—is hidden under the euphemism of *a beautiful anar-chy*, and structural heterogeneity is converted into the creative com-bination of the modern and the archaic, "our" peripheral incarnation and anticipation of the postmodern.[19]

This fetishization, or estheticization (Hopenhayn's term), can occur in many ways. One vivid example is presented by Nancy Scheper-Hughes in her *Death without Weeping*, where, in the context of widespread maternal and child death from poverty and hunger, "carnival" is proposed as a remedy for structural violation. True, it dissolves hierarchy and enables an outbreaking from many normal roles that are repressive (for women and others); and during the carnivalesque play normal orders are put in flux, and a "dancing against death" can become an artful resistance to daily oppressions.[20]

Nevertheless, without identifying and directly addressing the need to break *free from* structures of poverty, ludic practices like carnival in Brazil do not have in themselves the desired political consequence. To the contrary, they can mask and perpetuate the structures of violence and oppression, or, as in the case of Scheper-Hughes's context, they leave unaddressed the needs of the most violated who are ensnared in structures of oppression, those who cannot or do not participate in the carnivalesque: "How can I entertain myself when I have a house full of sick children? *Carnaval* is for men and cows," observed one mother to Scheper-Hughes in Bom Jesus da Mata in Brazil.[21]

What is needed along with, in, and maybe through postmodernist play and carnival, then, is a liberatory *a priori*. As an *a priori*, it is not a solid foundation, a clearly identifiable cause, or some always-formulated "first principle." It is more like a haunting, inescapable presumption that is difficult to deny, in spite of many postmodernist inclinations to do so. A liberatory *a priori* may seem like some throwback to a modernist, discredited world of first principles, first causes, nonconstructed essences, and all the rest; but, in fact, it is simply to name the way the desire and impetus toward full, structural freedom haunt the deep places of our thinking, our acting, our living. It is like a specter, to adapt one of Derrida's notions,[22] that shows itself occasionally, as when Foucault somewhat incoherently insisted under pressure of an interlocutor's questioning: "The guarantee of freedom is freedom."[23]

The liberatory *a priori* can be given a bit more structure than Foucault's announcement, of course, without losing a postmodern respect for flux and diversity. Perhaps, Hopenhayn opted for a bit too formalized an *a priori* when he posited "an emancipatory dynamic that runs beneath events or that guides the actions of humanity," but even this language is not the result of a simple modernist reason looking for a firm foundation for some grand narrative of liberation. No, for Hopenhayn, it was more a kind of refuge-taking under pressure, a presupposing based on certain practical demands posed by Latin American economies in crisis—all of which seemed necessary if any questioning of alienation and marginalization and other sufferings was to be sustained or even begun.[24]

In short the aporia of postmodernism, with respect to its political impact, consists of acute tension: on the one hand, postmodernist discourse (its theories and practices) can fruitfully unsettle dominative hierarchies of Western structures (the grand modernist metanarratives); on the other, it easily succumbs to being one more reinforcer of domination, especially in the context of recent neoliberal forms of transnational, capitalist hegemony (the current metanarrative of today's "globalization"). What can preserve postmodernism from its more negative function and thus guide it better through its aporia is a respect for a liberatory *a priori*, a respect that takes the form of giving attention and theoretical form to the haunting, spectral presence of human needs for liberation.

The Subaltern: Postmodernist Expression of a Liberatory *a Priori*

In the context of the aporia of postmodernism's politics, in which we are led to acknowledge a liberatory *a priori*, we can return to the notion of the subaltern and better understand its value. *Subaltern* is a valuable term for contemporary analysts seeking advocacy in support of oneself or of others suffering oppression. The term will also enable deeper reflections on the problems of advocacy and solidarity.

The very linguistic construction of the term *subaltern* bears witness to the way it can critically engage the world of postmodernist discourse and is itself a part of that world. Clearly, the term signals an interest in otherness (difference, diversity, deferral in a flux of signification and location) by way of its major linguistic unit, "-altern" (from Latin *alter*, "other"). Nevertheless, its prefix, "sub-," deepens and orients its interests in alterity to experiences of *subordination*. To study the subaltern is to study the subordinated others, usually, the others who have been subordinated because of their otherness or because their otherness was a convenient stigmatizing mechanism for organizing their subordination.

To use the notion of the subaltern is to engage and even affirm the interest of the postmodern milieu with otherness. More importantly, however, it also expresses an acknowledgment of a liberatory *a priori* that refuses to take subordination as simply one more mode of otherness. The term concerns, then, both "hybridity" as the intricate combining of forms in processes of othering, while retaining a binary character in its reference to subordinated peoples who are dominated by (and seeking liberation from) elite structures.[25]

A term that fuses the liberatory *a priori* with a concern for alterity has two advantages for theologians and other scholars seeking a rhetoric of resistance and solidarity with marginalized groups and peoples. Given what I have already discussed about the aporia of postmodern politics, these functional advantages will not be surprising. I do need, however, to make them more explicit.

First, there is *the advantage of unmasking*. By naming explicitly some among the sea of others as *subordinated* others, by identifying some dimensions of alterity as *sub*alterity, we take the mask off of the postmodern carnival-goers who not only play, but fetishize play, that is, those who celebrate every feature of their world as basically equivalent, simply a fascinating play of different entities. It is a way to resist what medical anthropologist Paul Farmer has termed the tendency of many scholars today to "conflate structural violence and cultural difference."[26] Naming, identifying, and respecting the presence of the *sub*altern has the advantage of unmasking the ideology of the postmodern milieu, which would prefer not to think about those whose labor makes possible their "play." It unmasks the reality that much of the postmodern play of First World academics in the trilateral North (Europe/North America/North Asia)[27] occurs in academic structures complicit in and dependent upon dynamics of subordination that cause suffering and trauma for those in "the South."[28]

Paradigmatic of this unmasking is, again, the way that Scheper-Hughes lifts the mask of carnival-goers in Brazil finds them so often to be mainly men and boys, which then also throws open the doors to reveal poor women left behind to care for sick children at time of *carnaval*.

For scholars seeking to attend to the world being studied, it is to their advantage to have a term that marks *precisely* this difference within alterity, the difference of those who are subordinated others, the subaltern. It should be noted that this entails not simply the unmasking of victims and sufferers. Indeed, that is so, but one of the advantages of the term *subaltern* is that its terminology includes not just suffering but also resistance. The subordinated, in diverse modes, struggle against the subordination. In this they disclose that liberatory drive, an effort to break free, even if only to gain some breathing space, some mode of survival under adverse conditions. When the subordinated others are revealed in the sea of alterity, what we view are the others who are both exploited and in resistance in some liberatory mode.

The second advantage in employing the notion of the subaltern is what I shall call *the advantage of complexity*. Here is an advantage that liberation theologians need to take more fully into their methodologies in understanding oppression, in analyzing the poor so often essentialized in their work.[29] The notion of the sub*altern* keeps us concrete, specific, manifold, hybrid, fully pluralistic in ever new ways, when speaking and acting in relation to experiences of subordination. As the very term *subaltern* suggests, subordination must be thought in relation to alterity, to the many and other diverse forms and manifestations.

To be sure, we might write and theorize about what subordinated peoples might share in common. We do not hear them, see them, or act with them, however, if we fail to acknowledge that they are of many kinds and forms. The Subaltern Studies Group regularly stressed that it was intent on emphasizing several key kinds of complexity in its study of oppression: for example, how the same people can be oppressed in one geographical region but not in another; how the same group can be transformed over time from oppressed to oppressor; how oppression works at not just two levels (oppressor vs. oppressed) but multilaterally, from many levels and sides.[30] More recently, John Beverley, writing in *The Latin American Subaltern Studies Reader*, suggests that subaltern studies is marked by a "radical heterogeneity" that keeps scholars ever attuned to complexities of difference.[31]

To these complexities, we might add still others and so remind ourselves of the teeming and multifarious worlds of alterity at work among subaltern peoples and their identities. Some of these additional complexities are obvious, but they have not always been attended to by those claiming to be reviewing or listening to the oppressed. Recall these complexities: (a) that oppressed peoples are characterized by different kinds of collective identities, as women, laborers, ethnic groups, cultural traditions, religious groupings and movements; (b) that the very notion of oppression is diversely related to other notions, which require careful theoretical elaboration, such as exploitation, marginalization, powerlessness, repression, and so on; (c) that oppressed peoples also have their own *individual* stories with distinctive psychological depths, turmoil, and insight that unfold along life histories that do not always mirror those of others in the same grouping; (d) that oppressed peoples are not the only others, but so also the oppressors are others who must be exposed in all their specificity (Apache joking rituals, for example, have yielded a new, richer, and fuller knowledge of "white male" others in North America); and (e) that oppressed peoples feature not only different spatial identities (cultural, national, social, sexual, etc.), but also different *temporal* identities produced by exposure to historical change, which often erode the essentializations of culture, nation, society, and sexual identity).

The two advantageous strategies emanating from employing the notion of the subaltern (of unmasking ludic views of otherness and embracing complexities) gives us a necessary rhetoric for expressing a liberatory *a priori* in theoretical analyses of the poor in postmodern contexts. Yet this is still not sufficient. Liberation theologians, or any theologians with intentions of thinking and acting in solidarity with the marginalized, must also face the problem of subaltern speechlessness.

The Problem of Subaltern Speechlessness

With this problem, we come into the heart of Gayatri Spivak's concerns in her essay "Can the Subaltern Speak?" When Spivak refers to the subaltern she is, as noted above, referring to those whom she terms "urban sub-proletarian women," those exploited by interacting forces of international capital, sexism, and racism, encountered often in urban areas, especially in the factories of many export zones throughout Asia, Latin America, and the Caribbean, and in rural areas. Exemplary of the subaltern about whom Spivak writes are also those about whom James Cockcroft writes in *Mexico's Hope*: "the super-exploited" women of Mexico, Asia, and Central America who are forced to live in the cities and to work the *maquiladoras*.[32]

The obstacles to the speaking of such as these are not simply the physical world-weariness of poverty and overwork, real as those impediments to speech, thought, and action may be. Nor is it that such subaltern women lack the resources, will, or powers of articulation and action to make themselves heard. Quite to the contrary, their powers of speech and action are very much in play, as evidenced by women's labor movements and acts of resistance worldwide, in many of the same factory worlds where their suffering seems most acute.[33] The problem is often that, in spite of the impressive articulation of voice and forging of resistance of subaltern woman, her opinions, as belonging to her, are denigrated, seen as "poor" and so "inexpert," "simple."

This, however, is too straightforward a way of characterizing the problem. It also has a more subtle form. I refer to a perhaps more debilitating dynamic that works even greater repression of subaltern voices than do the more straightforward modes of physical coercion and verbal disparagement. I refer to the ways speechlessness of the subaltern is reinforced, even created and shaped, by the allegedly well-meaning and benevolent First World intellectual, who would construct or point out the needs of groups called, for example, "poor women," "poor Third World women," or even "subaltern women." The program of the benevolent Western intellectual has regularly been to identify and then to assimilate Third World people as others, making a place for them, believing this to be the doing of good. This benevolence, in fact, can be seen as a key dynamic of imperialism.[34]

Imperialists' self-images often entail a vision of their colonizing societies as establishing the good society. As Spivak emphasizes about subaltern women, colonizers often spoke of the need to espouse the needs of women, to protect them amid their acute suffering. Unfortunately, with the racist and sexist postures of Western colonialist cultures, this did not mean protecting women from Western companies' exploitation of them as resource for cheap labor. It usually meant protecting "woman" from imagined dangers from her own kind. As Spivak writes, Western imperialists, with the intellectuals often to the fore among them, usually thought in terms of "white men [and sometimes white women] saving brown women from brown men."[35]

Even this, however, is too blatant an example of how imperialist logic can persist in elite discourses and practices, thus rendering subaltern peoples speechless. In the sheer act of pointing out these groups, here the subaltern, we have engaged in an activity that is a problematic one. The problem of subaltern speechlessness begins to emerge with this construction, for precisely in that construction we have exercised a kind of control. However radical or emancipatory may be our intentions, this exercise in control can make entitled advocates participants in the long-standing privilege of Western practices of control that are evident in imperialism and multiple modes of domination. It puts in place a mode of objectifying (here of the poor or subaltern) which, as Farmer has argued in social-science literature, is often a first step in the structural violence meted out to the poor.[36]

My point here is not simply some easily dismissable oversensitivity of "political correctness." Our desire to represent subaltern peoples' concerns— in the double sense of "representing" as offering words *about* and words *for and on behalf of*—easily becomes part of the overall process that Beverley exposed, whereby "literature and the university are among the practices that create and sustain subalternity."[37] Beverley is thinking of the way the very development of knowledge guilds, the funding of educational centers with rigorous admission criteria, and the careful teaching of disciplined argument in universities, all have a tendency to exclude. (When one considers the way systemic distortions by class, race, and gender often are at work in creating "literature and the university," Beverley's worry is all the more to the point.) Beverley's claim renders ever more acute the special quandary of the entitled advocate. The one who would in some way represent the concerns and identities of the subaltern becomes "self-contradictory,"[38] spinning discourse that perpetuates the very problem being lamented.

We become all the more enmeshed in self-contradiction if we claim to be able to remove ourselves, letting others speak through us. This more "dangerous benevolence," to continue Spivak's notion, surfaces especially when we pretend that we are absent, allowing oppressed others "to speak for themselves." We may, indeed, quote their writing or reported statements, record and reproduce their narratives (oral and written), but still we do not thereby generate a discourse free from our own personal and cultural constructions. In short, it is quite impossible for members working in an ethos of entitlement to undertake an erasure of themselves. The designators *poor* and *subaltern* are constructive activities by entitled scholars that implicate them in activities of control, replete with references to "them" or "their" struggle, "their" liberation. So it is that the benevolent intellectual, even if writing as a critic calling for liberation, is caught in a bind: how is it possible to hear and acknowledge the voice and speech of the subaltern without engaging in controlling exercises that reinforce their speechlessness?

Seeking Modes of Authentic Advocacy

There are no easy answers to the problem of subaltern speechlessness. Even though Beverley likened subaltern studies to liberation theology's "listening to the poor," both Beverley and that theology are challenged by the difficulty. The will to hear the poor, to listen to "the small voice of history," in Ranajit Guha's terms, poses a kind of crisis, and Beverley's long book *Subalternity and Representation* is one eloquent and diligent testimony to that crisis for the scholar—whether theologian, historian, or literary critic.

There is crisis, here, in two senses. First, the scholar who would engage in such studies and listening is confronted with his or her own involvement in preventing that hearing. Second, there is a crisis in not knowing how one could go forward at all with some kind of listening, study, and advocacy, given the complexities of complicity analyzed by Spivak and others. In fact, given this second sense of crisis, there is a penchant to just avoid advocacy and the whole pretense of being able to listen and "represent" at all. Indeed, within the academy, in addition to the usual elitism and blatant insensitivity to worlds outside the academic one, there is a kind of sophisticated awareness of the complexity in speaking or advocating about the worlds of the poor, which leads many to abstain from the attempt altogether.

I want to propose, nevertheless, that there is a way forward, one that does not solve all the problems but which can be taken and might constitute a kind of opportunity to understand anew theology's relation to the politics of hearing and advocating in relation to worlds of the subaltern. With this opportunity, then, the crisis might also have elements of *kairos*.

I will suggest for consideration here four modes of authentic advocacy that seem necessary if some way forward through crisis to opportunity is possible. By "authentic," I mean a kind of advocacy that avoids, as much as possible, the problems of subaltern speechlessness unfolded in the previous section. Each of the following four modes of advocacy are necessary and important. They build upon one another with the earlier modes making possible the later ones.

First, I suggest that it is crucial simply to acknowledge the problem that has been set before us, that when any of us as entitled advocates represent the subaltern, to speak of or for them, we are journeying along a route of a self-contradiction, through a scholars' kind of *via negativa*, along which we have to admit that we will be risking a kind of control and objectification of the subaltern that makes them un- or underrepresented even amid our attempts to represent them. We can never duck the fact, expressed so well by Beverley, that "academic knowledge is a practice that actively *produces* subalternity (it produces subalternity in the act of representing it)."[39]

This acknowledgment is all the more crucial if we are scholars who possess traditionally entitled places in the trilateral North and in other centers of power, while trying to study and develop arguments about the Third World, the poor, or any other group where similar power differentials are at work. Without this acknowledgment as a crucial first step, I see no way of moving forward given the critique and challenge Spivak sets before us. We male scholars, to take just one of many possible examples, especially if we would speak of and for women's movements and liberation, need to acknowledge that it is difficult to think and act in freedom from the patriarchal ways operative in the gendered political spaces within which we are entitled. Even if we somehow pass through this difficulty, we still risk rendering our subject matter speechless, as vociferous as may be our claims to some solidarity with women's task of being agents of their liberation.

With this first mode *of* advocacy—and I believe it should be seen as such and not only as a problem *to* advocacy—the way of advocacy begins in uncertainty. It is steeped in awareness of self-contradiction, a penchant for a *via negativa*. Talk of solidarity with the subaltern may be hard to sustain, suggesting, as that term often has, too sanguine a knowledge of the other, too pretentious an identifying with their plight, too presumptuous a connection to shared struggle with them. It may be, as anthropologist Diane Nelson suggests, that we should think of our relation to the subaltern, especially across cultural boundaries, as a relation of "fluidarity," in which there is little that is solid. Our identities are "stumped identities—open, bewildered, and political."[40] One of the most important boundaries confronted here is that between knowing and not knowing, even about whom, how, or whether we can speak of and for subaltern peoples at all.

Second, if speech and scholarship are to approach an authentic advocacy amid subaltern speechlessness, we who search for a way to speak about the subaltern anywhere must also be in resistance to the exploitation of the subordinated in our own academic and social locations. Our speech and participatory action with and for subaltern peoples must be embodied in a praxis of resistance *where we are*—in our institutions, in relation to the corporations in our cities, working with oppressed groups that are in our own neighborhoods, personal relationships, schools, and families. With this mode of authentic advocacy the need for local resistance becomes paramount.

I risk here, I know, the mere articulation of a well-worn moralism: something like, "Practice yourself at home what you preach for, or about, others elsewhere." Perhaps its well-worn character, and the accusatory manner that often accompanies it, makes it seem a moralistic exercise to be avoided. I do think, though, that it still needs to be said in numerous ways. There is something missing if we U.S. scholars support the work of Amnesty International for political prisoners in, say, Turkey, without focusing and working on the problems of political prisoners in the United States.[41] It is more than just an oversight if as U.S. theologians we lament the oppression of the poor in Latin America without focusing on the many in poverty in the United States, who constitute the largest group in poverty in any of the developed, industrialized nations.[42] It is unsatisfying if we speak of the repression at work in the Afghanistans, Sudans, and Colombias of the world without noting the way unprecedented levels of police brutality and the growth of a prison industrial complex have been deemed a systemic repression of human rights for citizens in the United States.[43] It is more than just inconsistent if we male scholars wax eloquent about women's movements for new freedoms abroad or in general without supporting vigorously the efforts of women in our departments and faculties for the institution of practices that support such freedoms.

The taking up of such local advocacies is more than just trying to obey some maxim of left culture that it is important "to act locally and to act globally." More to the point, the advocacy of subaltern peoples only in general or only abroad intensifies the problem of objectification that renders the subaltern speechless. It is to make the subordinated other into a distant object, exotic and often isolated from the scholar's world. Consequently, the scholar often becomes protected from critique by the subaltern and without a chance to develop the mutual play of critique and countercritique that come with local engagement. It may be fine to study distant subalterns, but without engaging the local subaltern, any advocacy easily becomes only the silencing and assimilating kind.

The third mode of authentic advocacy is somewhat difficult to articulate, but it too is an essential one. If entitled advocates of subaltern peoples are to avoid being the "dangerous, benevolent intellectuals," they must know that *their own* freedom and wholeness is at stake, not just that of some victimized subaltern other. We in the academies of the trilateral North or in other power centers, who would advocate action or theories for and about subaltern peoples, dare not conceive of ourselves as some more sophisticated kind of liberatory philanthropists who bring good arguments, data, resources for development or solidarity with the oppressed. Such a posture presupposes that we are the good bearers of fine gifts. This, though, is the lie. We are, within our worlds of entitlement, as subaltern peoples themselves sometimes know too well about us, something else: broken and insecure people, relentlessly and often viciously maintaining our identities and power out of fear and prejudice and often doing this on the backs of the poor's labor or on the basis of deeply ingrained stereotypes of racially stigmatized others, which reinforce our own inflated sense of self and group privilege.[44]

The process of objectification of the poor, which is so much a part of subaltern speechlessness, needs to be interrupted by entitled advocates' acknowledgments that their studies of subaltern others are part of their own pursuit of freedom and well-being. Again, this is a desirable interruption because it prevents the subaltern from being isolated as object, as object of suffering in need of liberation, with the scholar of the subaltern situated in some place of entitlement free of suffering and free of potentially being objectified as sufferer. With this acknowledgment, the myth of entitlement is at least qualified, if not countered outright. Any advocate of subaltern peoples' struggles who wishes to support the release of subaltern speech does well to have a sense of struggle and hope for him- or her*self*, as well as for the oppressed, the poor, the subaltern. Hence, Gustavo Gutiérrez once tried to interrupt the penchant of some North American audiences to talk of their "solidarity with the poor" by saying that he didn't want any North Americans working with the Latin American poor unless they were somehow in that struggle also *for them-selves*.[45]

This is not to argue that there is some kind of commensurability or, even less, some equality of suffering between the world of entitled advocates and the world of subaltern peoples. Not at all. It does mean, however, that enough connections exist between those worlds that a study of the dynamics of subaltern suffering can provoke *mutually* beneficial knowledge and action. Affirming that possibility, and working toward it, makes for another mode of authentic advocacy amid the problem of subaltern speechlessness.

The fourth and final mode of authentic advocacy may be a still more difficult one to articulate. It is, however, one especially relevant to theological advocacy of subaltern peoples. In addition, it opens up a mystical dimension at the heart of political struggle in relation to subaltern peoples, which has implications for Christian liberation theologians, other religious thinkers, and perhaps also for secular friends of liberation theology in subaltern studies. I stress that this final mode both presupposes and builds upon an understanding of the previous three modes of authentic advocacy. What I discuss in the fourth mode, below, will make little sense without having traversed the insights of the previous modes. This fourth mode of authentic advocacy is an embrace of a very specific kind of "delirium" that accompanies subaltern studies. What is this delirium? We can begin to understand it by noting that when an entitled advocate seeks practices and thinking that are both for them (the subaltern) and for him-/herself (the entitled advocate), as I suggested above in the third mode of authentic advocacy, then the voice of the subordinate other is, in a sense, no longer simply outside of the advocate. This other is also *in* us, as well as *outside* us.

When this experience comes to the advocate, there occurs a kind of doubling of voices. Amid this doubling, the voice of the subaltern speaks neither an easily comprehended nor a comfortable word. It will often be a confusing word, but one that remains fruitful—fruitful in the sense that the subaltern voice within the advocate ruptures and reorients the being of the advocate. At the very least, an entitled advocate's self is complexified, his or her identity is rendered problematic. The self of the advocate has regions discovered that are unfamiliar, perhaps unknown. In the disorienting and reorienting there is a whirl and destabilization.

It is Jacques Derrida from whom I have taken this term, "delirium." He helps describe the situation of living and working with the doubled voice, and he describes this situation as "rendering delirious that interior voice that is the voice of the other in us."[46] Derrida does not himself comment on the significance of this statement for scholarship in settings of entitlement and power, but the Indian critic of imperialism, Spivak, is right to suggest that acknowledging this delirium is crucial to a practice of struggle and advocacy with subaltern peoples against colonialism and imperialism. It is crucial, she suggests, for reducing the dangerousness in "benevolent Western intellectuals" who so often only reinforce their own power and identity by constituting the poor or the subaltern as other.[47] This doubling of voices may especially occur for sub-altern scholars, since, in spite of all their postmodern concerns with otherness and hybridity, they also work in a field that retains a certain binary structure, assuming a conflict of powers along an axis of "the elite" and "the subordi-nated."[48] The elite/subordinated binary means that "the voice of the other in us," as Derrida put it, is not just that of any other, but that of the subordinated other. The doubled voice within an entitled advocate of the subaltern, then, is a voice that inscribes a conflict within.

Perhaps Derrida's term, delirium, suggests a bit too much of the fetishized flux and play that so often leads to a carnivalesque ethos that rarely attends to a liberatory *a priori*. The kind of delirium that emerges from the subaltern scholar's experience of the doubled voice, however, retains a certain structural shape that saves it from sheer play and flux. To be sure, the unsettling quality of the doubling voice warrants the term *delirium*, suggesting frenzy, confusion, torment, disorder, and excited disturbance. But the delirium of the subaltern scholar does not lose its character as shuttling between voices, between the advocate's self and subaltern selves outside of the advocate or between the advocate's voice within and the subaltern's voice within. In both cases of this shuttling there is a certain patterned and structured movement. It is not a fetishized flux of pure carnival, because subaltern studies retains always a sense of the liberatory *a priori* that is intrinsic to the subaltern struggle amid subordination.

This kind of delirium has a kind of rhythm that is given by the laments, demands, worldviews of the subaltern, on one side, and the concerns, solidar-ities, scholarly projects of entitled advocates, on the other. The movement is perhaps like that of Stanford anthropologist Scheper-Hughes, who sees all the potential for epistemological and ethical pretense in her own work with starv-ing poor women in the *Nordeste* of Brazil, but then prefaces her 600-page book with these words:

> So despite the mockery that Clifford Geertz (1988) made of an-thropological "I-witnessing," I believe there is still value in attempt-ing to "speak truth to power." . . . Seeing, listening, touching, record-ing, can be, if done with care and sensitivity, acts of fraternity and sisterhood, acts of solidarity. Above all they are the work of recogni-tion. Not to look, not to touch, not to record, can be the hostile act, the act of indifference and of turning away.[49]

Maybe in the midst of this kind of delirium, the subaltern scholar is en-gaged in a kind of dance, the giving of one's life and body to the continuous and varied counterpoint of cry and response—a kind of binary two-step along

SUBALTERNITY AND ADVOCACY AS *KAIROS* FOR THEOLOGY   39

a presumed axis of elite/subaltern, which is also played out in a myriad of ever more complex spaces and varying gestures. This, we might say, in search of an analogy, makes up a kind of dance of the delirious subaltern scholar.

Not all advocates of subaltern peoples are willing to experience the tumult and abyss of self-questioning and self-doubting that emerge within this delirium. My major suggestion here is that if entitled advocates do not enter into that delirium, to embrace it as a necessary part of their representation of and for subaltern peoples, then they risk becoming mere benefactors who once again participate in colonizing and imperialist projects of objectifying and assimilating others, of muting and disabling the speech of the very subaltern ones they claim to hear.

The disorientations and reorientations worked by the doubled voices that produce delirium might also be interpreted as a region of mystery haunting the hermeneutical practice of subaltern studies. This mysterious dimension has many meanings. It is an experience of the subaltern other, but not only that. It is also a call to the self as already known; but again not only to the self, but also to a different, often surprising self, a self in a new, challenged, and often confusing self-other interplay. There may also be here a rising wonder about the kind of matrix in which selves and others might now be together in a newly pluralized, diverse, and always changing struggle, to explore if not a new solidarity, then some "fluidarity" wherein some real sharing evolves from the shaky ground of meeting one another amid difference. In all these ways and more, uncertainties and the unknown attach to subaltern studies and give it a quality of mystery.

I stress that authentic advocacy means embracing such mysteries, but entering this delirium does not replace or sidestep the need for disciplined scholarly endeavor in subaltern studies. By no means. Mystery and delirium concern merely one crucial dimension of subaltern studies, one that is especially crucial to acknowledge if we are to subvert the pretensions and assimilations to which entitled subaltern advocates are especially prone.

What good does the delirium do for subaltern studies? It subverts the secure status of the entitled advocate without doing away with the basic awareness of the relevance of a distinction between worlds of elites and worlds of the subordinated. The delirium is an important aspect of subaltern studies where a dance of relinquishment occurs—a relinquishment of objectification and assimilation that fosters rupture and reorientation so that the subaltern may find voice. I say "*may* find voice," because in the dance of this delirium, even though we have a better chance through it of rising above the problem of subaltern speechlessness, there is no guarantee that we will do so. Various concrete encounters and projects will always unfold differently when entitled advocates and subaltern groups risk coming together, and the outcomes will retain a certain unpredictability. There is no more guarantee that entitled advocates will successfully overcome problems of subaltern speechlessness than there is that two dancers who encounter one other on a dance floor will "dance well" together, to the satisfaction of each. The rhythms of both dancers, the capacity of both to be in step with one another, given the music, mood, and milieu of the night, will all conspire to shape the outcome. Without entering the dance, however, and without looking for the productive delirium that might arise from stepping out, there are few other ways forward. There certainly seem to be few other ways for the entitled advocate seeking a way through the co-nundrums of subaltern speechlessness.

Conclusion: A *Kairos* for Theology

This essay's exploration of subalternity and advocacy, culminating in a proposal of suggested modes of authentic advocacy, needs no lengthy conclusion. Any theologians with an interest in representing the subaltern (the marginal, the oppressed, the poor) will need to wrestle with the challenges posed by the subaltern who "cannot speak" (Spivak) and the challenge of subaltern speech-lessness itself. In so doing, theologians face a crisis encountered by any scholar of the subaltern, and liberation theologians, operating under their mandate and desire of listening to the poor, may face it more acutely than other theo-logians. The foregoing discussion of the problem of subaltern speechlessness was one attempt to understand that crisis.

A *kairos*, though, is more than just crisis. It is also an opportunity for transformation. For theology in the present, there is a distinct opportunity offered in the notion of the subaltern, unlocking as it does the advantages of unmasking ludic postmodernism and of rendering more complex liberation theologians' notion of the poor. If theologians also can receive the crisis of subaltern speechlessness as one that propels them toward a more authentic advocacy, then in this, too, is opportunity for transformation.

Of obvious concern to theologians, perhaps, is the fourth mode of authen-tic advocacy: the embrace of delirium and mystery. In this is a properly mystical dimension arising along the way of a search for authentic advocacy in political struggle with and for subaltern peoples. It is a dimension to which Christian liberation theologians would do well to attend more fully. The further questions for theology are many. What might be the relations between Christian under-standings of symbols like God, Jesus the Christ, Holy Spirit, and church to precisely *this* experience of the sacred? What is their relation to *this* encounter with the others who are the subaltern who often cannot speak?

Theologians might return to Derrida to clarify this other who is met in the state of delirium of subaltern studies. The other we meet in the dimension of delirium is not, in Derrida's words a "self-consolidating" other, but instead is, as he also says, the "quite other" (*tout-autre*).[50] This "quite other" is a very concrete and this-worldly mystery. It offers no license for easy theological talk about "the wholly other" or a "transcendent reality." It is, however, a region of mystery, an earthly locus of spirit, that invites reflection about the mythos that might enable us to encounter this "quite other" more profoundly and more surely.[51] Theologians might have a special future task in offering a mythos for the "quite other," the one(s) we meet in the delirium of finding our way forward in subaltern studies.

Outside Christian studies, we might wonder, as a final thought, if other traditions (religious or secular) might take up the task of reflecting on the dimension of delirium emergent when subalternity and advocacy are pondered together. Might there also be Maya, Iroquois, Muslim, Jewish, Buddhist, and other mythic modes of conceptualizing this kind of *tout-autre?* Is there a secular mythos that we might discern, enabling our journeying more deeply into understanding the delirium of subaltern studies? Beverley's proposal of some shared interests between secular studies and liberation theology, as noted in this essay's epigraph, suggests that those secular studies might find points of common concern with theology in that exercise where both together probe the deep places of their discourses and take on the complex challenges posed by listening to the poor.

If subaltern studies and advocacy entail a mystical dimension, as I have suggested they do, and if Beverley is correct about the likeness of subaltern studies and liberation theology, then the future may hold the promise of a multifaith dialogue about the challenges of subaltern studies, a dialogue that also fruitfully transgresses the boundaries of the secular and religious divide.

NOTES

1. Gayatri Chakravorty Spivak, *In Other Worlds: Essays in Cultural Politics* (New York: Routledge, 1988), 218. Spivak was born and educated (until the time of her doctoral studies) in India. She has been a distinguished visiting professor at institutions through the world and currently is at Columbia University. This book is on cultural theory, analyzing relationships between language, women, and culture in both Western and non-Western contexts.

2. Guha defines the notion of the subaltern as "a name for the general attribute of subordination . . . whether this is expressed in terms of class, caste, age, gender and office or in any other way." See Ranajit Guha, "Preface," in Ranajit Guha and Gayatri Spivak, *Selected Studies in Subaltern Studies* (New York: Oxford University Press, 1988), 35.

3. I first developed several of the thoughts on this topic in lectures at Ewha Womans University and am grateful to its community of scholars and students for offering critical and supportive dialogue at that time. See "The Postmodern Era in the Trilateral North," part 3, the 2d Distinguished University Lectures, Ewha Womans University, Seoul, Korea, May 26, 1992.

4. Gayatri Chakravorty Spivak, "Can the Subaltern Speak?" in *Marxism and the Interpretation of Culture,* ed. Cary Nelson and Lawrence Grossberg (Urbana: University of Illinois Press, 1988), 292.

5. For a critique of Spivak and poststructuralists along these lines, see Neil Larsen, "Postmodernism and Imperialism: Theory and Politics in Latin America," in *The Postmodernism Debate in Latin America*, ed. John Beverley, José Oviedo, and Michael Aronna (Durham: Duke University Press, 1995), 121.

6. Ihab Hassan, *The Postmodern Turn: Essays in Postmodern Theory and Culture* (Columbus: Ohio State University Press, 1987), 85ff.

7. David Harvey, *The Condition of Postmodernity: An Enquiry into the Origins of Cultural Change* (Oxford: Blackwell, 1989). Harvey argues persuasively, I think, that the conditions that generate what I call postmodernist discourse are in fact not best named postmodernity, but in fact, modernity in its most recent form, i.e., in a "post-Fordist" phase of capitalism using a new mode of more "flexible" accumulation of capital. On "Fordism" and "post-Fordism," see also Alain Lipietz, *Mirages and Miracles: The Crises of Global Fordism*, trans. David Macey (New York: Verso, 1987).

8. In addition to Harvey, see Beverley, Oviedo, and Aronna, *Postmodern Debate in Latin America*; Michael Hardt and Antonio Negri, *Empire* (Cambridge: Harvard University Press, 2000); and Fredric Jameson, *Postmodernism; or, The Cultural Logic of Late Capitalism* (Durham: Duke University Press, 1991).

9. Hal Foster, *The Anti-Aesthetic: Essays on Postmodern Culture* (Port Townsend, Wash.: Bay Press, 1983), 16–30, 31–42.

10. Mark C. Taylor, *Erring: Postmodern A/theology* (Chicago: University of Chicago Press, 1984), 112–13.

11. Linda J. Nicholson, "Introduction," in *Feminism/Postmodernism*, ed. Linda J. Nicholson (New York: Routledge, 1990), 1–16.

12. Lorraine Code, "Is the Sex of the Knower Epistemologically Significant," in Code's *What Can She Know? Feminist Theory and the Construction of Knowledge* (New York: Routledge, 1991), 1–26.

13. John Beverley and Marc Zimmerman, *Literature and Politics in the Central American Revolutions* (Austin: University of Texas Press, 1990), xii.

14. Manuel Castells, *The Rise of the Network Society*, vol. 1 of *The Information Age: Economy, Society and Culture*, 2d ed. (London: Blackwell, 2000), 448.

15. Hardt and Negri, *Empire*, 38, 138–39, 150; and on U.S. hegemony anchoring the transnational sovereignty, 309.

16. Susan Bordo, "Feminism, Postmodernism and Gender-Scepticism," in *Feminism/Postmodernism*, ed. Linda J. Nicholson (New York: Routledge, 1990), 151.

17. On this dynamic operative in postmodern critiques of indigenous "Maya" identities, see June C. Nash, *Mayan Visions: The Quest for Autonomy in an Age of Globalization* (New York: Routledge, 2000), 17–20, 261 n. 16.

18. I have argued elsewhere that in politically conscious vodou cultures of resistance in Haiti, one can see how an explicit commitment to liberation from slavery facilitated a polyform mode of play and differentiation that rivals what most ludic postmodernism in hegemonic Western powers today could only dream of. See Mark Taylor, "Vodou Resistance/Vodou Hope: Forging a Postmodernism that Liberates," in *Liberation Theologies, Postmodernity, and the Americas*, ed. David Batstone, Eduardo Mendieta, Lois Ann Lorentzen, and Dwight N. Hopkins (New York: Routledge, 1997), 169–87.

19. Martin Hopenhayn, "Postmodernism and Neoliberalism in Latin America," in *The Postmodernism Debate in Latin America*, ed. John Beverley, José Oviedo, and Michael Aronna (Durham: Duke University Press, 1995), 100 (emphasis added).

20. Nancy Scheper-Hughes, *Death without Weeping: The Violence of Everyday Life in Brazil* (Berkeley: University of California Press, 1999), 480–83.

21. Ibid., 495.

22. Jacques Derrida, *Specters of Marx: The State of the Debt, the Work of Mourning, and the New International* (New York: Routledge, 1994).

23. Michel Foucault, "Space, Knowledge and Power," in *The Foucault Reader*, ed. Paul Rabinow, trans. Christian Hubert (New York: Pantheon, 1984), 245.

24. Hopenhayn, "Postmodernism and Neoliberalism in Latin America," 99.

25. John Beverley devotes an entire chapter to the question of whether subaltern identities are binary or hybrid. See Beverley, *Subalternity and Representation: Arguments in Cultural Theory* (Durham: Duke University Press, 1999), 87–113.

26. Paul Farmer, *Infections and Inequalities: The Modern Plagues*, updated edition (Berkeley: University of California Press, 2000), 7, 82, 85, 95.

27. Mark Taylor, "The Postmodern Era in the Trilateral North," part 1: The Distinguished University Lectures, Ewha Woman's University, Seoul, Korea, May 24, 1992.

28. Beverley, *Subalternity and Representation*, 14, 34, 71.

29. For two critiques of the problematic reference to the poor in Latin American liberation theology, see Elina Vuola, *The Limits of Liberation: The Theology and Ethics of Reproduction* (London: Sheffield Academic Press, 2002); and Arthur C. McGovern, *Liberation Theology and Its Critics: Toward an Assessment* (Maryknoll, N.Y.: Orbis, 1993), 227–33.

30. Ranajit Guha, ed., *Subaltern Studies*, vol. 1: *Writings on South Asian History and Society* (Delhi: Oxford University Press, 1984), 8.

31. John Beverley, "The Im/possibility of Politics: Subalternity, Modernity, Hegemony," in *The Latin American Subaltern Studies Reader*, ed. Ileana Rodriguez (Durham: Duke University Press, 2001), 55.

32. James Cockcroft, *Mexico's Hope: An Encounter with Politics and History* (New York: Monthly Review Press, 1998), 368–69.

33. Ibid., 282–3, 318; Cynthia Enloe, *Bananas, Beaches, and Bases: Making Feminist Sense of International Politics* (Berkeley: University of California Press, 1990); cf. Annette Fuentes and Barbara Ehrenreich, *Women in the Global Factory* (Boston: South End Press, 1991).

34. Spivak, "Can the Subaltern Speak?" 298–99.

35. Ibid., 297.

36. On the "triple curse" that often befalls the destitute poor through scientific study and which starts with "objectification" before moving on to "institutionalized powerlessness" and then "blame for their own condition," see Farmer, *Infections and Inequalities*, 84.

37. Beverley, *Subalternity and Representation*, 71. About his entire book, Beverley writes, "I began this book with the question of the relation of the subaltern to the university as a knowledge center, because I believed that the project of subaltern studies was not just a question or representing (again, in the double sense of both 'speak-

ing about' and 'speaking for') the subaltern, *but of understanding how our own work in the academy functions actively to make or unmake subalternity"* (166, emphasis added).

38. Ibid., 30.

39. Ibid., 2 (emphasis in original).

40. For development of this notion of fluidity in relation to "Gringa positioning" and "vulnerable bodies" in Central America, see Diane M. Nelson, *A Finger in the Wound: Body Politics in Quincentennial Guatemala* (Berkeley: University of California Press, 1999), 41–73, 367.

41. On U.S. political prisoners, see Ward Churchill and J. J. Vander Wall, *Cages of Steel: The Politics of Imprisonment in the United States* (Washington, D.C.: Maisonneuve, 1992).

42. Richard Jolly, *The Human Development Report, 1998* (New York: Oxford University Press, 1998), 2.

43. Amnesty International, *United States of America: Rights for All* (London: Amnesty International, 1998).

44. For discussion of how the powers *and* very identities of entitled persons are often of this character and draw their power *from* dominance of the poor, see the chapter on white supremacism in Derrick Bell, *Faces at the Bottom of the Well: The Permanence of Racism* (New York: Basic Books, 1992); and Hardt and Negri, *Empire*.

45. Gustavo Gutiérrez, informal panel presentation at the American Academy of Religion, Annual Meeting, The Palmer House, Chicago, Illinois, November 21, 1989.

46. Jacques Derrida, "Of an Apocalyptic Tone Recently Adopted in Philosophy," trans. John P. Leavy Jr. in *Semia*, 71, cited from Spivak, "Can the Subaltern Speak?," 294.

47. Spivak, "Can the Subaltern Speak?" 294.

48. On this structural issue in subaltern studies, see John Beverley, "Hybrid or Binary? On the Category of 'the People' in Subaltern and Cultural Studies," in Beverley's *Subalternity and Representation*, 85–113.

49. Scheper-Hughes, *Death without Weeping*, 28. On the same page, Scheper-Hughes shares further insight on the problem discussed in this essay as subaltern speechlessness: "I grow weary of these postmodernist critiques, and given the perilous times in which we and our subjects live, I am inclined toward a compromise that calls for the practice of a 'good enough' ethnography. The anthropologist is an instrument of cultural translation that is necessarily flawed and biased. We cannot rid ourselves of the cultural self we bring with us into the field any more than we can disown the eyes, ears, and skin through which we take in our intuitive perceptions about the new and strange world we have entered. Nonetheless, like every other master artisan (and I dare say that at our best we are this), we struggle to do the best we can with the limited resources we have at hand—our ability to listen and observe carefully, empathetically and compassionately."

50. Derrida, "Of an Apocalyptic Tone Recently Adopted in Philosophy," 71, cited from Spivak, "Can the Subaltern Speak?," 294.

51. On the contribution of mythic discourse to concrete struggles for liberation, see my "The Need for Empowering Mythos," in Mark Kline Taylor, *Remembering Esperanza: A Cultural-Political Theology for North American Praxis* (Maryknoll, N.Y.: Orbis, 1990), 162–70.

2

On (Re)Centering the Margins: A Euro-African Perspective on the Option for the Poor

David N. Field

As we enter the twenty-first century, tectonic movements are taking place within Christianity as the numerical center of Christianity shifts from the countries of the North Atlantic Rim to the countries of the South. A significant contribution to this shift has been the dramatic growth of Christianity in sub-Saharan Africa. Christianity has become, in the words of Kwame Bediako, a "non-western religion."[1] More particularly it has become "the religion of the poor of the earth."[2] The consequences of the coming earthquake on the shape of future Christianity is not clear, yet the rumbles of the earthquake have already been felt in the rise of Third World theologies. Their contexts of poverty and powerlessness gave rise to their most significant contribution to a reconfigured Christianity, the affirmation of God's preferential option for the poor.

More generally it is widely held that we live in a time of global sociocultural change. Modernity, understood as the sociocultural order that has dominated the North Atlantic Rim and through its hegemony has affected the rest of the world since the Enlightenment, is in crisis. Out of this crisis has emerged a plethora of new ideas, cultural expressions, social conditions, new technologies, and experiences of life that have in various ways been conceptualized as postmodern.

Yet for the vast majority of Africans nothing has changed, or if it has changed it has changed for the worse. Wars continue to ravage our continent.[3] Poverty is increasing.[4] Two and a half million people are living with HIV/AIDS—thousands die each day[5]—while curable diseases such as tuberculosis and malaria kill hundreds of thousands more. Large segments of the population still do not have access to basic healthcare, clean water, and sanitation.[6] Corruption, inefficiency, and political intolerance plague many nations. Africa's share of the world economy continues to decrease.[7] Many of the new technological developments have left Africa behind—the majority of people do not have access to a telephone, let alone to a computer or the internet.[8] Within Africa itself there are substantial differences of wealth and power. The dominant economy, South Africa, contributes over a third of the GNP of sub-Saharan Africa. Within African countries, including South Africa, there are vast discrepancies between the relatively small economic and political elite and the masses.

Interpreting the Postmodern World

The continuing struggle of Africa and the emergence of postmodernities are not separate phenomena. They must both be understood in relation to the changes that have taken place in the global economic structures and relationships since the middle of the twentieth century. A sociocultural matrix always exists in dynamic interrelationship with the economy. Sociocultural changes are facilitated, made possible, and shaped by socioeconomic transformations; yet such changes in turn contribute to economic transformations. The contemporary economic changes are best understood as a complex of interrelated developments.

The first is the emergence of post-Fordist capitalism with its emphasis on flexibility, variety, and dynamism in relation to labor processes, products, and markets. One of the significant dimensions of post-Fordism is the centrality of consumption, the consumer as the focus of economic activity. Products are made with built-in obsolescence, rapid changes of design and fashions are emphasized, and demand is created through advertising. Consumerism and the increasing dominance of the market have led to the accelerating commodification of all dimensions of North Atlantic societies. Culture, religion, medicine, education, the academy, the news media have been turned into commodities to be shaped and reshaped by consumer demand. Whereas earlier capitalism was energized by the interrelationship of labor and capital, today the consumer has not only been added to this central dynamic but is given central significance through the new focus on the creation of desire and need. Thus, for example, "Michael Jackson earns as much for promoting Nike shoes as approximately 18,000 Indonesian workers who make these shoes."[9] Central elements of postmodernity, such as the emergence of multiple identities through changing and undetermined choices; experience as depthless, episodic, and ephemeral; the emphasis on heterogeneity, fragmentation, and difference; the centrality of pursuit of pleasure: and the focus on the aesthetic are all related to emergence of consumer capitalism. David Lyon thus argues that "the postmodern splits away from the modern when the production of de-mand—of consumers—becomes central."[10]

Second, the post-Fordist emphasis on flexibility has fed growing domi-nance of transnational companies who produce and market the consumer goods. They have assumed a new role as "a global aristocracy"[11] who are in the process of assuming supremacy but have not quite replaced the old aristocracy, the major industrialized nations. As Oswaldo de Rivero notes:

> Today 38,000 transnational corporations and their branches
> conduct two-thirds of the world's trade, and the combined sales of
> the eighty-six most powerful enterprises are larger than the exports
> of all the nation states that make up the international community.
> Only the exports of the nine most industrialised powers—the United
> States, Germany, Japan, France, Britain, Italy, Canada, Holland, and
> Belgium—exceed the sales of Shell, Exxon, General Motors, Toyota,
> Ford, Mitsubishi, Mitsui, Nissho Iwai, Sumimoto, Itoch Maruban,
> and Hitachi, the . . . most powerful transnational corporations.[12]

The policies and practices of these transnational companies decisively influ-ence the economies of nations and, hence, shape the culture and determine their well-being, as those companies decide "where, what, how, and for whom to produce."[13] They select the countries for investment based on the maximiz-ing of profit and not on the political, social, or environmental well-being of the countries concerned. Yet, as trade, development, and economic growth are virtually impossible without them, nations, particularly poor ones, are forced to shape their socioeconomic policies and laws in accordance with corporate demands rather than in accordance with the interests of their own people. The type of relationship with countries, and the level and nature of investments in them, will depend on their particular potential for maximizing profit. Manu-facturing that is labor intensive and potentially polluting will be situated in countries where there is cheap labor and limited or nonexistent labor and environmental legislation. Raw materials will be sourced where they are cheap and easily available, even if this means cooperating with oppressive regimes, rebels, and warlords.

The emergence of transnational capitalism has not diminished the cen-trality of North America, Europe, and Japan in the global economy. They still provide the major focus of transnational investment, as a consequence of their political stability, the wealth and numbers of their consumers, the availability of an educated and technically competent workforce, their superior levels of technological development, the strength of their financial systems, and the availability of investment capital. Many companies that originated in the Third World migrate to these centers once they have achieved transnational status, seeking primary listings on the London or New York stock exchanges. The result of this is a symbiotic relationship between the highly industrialized nations and the transnational companies. The powerful nations need the transnationals to maintain their position of dominance; hence, they shape their social, economic, foreign, and military policies in order to foster their well-being. The transnationals require the social and political environment that the powerful nations provide and, hence, will act to enhance that environment. The pursuit of profit requires expansion beyond the confines of these nations; thus a component of the activity of transnational companies is the fostering of the development of a consumer class within other nations where such investment contributes to the maximizing of profits. Hence, within many Third World nations is a political and economic elite who function as clients of the transnational corporations. The dominance of transnational companies is protected and enhanced by the policies and activities of the World Bank, the International Monetary Fund, and the World Trade Organization.

The transnationalizing of capitalism has contributed not only to the dominance of consumerism but also to the rise of a new pluralism and multiculturalism. The emphasis on the maximizing of profits demands the use of technical and management experts, regardless of ethnicity, nationality, race, gender, or sexual orientation. In turn, educated members of Third World elites have migrated to the North in search of employment and a superior lifestyle. Managers and technical experts from the North are sent to diverse locations to oversee parts of the transnational empires. Examples of economic success in different parts of the world become models for organizational development and management practice. The result is a greater awareness of and respect for diversity and otherness, as long as the diversity and otherness contributes to the maximizing of profits.

Third, while profits are maximized for the investors in the transnationals, in many cases these investors are anonymous and constantly changing. This is a consequence of a shift in patterns of ownership from individual investments to a variety of forms of managed investments. These changing patterns of ownership have been accompanied by the growth of financial markets and the development of computer and communications technology. In the financial markets, huge profits are made and lost through trade in currencies, bonds, and other financial instruments. Trade in both stocks and financial instruments is in the hands an elite group of fund mangers, brokers, and investment bankers who manage investments on behalf of others. This elite group moves money around the world at the touch of a computer keyboard, buying and selling with the aim of maximizing profit for investors and thus securing their own financial rewards. In the fast-changing markets, rumor, speculation, and sentiment are as important driving forces as economic fundamentals. The economic future of a distant country can be enhanced or destroyed at the touch of a button, on the basis of a rumor, for the benefit of people who will never even visit it. While the control of capital is in the hands of this select group, the ownership of capital has been democratized in the North Atlantic Rim. There are still extremely wealthy individual and institutional investors, but middle-class people have become significant investors in the stock and financial markets. Most of their investments take the form of managed investments such as mutual funds, insurance policies, and pension funds. While the owners of capital benefit (or suffer) from the consequences of the investments, they do not control them.

These developments in the global economy require us to reconceptualize relations of domination and exploitation. Simple binary oppositions between the oppressor and the oppressed, the exploiter and the exploited, the perpetrator and the victim, are inadequate constructs. Two other categories need to be added. First are the beneficiaries: consumers and investors who have no direct agency in the suffering of others that arises out of the production of their consumer goods, the behavior of the transnationals in which they have unknowingly invested, or the strategies of their investment managers. Yet they benefit from the exploitation and marginalization of others. Second are the abandoned: the people from areas deemed not worthy of investment. In such places transnationals extract resources using local warlords and rebels or a small group of expatriate workers, but have no interest in the local economy. This category also includes those who have lost jobs, education, medical care, and social benefits as a consequence of trade liberalization and World Bank–sponsored Structural Adjustment Programs. In a world of constantly changing relations, people exist in diverse and complex relations of exploitation, oppression, beneficiation, and abandonment, with the same person often relating in more than one way to others.

Returning to where we began, the shifts in the global economic systems that gave rise to postmodernity in the societies of those who benefit from them have led to the increasing exploitation, suffering, and marginalization of other people, particularly in Africa. In many cases the masses are oppressed and exploited directly or indirectly by local bourgeoisie, as well as by the dynamics of globalizing capitalism. Marginalized and exploited by modernity, Africans are now exploited, marginalized, and abandoned by postmodernity, despite its proclaimed intent of creating space for the other. This increasing marginalization of Africa and the suffering of its people in the context of globalizing capitalism raise significant challenges to our understanding of both postmodernity and the preferential option for the poor.

These challenges are multidimensional and context specific. The challenges experienced by the poor and marginalized African are quite different than those posed to members of the African elite or residents of the North Atlantic Rim. Hence, this essay adopts a specific stance and audience. The sociocultural stance from which the issue will be addressed is one that I designate Euro-African, that is, one characterized by the hybridity of one who is a descendent of the European colonizers of South Africa, whose cultural heritage has been decisively influenced by Europe, but who has deep roots in Africa, shares its pain, and is committed to its rebirth.[14] Such a stance is one of resistance to the colonizing and apartheid heritage, combined with a recognition of one's complicity with them and of one's position within the African elite as a consequence of such complicity. It is postcolonial and postapartheid in its commitment to the agency of the subjugated and marginalized subject, its resistance to the domination of the powerful, and its rejection of the hegemonic North Atlantic representations of the people of the South. Yet it recognizes that the conflict between the colonizer and the colonized, the North and the South, is internalized within one's self.[15] It is my contention that the particularity of this stance with its fracture between the colonizer and the colonized and its sense of straddling the fault line between Europe and Africa provides a significant location for a critique of the dominant theologies.[16] Thus the focus of this reflection is the significance of the option for the poor for the theology of the Third World bourgeoisie and that of the North Atlantic Rim in a postmodern and postcolonial context.

Postmodernity, God, and the Margins

> God always takes his stand unconditionally and passionately on this side and on this side alone against the lofty and on behalf of the lowly; against those who already enjoy right and privilege and on behalf of those are denied it and deprived of it.[17]

During the 1970s, theologies of liberation interrupted the placid normality of North Atlantic bourgeois theology. Radical theologians of the North Atlantic Rim were soon echoing liberation themes. Yet their popularity has waned as the consumers of radical theology have switched to the latest brands of postmodern theology. The preferential option for the poor has been replaced by a call for the rejection of all metanarratives. This move, it is claimed, leads to the decentering of the Western bourgeois subject and a radical openness to the other. Yet, as we have argued, postmodernities are the expressions of globalizing capitalism and thus an expression of the cultural shift that is taking place in the North Atlantic Rim and other centers of transnational capitalism. Thus the postmodern turn in theology continues to reflect the interests and context of the North Atlantic middle class. The majority of the world's population does not live in a context in which any form of postmodernity provides the primary conceptual framework. The very openness to the other claimed by postmodernity arises from an economic system that continues to exploit, marginalize, and abandon the poor and the vulnerable. Far from diminishing the significance of the option for the poor, the exploitative dimensions of postmodernity require its reassertion.

The preferential option for the poor has come to mean a lot of things, including an agenda for the church, a commitment to an alternative lifestyle, a hermeneutical strategy, a political stance, and an understanding of the gospel message.[18] But fundamentally it is a statement about the identity and purpose of God. The God who is revealed in the Exodus complex and in Jesus Christ is "in a special way the God of the destitute, the poor, and the wronged."[19] This God is sensitive to the cries of the oppressed and marginalized and responds to them. While this understanding has been a significant component of the traditional Christian interpretation of God's justice, liberation theologies have brought it to the center of theological reflection. This has led to the recognition that what defines authentic deity is not possession of certain incommunicable attributes but a commitment to justice for the poor and the marginalized. This understanding is powerfully expressed in Psalm 82's dramatic portrait of the right-sizing of the divine council, leading to the firing of gods who failed to take the side of the poor and oppressed. Hence, the preferential option for the poor "deals with nothing less than the heart of the Christian faith in and confession of God."[20]

The affirmation of God's preferential option for the poor entails not only that God's justice is characterized by a partiality toward the marginalized, but also that God works from the margins of the dominant sociocultural matrix, choosing to use the subjugated and the excluded as salvific agents. The biblical narratives are replete with examples of God's choosing the excluded, the victims, the underlings, the poor, the insignificant persons, and the oppressed.[21] In the patriarchal narratives God regularly defies the social conventions to choose a younger brother. In the Exodus Yahweh chooses "a rabble of slaves"[22] to become the instruments for bringing blessing to the world. Throughout its history, Israel remains a small and relatively insignificant nation. Yet the prophets have the audacity to proclaim, even after defeat and exile, that Yahweh orchestrates the history of other nations in relation to the covenant with Israel and, further, that Israel is central to God's redemptive purpose for all nations. This would be merely a case of national chauvinism if it were not for the prophets' withering critique of their own nation, their sensitivity to suffering, and their passion for justice that extends beyond Israel. The New Testament continues this emphasis with its critique of wealth and power, its affirmation that the gospel is good news to the poor, and its confession that the church, composed primarily of people from the underclasses, is the prime locus of God's redemptive action.

The centrality of this dynamic of God's choosing the margins is affirmed in the confession that in an "irruption smelling of the stable"[23] God became human in the backwaters of the Roman Empire. This poor carpenter was not only a member of a defeated and colonized nation but came from Galilee, an area despised by his fellow Jews. At the commencement of his ministry, Jesus abandoned the relative security of his trade and joined the landless poor; in so doing he "became an outcast by choice."[24] He rebuked the religious elite for their exclusionary and oppressive ideologies and praxis. He called on the wealthy to sacrifice their wealth for the good of the poor, proclaiming: "It is easier for a camel to go through the eye of the needle than for someone who is rich to enter the kingdom of God" (Mark 10:25). He denounced the pursuit of power, stating: "Whoever wants to be first, he must be the last of all and the servant of all" (9:35). Jesus' identification with the marginalized and oppressed culminated in his unjust trial and crucifixion as a traitor and criminal outside the gates of Jerusalem, abandoned by God and humanity. In Jesus, God has entered the world of the poor, the abandoned, and the colonized, identifying with their powerlessness, victimization, and suffering. In doing so God "transforms their situation into the privileged locus for the transformation of the world."[25]

The incarnation must radically transform our understanding of the economic, political, and social dynamics of global society. This goes beyond the postmodern affirmation of otherness and even the postcolonial affirmation of the agency of the suffering subjugated subject. It affirms that the theological significance of both arises out of the prior redemptive grace of God that reconfigures our conceptualization of centers and margins and the relationships between them. In the words of Frank Chikane: "We need to understand that to God the bottom is the top and the top is the bottom. We must learn to start from the bottom."[26] Thus, from a theological perspective, the center of any sociocultural matrix is not to be found in its citadels of political and economic power but in the communities of those it exploits, subjugates, abandons, and victimizes. These communities are the focus God's concern and the centers of God's redemptive action.

Hence, the center of the postmodern global village is not to be found among the excesses of the Northern consumer societies nor in the affluence of the Third World bourgeoisie. Rather it is to be found . . .

- among those whose economies have been destroyed by fund managers speculating on their currency
- among those who cannot afford life-sustaining and life-saving drugs because of the excessive prices charged by pharmaceutical companies in their pursuit of maximum profits
- in the countries that are being ravaged by wars fueled by a demand for oil, diamonds, and other minerals
- among those who suffer under the rule of oppressive and corrupt governments
- among those who have been retrenched when companies are downsized or closed as a consequence of trade liberalization
- among those who endure a hand-to-mouth existence in order to produce consumer goods for the Northern markets

- among those whose schools and hospitals have closed down as a result of World Bank–imposed Structural Adjustment Programs

The centers of social, political, and economic power must thus be decentered and the margins recentered as the primary locus of theological reflection. An orientation to the other is not sufficient; it must be an orientation to the exploited, suffering, and subjugated or abandoned other. Theologies that ignore the option for the poor in favor of a more general orientation to otherness or that in other ways implicitly support the exploitative interests of the postmodern middle class must be understood for what they are—special-interest theologies. Such theologies are irrelevant to the lives of the vast majority of Christians. More profoundly Jean-Marc Éla asks: "Doesn't 'theo-ology' actually fail to speak about the God of the poor by shutting itself up in a universe of the culture of the rich and the powerful?"[27]

The Poor, the Excluded, and the Other

> No Person may unfairly discriminate directly or indirectly against anyone on one or more grounds . . . including race, gender, sex, pregnancy, marital status, ethnic or social origin, colour, sexual orientation, age, disability, religion, conscience, belief, culture language and birth.[28]

The debates between Latin American, black, and feminist theologies in the 1970s and 1980s demonstrated that there is no one categorization of the excluded, subjugated, and victimized. Yet in all these debates the option for the poor defined and described the marginalized groups in relation to an "ethicopolitical norm,"[29] focused on issues of class, race, and gender. The processes of globalization, the aftermath of the Cold War, and the growing awareness of cultural pluralism have brought a greater recognition of the complex conflictual dynamics within human society. Postcolonial African societies have been forced to grapple with tensions and conflicts arising from diverse factors, including, ethnicity, religion, race, modernization, gender, and the rural/urban divide. Most of these divisions were reinforced or even created by colonialism,[30] yet they cannot be reduced to a binary opposition between the oppressors and the oppressed. Hence, we are constrained to pose the question as to whether the postmodern discourse on otherness and difference provides a more adequate tool for analyzing them.

However, Africans have good reason to be wary of a discourse of otherness. Western history is full of occasions when Africa and its people have functioned as the archetypal other against which Europeans have defined themselves. Africa was uncivilized, Europe was civilized; Africa was pagan, Europe was Christian; Africa was black, Europe was white; and so on. This archetypal otherness has negated African identity and has been an integral component of the colonial subjugation of African people through policies of enslavement, assimilation, discriminatory objectification, genocide, or some combination of these.[31] The archetype continues to function in the postmodern commodification of "African culture" and wildlife for the foreign tourist[32] and in the objectification of Africa as "barbaric," expressed through the hyperreal images of violence and chaos conveyed by the transnational news media. The distorting dimension of the latter functions in three other ways. First, it obscures the complicity of the North Atlantic Rim in Africa's suffering.[33] Second, it neglects the achievements of many Africans in the face of incredible hardship. Third, African conflicts gain major international media attention only when they have an impact on the descendents of the European colonists or on North Atlantic interests.[34]

This archetypal otherness was powerfully expressed in South African apartheid laws that sought to maintain white hegemony not only by dividing whites and blacks, but by further dividing blacks into separate ethnic identities. The ideological and theological justification of apartheid in South Africa was premised on a strong notion of otherness. Affirming that differentiation was God's normative order for creation, apartheid theologians argued that racial integration would lead to assimilation and, hence, was antinormative. It was thus argued that this necessitated the creation of social structures appropriate to the particularities of each ethnic group in order to maintain their own identity.[35] The reality of apartheid, however, lay not in respect for the other, but in massive social engineering, deprivation, and death.[36] The discourse of otherness and difference is not necessarily liberative; it can be oppressive and even genocidal.

However, the destructive and oppressive potential of the discourse of otherness must not be allowed to obscure its potential for deepening and broadening the conceptualization of the option for the margins. The interfacing of the postmodern emphasis on difference and otherness with the various liberation theologies' emphasis on the option for the oppressed raises the possibility of a more inclusive and complex interpretation of the margins. Such an interpretation will enable theologies of liberation to transcend their ethicopolitical concentration and a simple binary opposition between the oppressors and the oppressed, thus creating space for theological reflection on exclusion and otherness.

This leads to a new awareness that the biblical witness provides a diverse and complex portrayal of the dynamics of God's option for the excluded that cannot be comprehended within a sociopolitical categorization of the option for the poor. In the Exodus narratives, early Israel is portrayed as "a mixed crowd" (Exodus 12:38) whose membership was open to those who were not descendents of the patriarchs and matriarchs on condition that they were circumcised (Exodus 12:43–49; cf. Deuteronomy 29:10–15). Yahweh reacts strongly against the questioning of Moses' leadership on the basis of his marriage to a Cushite (Numbers 12). Yet this hospitality toward the other is contested as Israel struggles to work out what it means to be the people of the God of the Exodus. Deuteronomy, while keeping a strong emphasis on the poor, places restrictions on membership in the assembly of Yahweh in terms of physical mutilation, birth from an "illicit union" (probably incest), and ethnicity (Deuteronomy 23:1–8). Ezra and Nehemiah in their attempt to maintain Israel's identity as the covenant people in a hostile world act vigorously to root out the exploitation of the poor. Yet they are equally vigorous in enforcing the exclusion of non-Israelites from the community (Ezra 9–10; Nehemiah 5; 13). In contrast to this is a dynamic of welcoming the other. Amos describes Yahweh's work in the history of non-Israelite nations as parallel to Yahweh's action in Israel's history (Amos 9:7). Ruth describes the welcoming of a Moabite woman who becomes the ancestor of David. Jonah engages in a polemic against exclusivism with its portrait not only of Yahweh's accepting the repentance of the oppressive Ninevites but with its declaration that this is characteristic of Yahweh (Jonah 4:2). Interestingly, the Ninevites in their repentance use the generic term God (*Elohim*) rather than Yahweh. Some of the prophets anticipated a future welcoming of the Gentiles. Isaiah 19 hopes for a day when Assyria and Egypt will together with Israel be the people of God through whom the earth will be blessed. Yet they are not portrayed as being absorbed into Israel. Isaiah 56:1–8, in direct contrast to Deuteronomy, Ezra, and Nehemiah, looks forward to the presence within the worshiping community of eunuchs and foreigners who keep the Sabbath and the covenant.[37]

This unresolved tension between a welcoming and an excluding understanding of the people of God provides the context for the ministry of Jesus. In a radical interpretation of the emphasis on hospitality for the other, Jesus not only identified with the poor but also welcomed all who would repent and accept the good news of God's reign, including the poor, women, sinners, prostitutes, Gentiles, Samaritans, and tax collectors. The ethicopolitical paradigm of the option for the margins cannot comprehend this praxis, particularly with its inclusion of the tax collectors and Roman soldiers. While Jesus firmly maintained a preference for the victims of the political and economic system, this very commitment made it possible for him to include in the community of God's reign those who had been excluded from the people of God for other reasons. The early church, like postexilic Israel, continued to struggle with the dynamics of inclusion and exclusion. The Acts narrative describes the Spirit-directed inclusion of the Samaritans, an African eunuch, and the Gentiles. This inclusion rejects the division of creation into clean and unclean categories and the assumption that Gentiles must assume a Jewish cultural identity in order to be accepted by God. Paul affirms God's commitment to the poor, yet the emphasis of his ministry and theology falls on the welcoming of Gentiles into the new covenant people of God.[38] In his emphasis on inclusion he respects otherness, refusing to impose Jewish rituals on Gentiles and becoming as a Jew to the Jews and as a Greek to the Greeks. Yet his writings bear evidence of the struggle to work out what this inclusivity means in relation to the status of women and slaves.

This dynamic of welcoming the other is, however, not to be understood as a mere openness to difference. In the ministry of Jesus, inclusion takes diverse forms. It includes the rejection of all illegitimate divisions based on ritual purity; the healing and restoration of those whose lives had been distorted by powers of evil, by sickness, and by sin; the conversion of those who were involved in exploiting and oppressing others; and the repentance and transformation of all (including the victims) who would follow Jesus.[39] Paul's theology of inclusion rejects the demand that Gentiles deny their ethnic heritage and be assimilated into Judaism; yet it is based on union with Christ that transforms the ethical behavior of the Gentile converts. Thus, while the excluded are not defined by an ethicopolitical norm and cultural assimilation is rejected, the welcoming dynamic is not amoral. It demands a religio-ethical transformation in accordance with the irruption of the God's reign in Jesus among the excluded.[40]

The interfacing of the welcoming dynamic within the biblical witness to the God who "works righteousness and justice for all who are oppressed" (Psalm 103:6) with the multidimensional and multileveled exclusionary dynamics of contemporary society gives greater nuance and complexity to theological reconfiguration of the center and the margins. God's option for the margins embraces a whole variety of people excluded by the hegemonic powers at work in society, including religious society. The embrace of the excluded is attained not by the widening of the boundaries and thus through cultural assimilation, but rather through the emergence of a new center, Jesus Christ, who is to be found among the diverse groups of the excluded. Theology takes place as Christians join Christ "outside the camp," sharing in his exclusion.

Desmond Tutu's theology, with its roots in African understandings of humanness and Anglo Catholic spirituality, provides a suggestive, though not unproblematic, example of firm emphasis on both God's option for the oppressed and God's welcome of the excluded.[41] Central to Tutu's theology was the affirmation of God's preferential option for the poor and the oppressed. Yet in the height of the apartheid repression he wrote to the then–prime minister of South Africa, B. J. Vorster, "as one human person to another human person" and "as one Christian to another."[42] He argued that they were united by their common creation in the divine image, their common redemption through Christ, their common sanctification by the Spirit, and their common baptism into the body of Christ. During the (sometimes violent) uprisings against apartheid in the 1980s Tutu not only spoke against the killing of people accused of being police informers but intervened, risking his own life, to save the lives such persons. In the late 1980s and the 1990s he invoked the image of the "Rainbow People" to portray an inclusiveness that respected difference.

Tutu further demonstrated this inclusiveness in his sometimes controversial chairing of South Africa's Truth and Reconciliation Commission.[43] It was the same welcoming dynamic that led him, against the dominant trends in many African cultures, to become an advocate of women's ordination and, more controversially, the full inclusion of gay and lesbian people within the life of the church and thus the affirmation of gay and lesbian partnerships as legitimate forms of Christian sexual behavior.[44]

Otherness, Resistance, and the Margins

African Christian Thought: See Protestant Theology: South Africa.[45]

Paradoxically the concentration on the ethical and political dimensions of the option for the margins contributed to the marginalization of significant voices from the underside within the dominant theological discourse. Despite the phenomenal growth of African Christianity, the voices of popular Christianity (in this case the African Initiated Churches) and of African theologies (with the exception of South African liberation theologies) have been marginalized even within the progressive North Atlantic theological discourse. The concerns for the traditional African deity, the ancestral spirits, healing, and similar issues were totally alien to the conceptual world of progressive Western theologians and appeared to have little sociopolitical significance. Third World theology was interesting to the North Atlantic theological consumer only if it addressed the latest political fashion. South African theology, with its ethicopolitical focus, resonated with the interests of progressive North Atlantic theologians in a way which theology from the rest of Africa did not.

African theologies have been subjected to dominant definitions of poverty and liberation—and found wanting. This judgment is exemplified in Jürgen Moltmann's assertion that while African and Asian theologies are important, they are not "liberating theologies of the oppressed."[46] While liberation from socioeconomic poverty has not been a significant theme for many African theologians outside of Southern Africa, it has not been ignored.[47] However, the emphasis on inculturation that has characterized African theologies arises out of alternative experiences and conceptualizations of poverty, resistance, and liberation. The rise and dominance of the North Atlantic Rim as a politico-economic center was directly related to the exploitation of Africa through the slave trade and colonialism.[48] The centuries of violent, oppressive, and exploitative encounters between Europe and Africa have created a situation of poverty that extends far beyond the socioeconomic. Societies were disrupted, people enslaved, cultures were altered and even destroyed, land was stolen, and a new way of life was imposed. Hence, African poverty entails far more than socioeconomic poverty; it is, as Bénézet Bujo proposes, "a total loss of identity and a total alienation, since it involves a denial of humanity to the human person, down to the cultural roots."[49] This anthropological poverty has a particular theological significance as a consequence of the role played by missionaries in the suppression of African cultures and the establishment of the North Atlantic hegemony over Africa.

Hence, the emphasis on inculturation that has characterized African theology is an act of resistance against the hegemony of the North Atlantic Rim. While the focus has often been on liberating "African Churches in their theology, worship and structures"[50] it has not been limited to this. The alienation that has characterized the church is a reflection of the alienation and poverty that characterizes African society. Thus African theologies have "aimed at liberating the African from forces that hinder him [or her] from living fully as a human being"[51] through the recovery of and dialogue with African culture, tradition, and religion.[52] These traditions provide an integrated and holistic vision of the fullness of life that ensues when the human community lives in dynamic harmony with God and the spiritual world, the other human members of the community, and the earth.[53] This encounter between African traditions and Christian theology has led to a critical retrieval, reinterpretation, and re-evaluation of both. While African academics have theorized about integrating Christianity with African traditions, the most creative expressions of it have happened without their help within the African Initiated Churches. While the African Initiated Churches and African theologies should not be idealized, as churches and theologies of the subjugated and marginalized their symbolic and ideational resistance to the hegemonic forces of modernity provides a significant corrective to dominant forms of Christianity both within and outside of Africa.[54]

This process of recovery and reinterpretation is of crucial significance in the postmodern world. Globalizing consumer capitalism increasingly dominates and influences the production of culture, contributing to a continuing process of destroying and assimilating African culture through the mass media. African theology is a praxis of resistance not only against the destructive forces of modernity but also against the destructive forces of postmodernity. Hence, the hidden, subjugated, and ignored voices of Africa provide significant resources for transcending the negative dimensions of (post)modernity in order to develop an authentically postmodern theology. Yet they must be heard in all their otherness—recognizing that their voices will not necessarily resonate with the latest cultural and ideological fashion in the North Atlantic Rim.

A respect for otherness is not a sufficient criterion for ethical judgment. African cultures, religions, and traditions are characterized by tensions, diversity, and change as they interact with each other, other cultures, and changing material and environmental conditions.[55] The process of rooting theology in the real lives of African people engaged in the struggle for life has brought a greater awareness of the ambiguity of African cultures and traditions.[56] African women theologians, in particular, have emphasized that not all African traditions are liberative, particularly where African patriarchal traditions have been reinforced by North Atlantic patriarchy.[57] A liberative theology that respects otherness will be one that is rooted in the sociocultural realities experienced by ordinary Africans as they resist the forces of death and struggle for liberation and life.[58]

Journeying outside the Camp: The Options for the Margins
and a Theology for the Postmodern Middle Class

> The church as the possession of God must stand where [God]
> stands, namely against injustice and with the wronged, that in fol-
> lowing Jesus Christ it must witness against all the powerful and
> privileged who selfishly seek their own interests and thus control
> and harm others.[59]

It is one thing to argue theologically that in Christ the world has been turned upside down and that the socioeconomic margins are the theological centers; yet the reality is that the churches and the theology of the socioeconomic centers continue to dominate global Christianity. The reason for that lies precisely in the access these theologians have to economic resources and in their freedom from the struggles of life that characterize the life of the exploited and the abandoned. Yet if God's action reconfigures the centers and the margins, then we need to recognize that those of us who are part of the elite are at a severe theological disadvantage. If our theology is to be an authentic reflection on and witness to God who is revealed in Jesus Christ as the God of the excluded, then we need to embark on the often painful journey to meet with Jesus the Christ outside the camp, among the excluded. Such a journey will leave us uncomfortable and displaced in the "carnivalesque"[60] postmodern world.

The understanding that theology is a pilgrimage to the margins does not entail a neglect of the context of Christianity in the North Atlantic Rim or other centers of power. Rather it recognizes that a particular context must be analyzed primarily in relation to those it excludes and victimizes. The contextual specificity of theologies arises out of their diverse relations to the realities of the margins. As Douglas John Hall states:

> In order to approximate genuine understanding of the context
> in question, we must open ourselves to those at the center of it, its
> victims. Such growth in understanding can only be attained through
> participation . . . that is, through a process of recognizing existen-
> tially something of our own responsibility, as First World citizens

for this Third World condition—in other words, through a painful confrontation with the realities of *our own specific context*.[61]

It is the orientation of theology to the victims that provides the common dimension that links the diverse contexts of the contemporary world. It is or ought to be, to use Frederick Herzog's phrase, the "common interest"[62] of all contextual theologies.

As Hall indicates, the pilgrimage begins when we recognize and take re- sponsibility for our complicity in the forces that abandon, oppress, and exclude. In the complex web of economic and political relationships that characterize the globalizing society, all of us from the centers of power, whether as residents of the North Atlantic Rim or as members of the Southern bourgeoisie, share a common complicity in the suffering of the powerless. This complicity should not be understood in a binary fashion as that between the oppressors and the oppressed, but rather as a complex web of relationships entailing exploitation, oppression, exclusion, beneficiation, and abandonment in which individual persons may relate to others in a diversity of ways as perpetrator, victim, and/or beneficiary. Complicity in the suffering of the powerless is not confined to governments and big business. It is shared by the average middle-class citizen whose savings and pension funds are invested in the financial and stock mar- kets, whose desire for cheap consumer goods leads to the exploitation of the powerless, and who votes for governments that protect his or her own eco- nomic interest at the expense of poor countries and that support corrupt and oppressive elites when it suits their economic and geopolitical interests. There is no place for a psuedo-innocence for those who would be faithful to the excluded Christ, as our daily pursuit of life is dependent upon the exploitation of others.[63] There is always a danger of blaming the other. The economic and political elite of countries of the South often blame the suffering of their coun- tries on the policies of the countries of North Atlantic Rim, yet do not recognize their own involvement in corruption, exploitation, and oppression. Equally, the residents of the North Atlantic Rim lay the blame on corrupt and oppressive Southern governments, without examining their own complicity in the exploi- tation of the poor. In a globalizing society our action and inaction impact and exploit others; hence, it is imperative that we each examine our own complicity in the suffering of others rather than claiming innocence and seeking to blame others.

Our pilgrimage to the margins is not the journey of lone travelers; rather it is the process of acquiring new conversation partners as we enter into dia- logue with the victims and the abandoned. It is a process of listening to their reflection on God's actions, the articulation of their response in faith and praxis, and their critique of our faith, praxis, and theology.[64] Such conversations are always bound up with the complexities of power relations and inequalities of resources. It must always be recognized that "the voice of the other is a voice

that is skewed, silenced, subjugated not simply by other voices, but by structures of power."[65] This is so even when engaging academic colleagues marginalized by the centers of economic power—and much more so when we attempt
to engage poor and marginalized communities. As such it entails a deliberate
stepping back, the creation of space for the voice of the marginalized, and a
process of building trust. This can take place only when we recognize and
foreground our own interests, position, and resources.[66]

A postmodern theology that remains within the camp, isolated from the
realities of the exploited and the excluded, has failed to transcend the constraints of modernity. The dominant forces of modernity excluded the voices
of Africans because the traditions, presence, and praxis of Africans were a
threat to their hegemony. It is only when we privilege and hear the voice of
the victims of both modernity and the emerging postmodern era that it is
possible for theology to transcend modernity and become authentically postmodern—hence, popular and academic African theologies, as the reassertion
of the agency of African people in resistance to the dehumanizing forces of
modernity and globalizing capitalism.[67] These voices provide an alternative
vision of Christian faith and praxis that is a significant critique and corrective
to North Atlantic theologies. It is this critique and corrective that can instigate
their liberation from captivity to both modernity and the self-indulgences and
frivolity of postmodern consumer capitalism.[68]

If we recognize the diverse character of the excluded groups among whom
Christ has taken his place, then the reconfiguration of the center and the margins does not create a single new center. Rather it affirms the polycentric
character of theological reflection that takes place from, with, and about diverse
locations of exclusion.[69] While not all the grounds of exclusion referred to in
the South African constitution, quoted above, are legitimate locations for Christian theological reflection, they are all legitimate interlocutors for a liberative
theology. However, the welcoming dynamic with its respect for otherness and
the option for the poor cannot be reduced to each other. As Robin Petersen
argues: "All difference is not equal. Some difference carries a freight of oppression and subjugation, as well as a history of repression."[70] In giving attention to the multiplicity of locations of exclusion, theological reflection cannot
neglect the subjugated person. Dietrich Bonhoeffer's notion of the *cantus firmus* provides a fruitful tool for relating a theologizing of difference and the
option for the margins that does not dissolve the option for the poor into mere
openness to difference. In his discussion of the relationship between love for
God and love for life, Bonhoeffer uses the musical analogy of the relationship
between the *cantus firmus* and the polyphony of contrapuntal themes. He argues that "where the *cantus firmus* is clear and plain, the counterpoint can be
developed to its limits"[71] In relation to the option for the excluded, the *cantus
firmus* must always be a commitment to the victims of a given socioeconomic
and political matrix. Once that is strongly and clearly emphasized, then the

polyphony of other dimensions of otherness and exclusion can be fully addressed. Theology thus becomes a dynamic dialogue (or multilogue) between the centers interrelated by their common *cantus firmus*.

The pilgrimage beyond the camp is fundamentally kenotic in character.[72] It arises out of a commitment to a twofold solidarity. The first is an identification with our fellow inhabitants of the centers of socioeconomic power in our complicity in the exploitation and oppression of the excluded other. The second is a solidarity with the excluded others. This leads to a praxis characterized by self-giving, self-withdrawing, and receiving from the other. *Kenosis* is often understood in terms of self-giving and thus the self-sacrificial giving of one's possessions, talents, resources, comforts, and even of one's very self in the service of the poor and excluded. While this is an integral component, mere self-giving can easily be a patronizing paternalism rather than a genuine solidarity with the other. Thus self-giving must be accompanied by self-withdrawal to create space for the excluded other. The exact dynamics of this will vary from context to context and person to person. It could include the withdrawal from positions of power and influence to make way for someone who has been excluded, the refusal to exercise control and power over others or over resources given for the benefit of others, and the creative transformation of institutional structures to make space for the voice and presence of the excluded. Self-giving and self-withdrawing will be authentic expressions of *kenosis* to the extent that a reception from and a listening to the excluded other accompany them. It is the movement from giving to receiving which transforms the relations of power and affirms in praxis that the sociopolitical margins are the centers from which God acts in blessing and salvation. While self-giving, self-withdrawing, and receiving from the other are dimensions of personal discipleship, they must not be restricted to this. If they are to have a significant impact on the life of the excluded, they must be expressed in structural change and renewal. Hence, to journey outside the gate is to engage in a discipleship of social transformation.

Conclusion

The pilgrimage beyond the camp is not easy, but the alternative is theologies that merely reflect the special interests of the powerful. Yet it is easy to remain in the ghettos of power and privilege and mistake them for the world. White South African theologians have had an advantage in that we have been confronted with a dramatic process of change in the past ten years, through which the margins are being recentered. Even though we have still maintained economic power, we have lost political power. The Truth and Reconciliation Commission has confronted us with our complicity in apartheid, affirmative action has threatened our employment prospects, and our sociocultural interests no longer dominate. Those who have left the security of the white ghettos and engaged a journey outside the camp have discovered it to be the source of profound spiritual and theological renewal. The affirmation of God's option for the margins challenges us all to embark on a similar journey in the diverse contexts in which we find ourselves.

NOTES

I would like to thank two colleagues at Africa University, Drs. Paul Gundani and Philemon Chikafu, for their comments on an earlier draft of this essay.

  1. Kwame Bediako, *Christianity in Africa: The Renewal of a Non-Western Religion* (Maryknoll, N.Y.: Orbis, 1995).

  2. Ibid., 126.

  3. There are at present seventeen armed conflicts on the continent, the majority of which are civil wars. An estimated one million people have died in three years of war in the Democratic Republic of the Congo alone. It is estimated that there are approximately six million externally and internally displaced refugees throughout the continent. An additional legacy is the approximately thirty-three million land mines that continue to kill and maim long after war has ended.

  4. Of the 174 countries listed in the United Nations' *Human Development Report, 2000*, the bottom 24 are African. There has been a constant decline in real income: it is estimated that the average income per head has fallen 1 percent every year for the past 25 years. In 1999 the GNP of sub-Saharan Africa was $320.6 billion (of which South Africa contributed $133.2 billion), compared with the Netherlands' $384.3 billion and the United States' $8,351 billion. The GNP per capita growth rate for 1998–99 was–0.3. Sub-Saharan Africa was the only region listed in the same report where there was a decline in supply of calories per person from 1970 to 1997 (from 2,271 to 2,237). It is the only region where between 1985 and 1995 there was an increase in the number of malnourished children (33 percent of children under age five malnourished). In 1997, 42 percent of the adult population was illiterate; this is an improvement from 50 percent in 1990. Only 56.2 percent of the relevant children were in primary education, and 41.4 percent in secondary education. According to the World Bank, sub-Saharan Africa had a total external debt in 1998 of $230.1 billion, compared to $176.9 billion in 1990. The majority of these figures and those that follow are from the United Nations Development Program, *United Nations Development Program Poverty Report, 2000—Overcoming Human Poverty* (New York: UNDP, 2000); United Nations Development Program, *Human Development Report, 2000* (New York: Oxford University Press, 2000); and World Bank, *World Development Report, 2000/2001: Attacking Poverty* (New York: Oxford University Press, 2000).

  5. Antiretroviral drugs have made AIDS a manageable disease in Europe and North America. However, the cost of drugs and the lack of health infrastructure puts treatment out of the reach of the majority of Africans.

  6. In sub-Saharan Africa there are 32 doctors per 100,000 people, whereas in the United States there are 245. The infant mortality rate for sub-Saharan Africa is

106 per 1,000 live births; in the United States it is 7. In sub-Saharan Africa 46 percent of the population does not have access to safe water, and 52 percent does not have access to sanitation.

7. Sub-Saharan Africa's share of world trade continues to decline. In 1985 it contributed 3.1 percent of the world's exports of primary commodities and 0.4 percent of manufactured goods. By 1998 this had fallen to 2.6 percent and 0.2 percent, respectively. In 1985 Africa contributed 1.1 percent of the world's imports of primary commodities and 1.4 percent of manufactured goods. By 1998 this had fallen to 0.9 percent and 0.7 percent, respectively. Sub-Saharan Africa contributes only 1.09 percent of global GNP (1999). This is despite substantial increase in net foreign direct investment from 1990 ($834 million or 0.43 percent of the global) to 1998 ($4,364 million or 0.7 percent of the global total).

8. In 1996–98 there were 14 landline telephones per 1,000 people in sub-Saharan Africa compared to the United States' 661 per 1,000 (this has to some extent been offset by increases in the use of mobile telephones). There were 198 radios per 1,000 compared to the United States' 2,146 per 1,000. There were 52 televisions per 1,000 compared to the United States' 847 per 1,000. There were 7.5 computers per 1,000 compared to the United States' 459 per 1,000.

9. Ronald Sider, *Rich Christians in an Age of Hunger: Twentieth Anniversary Edition* (London: Hodder & Stoughton, 1997), 144.

10. David Lyon, *Postmodernity* (Minneapolis: University of Minnesota Press, 1994), 57. Lyon argues this in relation to the analysis of a number of postmodern theorists (54–69). Cf. Hans Bertens, *The Idea of the Postmodern* (New York: Routledge, 1995), 209–37.

11. Oswaldo de Rivero, *The Myth of Development: The Non-Viable Economies of the 21st Century* (New York: Zed, 2001), 45.

12. Ibid., 46.

13. Ibid.

14. I have explored the significance of the term *Euro-African* in "On Being a Euro-African Theologian: Identity and Vocation in Post Apartheid South Africa," *Journal of Theology for Southern Africa* 201 (1998): 45–59. See also my "Participating in the Kenosis of God: Christology and Discipleship in Euro-African Perspective," in *Religion im Erbe: Dietrich Bonhoeffer und die Zukunftsfähigkeit des Christentums*, ed. Christian Gremmels and Wolfgang Huber (Gütersloher: Gütersloher Verlagshaus, forthcoming). The term is not unproblematic and has been used in some parts of Africa to designate people of mixed racial origins.

15. See the discussion in Stephen Slemon, "Unsettling the Empire: Resistance Theory for the Second World," *World Literature Written in English* 30.2 (1990): 30–41.

16. See my "On Being a Euro-African Theologian" and "Participating in the Kenosis of God." This also has a personal dimension, as this essay is being written as I am preparing to temporarily leave Africa.

17. Karl Barth, *Church Dogmatics*, vol. 2: *The Doctrine of God*, part 1 (Edinburgh: Clark, 1957), 386. This conceptualization is not an isolated proposition but is rooted in Barth's Christology. See Takatso A. Mofokeng, *The Crucified among the Crossbearers: Towards a Black Christology* (Kampen: Kok, 1983), 112–85; and Dirkie Smit, "Para-

digms of Radical Grace," in *On Reading Karl Barth in South Africa*, ed. Charles Villa-Vicencio (Grand Rapids: Eerdmans, 1988), 17–43.

18. See, for example, Albert Nolan, "The Option for the Poor in South Africa," in *Resistance and Hope: South African Essays in Honour of Beyers Naude*, ed. Charles Villa-Vicencio and John de Gruchy (Cape Town: David Philip/Grand Rapids: Eerdmans, 1985), 189–98.

19. Belhar Confession, article 4. The full text can be found in G. D. Cloete and D. J. Smit, eds., *A Moment of Truth: The Confession of the Dutch Reformed Mission Church, 1982* (Grand Rapids: Eerdmans, 1984), 1–6.

20. D. J. Smit, "In a Special Way the God of the Destitute, the Poor, and the Wronged," in *A Moment of Truth: The Confession of the Dutch Reformed Mission Church, 1982*, ed. G. D. Cloete and D. J. Smit (Grand Rapids: Eerdmans, 1984), 59.

21. The challenge posed by Intumeleng J. Mosala in his *Biblical Hermeneutics and Black Theology in South Africa* (Grand Rapids: Eerdmans, 1989) to any simplistic assertion that the biblical material unambiguously takes the side of the poor and the excluded must be recognized. The biblical writers were embedded in particular sociohistorical contexts, so that their writings both obscure and reveal the understanding of God as taking the side of the poor and oppressed. Yet I would argue that such an understanding of God is crucial to the significance of the narrative centers of the biblical traditions. See my "On Being a Euro-African Theologian." See also the discussion of biblical material in Jean-Marc Éla, *My Faith as an African* (Maryknoll, N.Y.: Orbis, 1988), 102–12; Gustavo Gutiérrez, *The God of Life* (Maryknoll, N.Y.: Orbis, 1991); Jorge Pixely and Clodivis Boff, *The Bible, the Church, and the Poor: Biblical, Theological, and Pastoral Aspects of the Option for the Poor*, trans. Paul Burns (Turnbridge Wells: Burns & Oates/Maryknoll, N.Y.: Orbis, 1989), 17–122; Sider, *Rich Christians in an Age of Hunger*, 41–121; and Smit, "In a Special Way the God of the Destitute, the Poor, and the Wronged" (in particular the appendix to this essay on pp. 127–40).

22. Desmond Mpilo Tutu, *Hope and Suffering: Sermons and Speeches* (Johannesburg: Skotaville, 1983), 60.

23. Gutiérrez, *God of Life*, 84.

24. Albert Nolan, *Jesus before Christianity* (Cape Town: David Philip, 1986), 27.

25. Mofokeng, *Crucified among the Crossbearers*, 167 (Mofokeng is commenting on Barth's Christology). Cf. Frank Chikane, "The Incarnation in the Life of the People in Southern Africa," *Journal of Theology for Southern Africa* 51 (1985): 37–50.

26. Chikane, "Incarnation in the Life of the People in Southern Africa," 49.

27. Éla, *My Faith as an African*, 111.

28. Constitution of the Republic of South Africa, 1996, clauses 9.4 and 9.3.

29. Robin Petersen, "Liberation Theology beyond Modernity," *Journal of African Christian Thought* 2.1 (1999): 31.

30. The conflict between Hutus and Tutsis in Rwanda is often portrayed as epitomizing African ethnic conflict; yet the creation of distinct Hutu and Tutsi ethnic identities was a product of colonial anthropologists and missionaries. See Laurent Mbanda, *Committed to Conflict: The Destruction of the Church in Rwanda* (London: SPCK, 1997).

31. Cf. Miroslav Volf's categories of exclusion as elimination, assimilation, domi-

nation, and abandonment in *Exclusion and Embrace: A Theological Exploration of Identity, Otherness, and Reconciliation* (Nashville: Abingdon, 1996), 75.

32. See my "Snakes in an African Eden: Towards a Theological Ethic for Ecotourism and Conservation," *Scriptura* 69 (1999): 165–80.

33. For example, the present civil war in the Democratic Republic of the Congo can be understood only in relation to the role played by the United States in supporting the kleptocratic and oppressive regime of Mobutu Sese Seko. North Atlantic banks and their shareholders are significant beneficiaries of corrupt African rulers such as Mobutu. They lend money at high interest rates and receive back far more than the original loan. Yet at the same time, significant portions of the money stolen from these loans by the corrupt rulers are redeposited on occasion in the same banks from which it had been borrowed.

34. In most international media reports on the present political crisis in Zimbabwe, references to the death of the government's opponents usually include a parenthetical statement such as "including eight white farmers," as if their deaths are more significant than the approximately one hundred others.

35. See John de Gruchy and Charles Villa Vicencio, eds., *Apartheid Is a Heresy* (Cape Town: David Philip/Guildford: Lutterworth, 1983); J. A. Loabser, *The Apartheid Bible: A Critical Review of Racial Theology in South Africa* (Cape Town: Maskew Miller Longman, 1987); and A. J. Botha, *Die Evolusie van 'n Volks Teologie*, Teks en Konteks 4 (Belville: University of the Western Cape Press, 1994).

36. See *The Truth and Reconciliation Commission of South Africa Report*, vols. 1–5 (Cape Town: Truth and Reconciliation Commission, 1998). Summarized presentations can be found in Desmond Mpilo Tutu, *No Future without Forgiveness* (London: Rider, 1999); and Antjie Krog, *Country of My Skull* (Johannesburg: Random, 1998). See also Kader Asmal, Louise Asmal, and Ronald Suresh Roberts, *Reconciliation through Truth: Reckoning with Apartheid's Criminal Governance* (Cape Town: David Philip, 1996).

37. See the discussion in Paul D. Hanson, *The People Called: The Growth of Community in the Bible* (San Francisco: Harper & Row, 1986), 253–324.

38. Note how in Galatians 2:7–10 the acceptance of Paul's ministry to the Gentiles is conditional upon his commitment to remember the poor.

39. See Volf, *Exclusion and Embrace*, 72–74, 111–19.

40. The New Testament also describes disciplinary exclusion, where disciples are excluded from the community in order to bring their behavior into conformity with the ethos of God's reign. This is not intended as a permanent exclusion but is directed toward the reinclusion of the repentant disciple. The conditionality is ethical and, in the perspective of the New Testament authors, does not arise from factors beyond the person's control.

41. See his *Hope and Suffering* and *The Rainbow People of God* (London: Doubleday, 1994).

42. Tutu, *Rainbow People of God*, 8.

43. See Tutu's *No Future without Forgiveness* for a theological critique of the Truth and Reconciliation Commission. See Tinyeko Sam Maluleke, "Truth, Unity and Reconciliation in South Africa: Aspects of the Emerging Theological Agenda," *Missionalia* 25 (1997): 59–86; idem, " 'Dealing Lightly with the Wound of my People'?

The TRC Process in Theological Perspective," *Missionalia* 25 (1997): 324–43; and idem, "The Truth and Reconciliation Discourse: A Black Theological Evaluation," in *Facing the Truth: South African Faith Communities and the Truth and Reconciliation Commission*, ed. James Cochrane, John de Gruchy, and Stephen Martin (Cape Town: David Philip/Athens: Ohio University Press, 1999), 101–13.

44. See his "Foreword" to Paul Germond and Steve de Gruchy, *Aliens in the Household of God: Homosexuality and Christian Faith in South Africa* (Cape Town: David Philip, 1997), ix–x. A discussion of the relevance of a theology of welcome in relation to gay and lesbian people lies beyond the scope of this essay. For the conclusion that such a theology requires their full acceptance and thus the affirmation of gay and lesbian partnerships as normative forms of Christian sexual behavior, see Germond and de Gruchy, *Aliens in the Household of God*. For the conclusion that a theology of welcome requires acceptance of gay and lesbian people but not the affirmation of gay and lesbian partnerships, see Stanley J. Grenz, *Welcoming but Not Affirming: An Evangelical Response to Homosexuality* (Louisville: Westminster/John Knox, 1998). For the post-Christian conclusion that Christianity is irredeemably heterosexist and does not offer good news to gay and lesbian people, see Heather Garner and Michael Worsnip, "Oil and Water: The Impossibility of Gay and Lesbian Identity within the Church," in *Towards an Agenda for Contextual Theology: Essays in Honour of Albert Nolan*, ed. Mc-Glory T. Speckman and Larry T. Kaufmann (Pietermaritzburg: Cluster, 2001), 205–30.

45. Alistair McGrath, ed., *The Blackwell Encyclopedia of Modern Christian Thought* (Oxford: Blackwell, 1993), 3.

46. Jürgen Moltmann, *Experiences in Theology: Ways and Forms of Christian Theology* (London: SCM, 2000), 183.

47. See, for example, Éla, *My Faith as an African*; idem, *African Cry* (Maryknoll, N.Y.: Orbis, 1986); and Kwesi A. Dickson, *Theology in Africa* (London: Darton, Longman & Todd/Maryknoll, N.Y.: Orbis, 1984), 129–40. In the post–Cold War environment, the emergence of theologies of reconstruction has refocused attention on the sociopolitical dimensions of the African context. See J.N.K. Mugambi, *From Liberation to Reconstruction: African Christian Theology after the Cold War* (Nairobi: East African Educational Publishers, 1995); J.N.K. Mugambi, ed., *The Church and the Reconstruction of Africa: Theological Considerations* (Nairobi: All Africa Conference of Churches, 1997); and José B. Chipenda et al., *The Church in Africa: Towards a Theology of Reconstruction* (Nairobi: All Africa Conference of Churches, 1991).

48. See among others Andre Grunder Frank, *World Accumulation, 1492–1789* (London: Macmillan 1978); J. H. Parry, *Europe and the Wider World, 1415–1715* (London: Hutchinson, 1966); Walter Rodney, *How Europe Underdeveloped Africa* (Nairobi: Heinemann, 1989); Immanuel Wallerstein, *The Modern System*, vol. 1: *Capitalist Agriculture and the Origins of the European World Economy in the Sixteenth Century* (New York: Academic 1974); and idem, *The Modern System*, vol. 2: *Mercantilism and the Consolidation of the European World Economy, 1600–1750* (New York: Academic 1980).

49. Bénézet Bujo, *The Ethical Dimensions of Community: The African Model and the Dialogue between North and South* (Nairobi: Paulines Publications Africa, 1998), 136.

50. J. S. Pobee, *Skenosis: Christian Faith in an African Context* (Gweru: Mambo,

1992), 41. See also Dickson, *Theology in Africa;* John S. Pobee, *Toward an African Theology* (Nashville: Abingdon 1979); and J.N.K. Mugambi, *African Heritage and Contemporary Christianity* (Nairobi: Longman, 1989).

51. J.N.K. Mugambi, *African Christian Theology: An Introduction* (Nairobi: East African Educational Publishers, 1989), 12. Mugambi has since argued that in the post–Cold War era the motif of reconstruction is a more appropriate one for African theology. See his *From Liberation to Reconstruction.* This alternative has been problematized by Tinyeko Sam Maluleke, "Recent Developments in the Christian Theologies of Africa: Toward the 21st Century," *Journal of Constructive Theology* 2.2 (1996): 33–60; and idem, "Half a Century of African Christian Theologies: Elements of the Emerging Agenda for the Twenty-First Century," *Journal of Theology for Southern Africa* 99 (1997): 4–23.

52. See Bénézet Bujo, *African Theology in Its Social Context* (Maryknoll, N.Y.: Orbis, 1992).

53. See Laurenti Magesa, *African Religion: The Moral Traditions of Abundant Life* (Maryknoll, N.Y.: Orbis, 1997).

54. With reference to the African Initiated Churches, see Petersen, "Liberation Theology beyond Modernity"; idem, "Articulating the Prophetic and the Popular: Proposals for a Neomodernist Liberation Theology," *Bulletin for Contextual Theology in Southern Africa and Africa* 5.1–2 (1998): 36–43; idem, "The AIC's and the TRC: Resistance Redefined," in *Facing the Truth: South African Faith Communities and the Truth and Reconciliation Commission,* ed. James Cochrane, John de Gruchy, and Stephen Martin (Cape Town: David Philip/Athens: Ohio University Press, 1999), 114–25; Pobee, *Skenosis,* 71–94; and M. L. Daneel, *African Earthkeepers,* vol. 1: *Interfaith Mission in Earth-Care* (Pretoria: Unisa, 1998) and *African Earthkeepers,* vol. 2: *Environmental Mission and Liberation in Christian Perspective* (Pretoria: Unisa, 1999).

55. See Pobee, *Skenosis,* 23–41, 58–70; Bénézet Bujo, *African Christian Morality at the Age of Inculturation* (Nairobi: St. Paul Publications–Africa, 1990), 119–30; and Tinyeko S. Maluleke, "African Culture, African Intellectuals and the White Academy in South Africa: Some Implications for Christian Theology in Africa," *Religion and Theology* 3 (1996): 17–42.

56. See Simon S. Maimela, ed., *Culture, Religion and Liberation: Proceedings of the EATWOT Pan African Theological Conference, Harare, Zimbabwe, January 6–11, 1991* (Pretoria: All Africa Conference of Churches, 1994).

57. See Mercy Amba Oduyoye and Musimbi R. A. Kanyoro, *The Will to Arise: Women Tradition and the Church in Africa* (Maryknoll, N.Y.: Orbis, 1992); and Mercy Amba Oduyoye, *Daughters of Anowa: African Women and Patriarchy* (Maryknoll, N.Y.: Orbis, 1997).

58. See Éla, *My Faith as an African* and *African Cry;* and Xolile Keteyi, *Inculturation as a Strategy for Liberation* (Pietermaritzburg: Cluster, 1998).

59. Belhar Confession, clause 4.

60. J. Richard Middleton and Brian J. Walsh, *Truth Is Stranger Than It Used to Be: Biblical Faith in a Postmodern Age* (Downers Grove, Ill.: InterVarsity, 1995), 42.

61. Douglas John Hall, *Thinking the Faith: Christian Theology in a North American Context* (Minneapolis: Fortress, 1991), 80 (emphasis original).

62. See Frederick Herzog, "United Methodism in Agony," in *Doctrine and Theol-*

ogy of the United Methodist Church, ed. T. A. Langford (Nashville: Kingswood, 1991), 33–34. Joerg Rieger has expanded on this in "Developing a Common Interest Theology from the Underside," in *Liberating the Future: God, Mammon and Theology*, ed. Joerg Rieger (Minneapolis: Fortress, 1998); and idem, *God and the Excluded: Visions and Blind Spots in Contemporary Theology* (Minneapolis: Fortress, 2001), 124–41.

63. See Karl Barth, *Ethics* (New York: Seabury, 1981), 164–65.

64. See James R. Cochrane, *Circles of Dignity: Community Wisdom and Theological Reflection* (Minneapolis: Fortress, 1999); Gerald West, *The Academy of the Poor: Towards a Dialogical Reading of the Bible* (Sheffield: Sheffield Academic Press, 1999); idem, "Contextual Bible Study in South Africa: A Resource for Reclaiming Land, Dignity and Identity," in *Towards an Agenda for Contextual Theology: Essays in Honour of Albert Nolan*, ed. McGlory T. Speckman and Larry T. Kaufmann (Pietermaritzburg: Cluster, 2001), 169–84; Piet Naudé, *The Zionist Christian Church: A Case Study in Oral Theology* (Queenston: Edwin Mellen, 1995); Graham Philpot, *Jesus Is Tricky and God Is Undemocratic: The Kin-dom of God in Amawoti* (Pietermaritzburg: Cluster, 1993).

65. James R. Cochrane, "Questioning Contextual Theology," in *Towards an Agenda for Contextual Theology: Essays in Honour of Albert Nolan*, ed. McGlory T. Speckman and Larry T. Kaufmann (Pietermaritzburg: Cluster, 2001), 75.

66. For an account of what it means to authentically encounter the excluded, see Anthony Bellagamba, "Christian Journey toward Discovering the Struggling Poor," in *Towards African Christian Maturity*, ed. Aylward Shorter et al. (Kampala: St. Paul Publications–Africa, 1987).

67. See Tinyeko S. Maluleke, "The Rediscovery of the Agency of Africans: The Emerging Paradigms of Post–Cold War and Post-Apartheid Black and African Theology," *Journal of Theology for Southern Africa* 108 (2000): 19–37. While Maluleke's focus is on contemporary developments, I would argue that the emphasis on African agency can be found in earlier developments.

68. See, for example, Neville Richardson, "Can Christian Ethics Find Its Way, and Itself, in Africa?" *Journal of Theology for Southern Africa* 95 (1996): 37–54; idem, "Community in Christian Ethics and African Culture," *Scriptura* 62 (1997): 373–85; Peter Fulljames, *God and Creation in Intercultural Perspective: Dialogue between the Theologies of Barth, Dickson, Pobee, Nyamiti, and Pannenberg*, Studies in the Intercultural History of Christianity 86 (Frankfurt am Main: Peter Lang, 1993); and Lee E. Snook, *What in the World Is God Doing? Re Imagining Spirit and Power* (Minneapolis: Fortress, 1999).

69. See Frans J. Verstraelen's argument for a polycentric approach to theology in *Christianity in a New Key: New Vistas and Voices through Intercontinental Communication* (Gweru: Mambo, 1996). Verstraelen's focus is on diverse geographical centers and not on the diverse centers of exclusion within a geographical location.

70. Robin M. Petersen "Towards a South African Theology of Non-Racialism," *Journal of Theology for Southern Africa* 77 (1991): 25.

71. Dietrich Bonhoeffer, *Letters and Papers from Prison* (New York: Macmillan, 1972), 303.

72. I have explored this in more detail in "Participating in the Kenosis of God."

3

Liberation Theology in the Twenty-First Century

Kwok Pui-lan

Entrance into the world of the poor is a long and sometimes painful process, but it is there that we find the One of whom theology is called upon to speak.

—Gustavo Gutiérrez, *The Truth Shall Make You Free*

Every theology implies a conscious or unconscious sexual and political praxis, based on reflections and actions developed from certain accepted codifications.

—Marcella Althaus-Reid, *Indecent Theology*

I first encountered liberation theology in the mid-seventies when I was a college student studying theology in the British colony of Hong Kong. The seventies were a turbulent period of social ferment and protest as students around the world organized sit-ins, occupied campus buildings, and challenged authorities to demand radical changes in social policies, to end the Vietnam War, and to clean up the government. The students in Hong Kong organized themselves and took to the streets to fight for the adoption of the Chinese language as an official language, along with English. More than 90 percent of the population in Hong Kong were Chinese, and many could not read government notices or fill out official forms because they could not understand English. Living in such a repressive colonial situation, I found liberation theology relevant to the burning issues of the day and Gustavo Gutiérrez's work, *A Theology of Liberation*, a critical intervention in theological discourse.

Today, liberation theology has developed not only in Latin America but also in many different parts of the world. It has become a multicultural and multilingual theological movement, articulating the hopes and aspirations of the poor and the marginalized from the black townships in South Africa to the poverty-stricken villages in India, where women need to search even for clean drinking water. However, recent happenings in world politics and a changing intellectual climate in academia have called into question some of the premises and presuppositions on which liberation theology was predicated. For example, the political transformation of Eastern Europe and the disintegration of the former Soviet Union challenged the efficacy of Marxist social analysis in liberation theology. The postmodern turn in academia has proclaimed the end of the subject, the collapse of metanarratives, and the indeterminacy of meaning and has cast doubt on whether poor can be the subjects of history. What will be the future of liberation theology? In this essay, I discuss three important issues that will have an impact on liberation theology in the twenty-first century. The first section focuses on the relation between postmodernity and liberation theology and explores the extent to which the option for the poor is still viable in postmodernity. The second section points out that many of the world's poor are non-Christians and calls attention to the challenge of postcolonial theory in the study of religion. The last section challenges patriarchy and heterosexuality in liberation theology and shows why gender and sexuality must be fully integrated in the discourse.

Postmodernity and Liberation Theology

In his recent book *The Density of the Present*, Gutiérrez acknowledges the changing political situation and urges us to discern the signs of the times, "signs which must be perceived in order to proclaim the Gospel, and whose call to commitment demands to be heard."[1] What are the signs of our time and how can we offer a "thick description" of the density of the present? Should we use a temporal or historical narrative, calling the present moment modern, postmodern, or transmodern? Should we deploy spatial metaphors, such as the global village, the world wide web, and cyberspace? Are the labels First, Second, Third, and Fourth World still relevant? Who are the new rich and the new poor in today's economy, in which the First World exists within the Third World, and the Third World within the First World?

As we face the beginning of a new millennium, the major challenge for those committed to the struggle of the poor will be to assess and address the impact of neoliberal capitalism on the lives of the majority of the world's population. Following colonialism and development, this new wave of globalization aims to extend and intensify the market to such an extent that the logic of the economy will become the logic of society itself.[2] With the collapse of the former Soviet Union and the disintegration of the Eastern Bloc, economists and politicians have predicted capitalism as the final point of human ideological evolution and the universalization of Western liberal democracy as the final form of human government. Indeed, much of the rhetoric of the "New World Order" that has been promulgated by the United States since the end of the Cold War has been marked by blatant self-congratulatory triumphalism and a renewed sense of purpose and responsibility to lead and possibly even save the world.

The rapid transformation of the Eastern Bloc and the introduction of capitalist economies in former socialist strongholds, such as China and Vietnam, have challenged the promise and legitimacy of socialist analysis. The 1990s saw the realignment of world powers according to their geo-economic interests. The market is not now subjected to the control of individual nation-states, but is rather dictated by transnational economic powers defined by greed and corporate interests. The huge international debt accumulated during the past decade adds an additional burden to many small countries, which have to spend more money in servicing national debts than in providing social services and education for their people. The widespread poverty that prompted the development of liberation theology in the 1960s still exists, and it has taken a new insidious turn. Theologian Pablo Richard describes the dire situation: "The great majority of the South is in total abandonment. It can no longer be called dependent, but is simply nonexistent. We have moved from dependency to dispensability; today being dependent even seems to be a privilege."[3]

Politically, the world has entered a stage of history much more insecure, unsettled, and volatile than was the Cold War era. According to political scientist Samuel Huntington, the end of the Cold War has not brought peace on earth and good will to humankind. Instead, there has been an increase in warfare and the number of armed struggles fought, not among former ideological rivals, but along the new fault lines of religious conflict, ethnic cleansing, and renewed tribalism.[4] Today the two strongest forces shaping our cultural politics are the global and the local. On the one hand, globalization has influenced many arenas of cultural production, including academic research, media, entertainment, arts, and sports. The McDonaldization of the world creates a homogenous consumerist culture shaping the taste of the popular masses. On the other hand, there is a renewed search for cultural, religious, and ethnic identity among former colonized and subjugated peoples in an attempt to resist the forces of globalization. Such a quest for cultural roots and tradition often attaches great importance to location and cultural uniqueness, and it values difference and the right of each group to pursue specific ways of living and being. In its extreme forms, cultural and religious fundamentalism has led to intolerance, the breaking down of civil society, and the increasing fragmentation of the world.

How has liberation theology responded to this rapidly changing world situation? Is the liberationist paradigm adequate and comprehensive enough to analyze the social, economic, political, and cultural changes in the beginning of the twenty-first century? Some have argued that liberation theology is in crisis because Marxist jargons and class analysis are outdated in today's post-Marxist world. They point out that as liberation theology begins to address the issues of gender, race, culture, and ecology, it will need to broaden its analytical framework and employ newer tools. Others have insisted that more than ever liberation theology needs to commit to the preferential option of the poor and continue to speak of both the "God for the poor" and the "church for the poor." But they also understand that the collapse of the Second World has narrowed both the theoretical and political space for social activists, community organizers, and progressive theologians in the Third World.

The heart of the debate is over how liberation theology will respond to the postmodern challenge, which has dominated so much of the current cultural and intellectual landscape.[5] Postmodernism questions some of the most basic assumptions of modernism: the constitution of the self as unified and coherent, the representative nature of language, the belief in human reason and universal truth, the commitment to liberal humanism, and optimism vested in technology, development, and progress. Some commentators have argued that liberation theology, at least in its classical form in Latin America, shares much with modernist thinking, as it is also an heir of the Enlightenment. Deploying the rhetoric of the European Enlightenment, liberation theology shares the modernist belief in humanism, which is grounded in the inherent dignity of all human beings and their inalienable right to shape their own destinies. Liberation theology makes use of Marxist analysis in its critique of the industrialized society and in its attack on bourgeois religion; such analysis is seen as an integral part of modern thought. Liberation theology also relies on the use of metanarratives, such as the liberation of the poor, to mobilize the masses. Furthermore, liberation theologians project a teleological utopian dream, not of a Marxist classless society, but of one couched in religious language, of the kingdom of God. The difficulty is that the grand narratives of emancipation and utopia have lost much of their appeal and legitimation in the postindustrial and postmodern society.[6]

Facing this postmodern challenge, liberation theologians have had various responses, three of which will be briefly discussed here: (1) liberation theology, as it has developed to be a global movement, has a close relationship to both postcolonialism and postmodernism; (2) the liberationist paradigm has outgrown its usefulness and should be replaced by postmodernist and postcolonial paradigms; and (3) postmodernist thought sidetracks us from our commitment to sociopolitical struggles, and its proposed dissolution of the subject aims to curtail the agency of the oppressed.

Those who argue that liberation theology and postmodernism can work hand in hand stress the plurality and diversity within liberation theology, especially in the works of the second-generation theologians. In fact, some commentators have suggested that Third World theologies of liberation have undergone what amounts to a paradigmatic shift—from socioeconomic analysis to cultural analysis and from modernity to postmodernity.[7] Indeed, some theologians do not hesitate to employ some of the critical tools of postmodern thought. For example, Fernando Segovia, a Cuban American theologian, regards postmodernism as useful in challenging many forms of essentialism and universalism, for it emphasizes the situated perspective of the observer and the construction of all knowledge, including theology. He writes:

> At the heart of postmodernism . . . lies the fundamental myth or
> narrative of radical diversity and pluralism, quite different from that
> of modernism, with its emphasis on universality and objectivity.
> From the point of view of postmodernism, therefore, there is no re-
> ality as such but rather a multitude of "realities"; in other words,
> "reality" is always seen in terms of perspective.[8]

Segovia notes that the theology of liberation, as it has expanded to different parts of the world, has gone beyond the overriding socioeconomic focus to include other socioreligious and sociocultural concerns. Furthermore, liberation theology has always put its contextual character and multiplicity of perspectives in the foreground as it asserts the position of the marginalized. Segovia sees that liberation theology is fundamentally related to postmodernism and postcolonialism: "The theology of liberation has shared in both the postmodernist myth or narrative of radical pluralism and the postcolonial process and project of decolonization."[9]

Some argue that the time has come for the liberationist paradigm to be replaced, as it has too many problems to be repaired. One radical interlocutor is Marcella Althaus-Reid, who states: "The flirtation of Systematic Theology with Liberation Theology may be coming to an end. It may be moving from the liberationist paradigm towards a postcolonial or postmodern perspective."[10] She critiques liberation theology's overemphasis on economic liberation of the poor, to the exclusion of their other needs. Latin American liberation theology, she charges, has constructed the theological subject of the poor as a contrast to the North Atlantic theological subject. But the category of the poor has been so flattened and homogenized that it is taken to mean male peasants who belong to the church. It does not include women and does not refer to the urban poor or to lesbian, gay, transgendered, and bisexual people. Althaus-Reid accuses liberation theologians of repeating the homogenizing tendency found in much of the Western framework of thinking.[11] Furthermore, male liberation theologians have largely remained silent on women's liberation and have not questioned the patriarchal and sexual implications of the theology they espouse. I will examine this issue in more detail below.

But not everyone welcomes postmodernism as a blessing for, or a potential ally to, liberation theology. Those who follow strict Marxist criticism insist that the structural oppression of a political economy takes precedent over other forms of exploitation. They feel that diverting attention from the struggle against the basic poverty of the people betrays the liberationist commitment. And they favorably cite Fredric Jameson's critique of postmodernism as the cultural logic of late capitalism and point out that "culture" has been so integrated into commodity production that it does not further the cause of the poor and oppressed, but instead sidetracks the real economic struggle.[12] They are also suspicious of yet another overarching Western-based theory superimposed onto the theological projects of the Third World.

Other theologians are hesitant to accept postmodern thought because of some of its playful reading strategies and its dissolution of subjectivity and agency at a time when women and other oppressed groups are just beginning to claim their voices and places in history. For example, feminist biblical critic Elisabeth Schüssler Fiorenza expresses concerns about a postmodernist approach to the Bible, because such an approach has the potential to reduce women to textuality or to use the term *woman* simply as a figure of speech. She refuses to follow a kind of "ludic (playful) postmodernism" which undermines the political implications of feminist reading of the texts.[13] Instead, she develops a critical feminist interpretation based on dialogue with critical theory and liberation theology. She warns that feminist theology and biblical studies should not claim male figures as their "Godfathers"—whether they are Jerome, Thomas, Bultmann, and Albright or such postmodernist thinkers as Derrida and Foucault. She urges feminists to scrutinize all "malestream" thinkers, including the postmodernists, before they use those frameworks for their own thought.[14]

From another perspective, Hispanic theologian Roberto S. Goizueta also criticizes the timing of the postmodern argument for the dissolution of the subject. The denial of subjectivity is seen as detrimental to marginalized peoples in their struggle to claim a voice and position from which to present their oppositional worldview. He writes:

> The deconstruction of the subject is similarly suspect. For centuries, the modern Western, rational subject has been the axis of history, in relation to whom Third World peoples were simply heathens, barbarians and nonpersons. Now that we heathens, barbarians and nonpersons have finally begun to enter the historical stage as rational subjects in our own right, we are informed that the stage has been disassembled, or deconstructed.[15]

From the above discussion, it is clear that there is no consensus or simple agreement regarding the relationship between liberation theology and postmodernity. While some are more optimistic about the intersection, others express strong political and philosophical reservations. My own observation is that one's assessment of an intellectual current as diverse as postmodernism need not be either a wholesale rejection or an indiscriminate embrace. Insofar as postmodernism represents the serious self-reflexity of modernity, it will help debunk the universal "man of reason" and logocentrism in much of Western thought. Since modernist thinking has been superimposed onto the world because of colonial education and pedagogy, postmodern theory enables Third World theologians to dislodge themselves from familiar habits of thinking and be self-critical of their collusion with modernist, universalistic, or even imperialistic frameworks.

On the other hand, much of the world is not yet postindustrial and post-modern, as are the societies in Europe and America. We have to safeguard against making postmodernism another globalized theory that suppresses all local contexts and differences. There is a material difference between theoreticians working out sophisticated postmodern arguments in Western academies and women and men struggling to live in subsistence-level realities. Postmodern thought can become another sophisticated theory with currency in the academic world, but without much political importance in changing the social world. The endless deferral of meaning and the intense suspicion of agency will also make collective action against injustice difficult. Liberation theology that is grounded in concrete social realities, with pragmatic strategies for social and political change, will still be needed in the twenty-first century. But it must broaden its scope and pay attention to the diverse "life-worlds" of the poor, which are shaped by gender, race, culture, religion, and sexual orientation.

The Study of Third World Religiosity

One of the challenges of postmodernity is how to preserve differences without collapsing them into sameness. When we consider the diversity of the poor and oppressed in the world, we must reckon with the fact that the majority of them are non-Christians. Within the Ecumenical Association of Third World Theologians, the Asian and African theologians have always emphasized the religio-cultural dimension of liberation, in addition to the transformation of social and economic structures. Sri Lankan theologian Aloysius Pieris has said:

> The irruption of the Third World is also the irruption of the non-Christian world. The vast majority of God's poor perceive their ultimate concern and symbolize their struggle for liberation in the idiom of non-Christian religions and cultures. Therefore, a theology that does not speak to or through this non-Christian peoplehood is an esoteric luxury of a Christian minority.[16]

Thus, these theologians have criticized Christian imperialism, called for inter-religious dialogue, and promoted action-oriented solidarity across religious differences.

If we think in terms of a history of religions, of Third World religiosity as an important resource for theological reflection in liberation theology, we have to pay attention to how religion has been studied in the past. The academic study of religion, which had its beginning in the mid-nineteenth century, was thoroughly embedded in the colonial ethos and political configurations of its time. Claiming to be objective, *Religionswissenschaft* was supposed to be an impartial and scientific comparison of the religions of humankind. But in practice, the study of religion in the nineteenth century relied on colonial power for support and provided justification for the "civilizing" mission of the West. For example, the study of Hinduism and Buddhism was greatly assisted by the acquisition of ancient manuscripts by missionaries and colonial officials in Asia. Early ethnographic studies and field research were made possible because of the power and control that white men enjoyed over their native informants.

One of the founding figures in the study of religion was Friedrich Max Müller, who became a professor of comparative philology at the University of Oxford, a crucial site of knowledge production in the British Empire. Müller was instrumental in editing and partially translating the fifty-volume *Sacred Books of the East* (1879–1910). The publication of these books promoted the impression that the classic golden age of these Hindu and Buddhist civilizations was long gone and that their present cultures represented a degeneration from past ideals. Such orientalist tendencies justified both the ethnocentric claim of superiority by Western culture, as well as the missionizing efforts of Christianity in other parts of the world. And just when these classics from the literary Far East were published, scholars studying the oral cultures and traditions coined the term *primitive religions*. The adaptation of the evolutionary framework to the comparative study of religions and the presupposition that Christianity was the highest of all religions fueled, in Europe, both a colonial impulse and an anti-Semitic posture.

Although the study of religion has changed since the early days of the founding "fathers," colonialist representations and orientalist approaches remain strong in Western academies to this day, although often under a different, subtler disguise. In their recent books, Donald S. Lopez Jr. and Richard King document the entrenched orientalism in the study of Buddhism and Indian religions in the West.[17] Such self-reflexivity, however, is rare, due in part to the Eurocentric biases in the study of religion and in part to the continued claims of objectivity and neutrality. Claiming to present objective and demonstrable data, researchers may not want to deal openly with the politics of studying other people's myths and religions. And some scholars, positioning themselves as the experts or spokespersons for Hinduism, Buddhism, or Confucianism, find it inconvenient to discuss the politics inherent in representing the other. Even as these issues are gaining attention and importance, many view them as merely a challenge to refine methodologies, rather than an as opportunity to scrutinize existing paradigms or even overhaul the entire discipline.[18]

Unfortunately, many religion scholars in the Third World have been socialized or disciplined in orientalist ways of thinking by their professors. Likewise, the works of Otto, Eliade, and Malinowski are digested as foundational texts for religion studies in the Third World, as well as in the First World. Many have not benefited from the insights of the critique of orientalism by Edward Said,[19] nor have they engaged the body of postcolonial theory and literature. Since the 1990s, scholars who have borrowed insights from postcolonial studies have raised fundamental issues regarding the definition of religion and the constitution of religion as fields of study. Many scholars have pointed out that religion has largely been defined by people who use Western Christian religion as their model. But this Christianized model overemphasizes the belief system of religion and often neglects the ways in which religion permeates and infuses other aspects of communal life. A central component of this model is theistic belief, which posits a fundamental dualism between the sacred and the human world.[20] The perennial discussions of mono-, poly-, and pantheism are foreign concepts superimposed on other religious traditions. Since Christian scholars in the modern West have emphasized the study of sacred Scriptures, the tendency to textualize the "world religions" is pervasive. The study of Buddhism and Hinduism in the West, for example, have been constituted as the study of ancient texts, rather than of living traditions.

These critics question the complicity of early scholars with colonialism, the use of universalistic and essentialist paradigms in the comparison of religions, the construction of India as the "mythic East," the limits and biases employed in studying the other, the misappropriation of spiritual resources from Native cultures, and the privileging of textual studies over the vernacular. In a ground-breaking book, *Curators of the Buddha*, scholars in Buddhist studies debunk the long-cherished views that Zen Buddhism is conceived as "unmediated" experience, that Tibetan Buddhism is polluted, that Jung really knows about oriental wisdom, and that the Buddha image is of Greek or Roman origin.[21] In Hindu studies, scholars have questioned the construction of Hinduism as a pan-Indian tradition, the claim by nineteenth-century Western scholars that orientalist studies done in Europe could offer back to Indians their past, the use of orientalist studies of the Vedas by colonial officials to undermine local authority, and the New Age appropriation of Hindu goddesses.[22] And scholars in Islam have pointed to the Western stereotypes of Muslim culture and religion, challenged "colonial feminism" imposed by Christian missionaries and colonial administrators, and discussed multiple critiques employed by postcolonial Arab women in negotiating their complex transcultural religious identities and national loyalties.[23] In addition, two recent important books, *Savage Systems* and *From Savage to Negro*, present thought-provoking and substantial critiques of the construction of the "savage" from Southern African and African American perspectives. Both works condemn racist ideology and social Darwinism in anthropology, and *Savage Systems* contrasts the strategies of the imperialistic comparative study of religion at the metropolitan centers with religion scholarship on the colonial frontier.[24]

The application of postcolonial theories to the study of Christianity is quite recent and concentrates on the study of the Bible. Currently, postcolonial studies of the Bible are being conducted on many different levels and involve scholars from diverse disciplines. First, there are those who focus on the biblical text, following the "Saidian exhortation to peruse the texts for gaps, absence and ellipses, the silences and the closures, and so facilitate the recovery of history or narrative that has been suppressed or distorted."[25] Others discuss the imperial motives of canonization and subjugated biblical histories and compare the Bible with other imperializing texts.[26] Second, scholars such as R. S. Sugirtharajah have challenged orientalist interpretations of the Bible and Eurocentrism in the field of biblical studies. Sugirtharajah further points out that even the "natives," or the "colonized," internalized such an approach to the Bible, to the extent that the orientalist mode of thinking could be found both in the metropolis and among colonial elites.[27] Third, scholars from minority communities in the United States have applied postcolonial theories to the study of the ways the Bible has been used in their respective communities to challenge the hegemony of Eurocentric interpretations. The works of Fernando Segovia, Hector Avalos, Randall Bailey, and Jace Weaver are examples.[28]

Although this nascent body of scholarship, coming from many religious traditions, has created ferment and excitement, feminist religious scholars have yet to participate in the discussion in significant ways. The early works of feminist scholars in religion critiqued patriarchy as a "universal" phenomenon and aimed to include essentialized "women's experiences" in their analysis. Although feminist scholars have challenged the authority of the "founders" and the "fathers" in their fields, much of their work is still based on white male liberal scholarship. Since there has not been a sustained discussion on how white male scholarship has colluded with colonialism, a mere inclusion of gender as a category of analysis is not sufficient to dissociate feminist scholars from the colonialist stance. Moreover, the construction of Western women as subject is often predicated upon the denial of subject status to the other women (Natives, Asians, and Muslims). The worship of ancient goddesses, such as Isis and Aphrodite, has been reappropriated by white women to compensate for their lack of feminine images. The feminine figures in Hinduism, Buddhism, and the Native traditions have been colonized to serve white women's psychological and emotional needs for the "mother."

Feminist liberation theologians and religious scholars have an important role to play in studying the symbolic universes of women in the Third World, providing for women's religious leadership in faith communities, elevating the status of women in popular religious movements, and facilitating the passage of culture and religion from one generation to another. Such efforts will enable us to better understand Third World women's religiosity and enrich the theological imagination of feminist liberation theology. Some work has already been done in this area. For example, Mercy Amba Oduyoye from Ghana has examined the ways in which proverbs, legends, and myths have shaped the religious and cultural worldview of African women.[29] Asian feminist theologians have paid attention to how religious pluralism has shaped the images of God among Christian women in Asia.[30] Latin American feminist theologians have emphasized women's popular religiosity, especially their devotion to the Virgin Mary.[31] But a lot more needs to be done.

Engendering Liberation Theology

Although male liberation theologians have supported a preferential option for the poor, they have not always listened to the outcries of poor women. Mercy Amba Oduyoye has called the intervention of women in the movement of liberation theology the "irruption within an irruption" of the Third World.[32] Almost twenty years after the first irruption in 1981, at an assembly of the Ecumenical Association of Third World Theologians, a few male theologians have begun to mention women's oppression in their writings. However, women's issues have largely remained on the periphery of liberation theology, and male theologians have not taken significant steps to modify their analytical framework.

The persistence of the masculinist paradigm in liberation theology is not a simple oversight or a theoretical blind spot, but is rooted in the deeper social, cultural, and political configurations of its time. Liberation theology emerged in the 1960s during a period of intense struggle for the political and economic independence of the Third World. Colonialism superimposed the will of the master and deployed the rhetoric of gender to describe a relationship characterized by domination and submission. Since colonized people were described in feminine terms, colonized men felt their manhood in doubt and their pride diminished. Not surprisingly, the rhetoric of the Black Power and nationalist movements in the 1960s was full of anger, disgust, and hatred. It was Frantz Fanon who first articulated the complex psychodynamics of why a black man desires to be a white man under the conditions of colonialism: the colonized and subjugated man wants to usurp the white man's power while preserving his patriarchy.[33]

As a result of the cultural and political climate of the 1960s and 1970s, male liberation theologians began to attack racism and poverty and to criticize

white, European Christianity for its complicity in racial oppression and colonialism. The image of the black Christ proposed by black liberation theologians
demystifies the power behind the symbol of the white Christ, while celebrating
the beauty and dignity of the black man. The image of Christ the liberator
dispels the myth of a meek, obedient, vulnerable Jesus and brings hope and
expectation to the subjugated poor who are longing for freedom. The liberator
can be imagined to be a masculinist fighter—in the person of a guerrilla, a
revolutionary, or a political dissenter. What is missing, however, is the concomitant critique of male dominance in society and the patriarchal and heterosexual assumptions of Christianity.

In her provocative book *Indecent Theology*, Althaus-Reid has challenged
that liberation theology remains trapped in the binary and dualistic construction of gender and heterosexual norms. Liberation theology may have deviated
from traditional theology in terms of its solidarity with the poor, but it continues to perpetuate the same sexual hierarchy and compulsory heterosexuality
found in most theologies. She argues that much of liberation theology is *decent*—meaning that it supports the sexual codification of society and heterosexual norms. Even feminist liberation theology in its analysis of human anthropology tends to accept this codification. Feminist theologians in the Third
World may be willing to talk about gender, but are less prone to talk about sex
and the sexuality of women. Liberation theologians portray images of Christ
and Mary that are decent and safe and do not disrupt conventional sexual
norms. Jesus can be seen as a social radical, but only as an asexual or celibate
human being. The motherhood of the Virgin Mary is affirmed, and she can
even be seen as the mother of the poor, yet she has to remain a virgin in the
popular imagination.

Althaus-Reid's work on the intersection between sex, politics, and theology
has demonstrated that gender and sexuality are not tangential to economics
and politics and should not be relegated to the private realm or construed as
affecting the lives of women alone. Much of the male theologians' reluctance
to treat gender and sexuality as priority issues has resulted from the regard of
them as separable from and secondary to their socioeconomic analysis. But
Althaus-Reid turns the argument upside down by arguing that sexual ideology
pervades economic and political theories and undergirds the epistemological
foundations of theology, including liberation theology.[34] Therefore, a social
analysis that understands poverty only in economic terms but not in genderized and sexual terms is not only incomplete, but mystifies the complex web
of human relations that both constitute and sustain the social conditions that
effectively keep people poor.

Engendering liberation theology means that we have to integrate gender
and sexuality into major theological concerns, whether it is gospel and culture
or globalization or political theology. For example, in the ecumenical discussion on gospel and culture, a genderized perspective will indicate that Third

World women and men are positioned differently in their cultures. Kenyan theologian Musimbi Kanyoro has called for a "cultural hermeneutics" to unpack the layers upon layers of tradition that women have inherited.[35] She says that missionaries and Westerners often condemn the cultures of Africa as "totally barbaric" and "undeveloped." This has perpetuated the colonialist paradigm which often purports the inferior status of women in native lands and holds up the sexual and genderized practices of footbinding, polygamy, and veiling to justify the "civilizing mission" of the West. Colonial feminism, which claims to lift up the colonized women from darkness, is an integral part of the colonialist paradigm. The reversion to the traditional patriarchal culture was seen by those involved in nationalistic struggles as a way to reclaim their cultural pride. Likewise, in the theological movements of inculturation or indigenization, male theologians have attempted to recover their Asian or African cultural roots, but have left the women's culture and women's suffering out of their equation.

It is time that we begin to look at complex cultural politics not only in terms of cultures of the West/Third World but also in terms of the multilayered cultures existing within the Third World and to examine how women fare in each of these layers. Elsa Tamez, a leading Latin American feminist theologian, distinguishes four levels of Latin American culture: indigenous, black, mestizo-white, and globalized culture of the rich nations. While the mestizo-white culture exerts hegemony over indigenous and black cultures, it is in turn dominated and influenced by European and American cultures. She suggests that women in different cultures must both question the elements of their traditions that legitimize violence against women and work together with women of other cultures and races through intercultural dialogue and international alliances.[36]

Feminist liberation theologians also insist that a genderized understanding of globalization is necessary. A Marxist approach to social analysis may be adept at examining the oppression of poor men, but it is ill equipped to understand the roles of women in rural and subsistence economies or the growing division of gender in international labor. The widely acclaimed work of Indian physicist and ecologist Vandana Shiva has documented the effects caused by multinational corporations building large dams and clearing forests in Africa. Such large-scale developmental projects threaten the survival of subsistence economies. She clearly shows that women's roles as creative managers of forests, the food chain, the water resources, and the livelihood of a household are eroded in poor neighborhoods in India and Africa.[37] In East Asia, the so-called Asian miracle that took place in the late 1980s and early 1990s was built on the availability of cheap female labor. Globalization brought about a new international division of labor, with multinational corporations relocating factories and manufacturing plants in the Third World. Many Asian women work for long hours in low-paying, labor-intensive manufacturing jobs in the textile and garment industries and in electronics and toy factories. Similar exploitation also takes place among the Asian and Latina immigrants, who provide cheap unskilled labor for the booming U.S. economy.

Another category of women's labor that male liberation theologians have largely overlooked is sexual labor. Vietnamese scholar Thanh-dam Truong has called prostitution a form of sexual labor, which has become lucrative and highly institutionalized in Southeast Asia. After the Asian economic crisis in 1997–98, sex tourism became even more important for Southeast Asian countries because it brought in much needed foreign capital. Truong has documented the vast international network that sustains the sex industry, including local police, government officials, gangs and pimps, the airlines, travel agencies, and hotel and food-service industries.[38] In their critical study of prostitution in Asia and in the United States, Rita Nakashima Brock and Susan Brooks Thistlethwaite charge Christian theology itself with positioning prostitutes as archetypal sinners, as it has not yet acknowledged how its own dualistic construction of mind and body, male and female, and individual sin and social evil has contributed to the problem of male privilege.[39]

Liberation theology must come to a deeper understanding of the interplay between sexuality, power, and violence in order to fully analyze the relationship between sexual politics, male privilege, and state terror. Violence against women and girls has been a persistent tool in maintaining male power and state control over women. Physical and domestic violence against women takes many different forms across the world. From dowry death and dieting to genital mutilation, female bodies are subjected to unspeakable torture, dismemberment, and coercive control. Wife beating and domestic abuse are justified and condoned in some cultures, and many battered women silently suffer because of internalized shame or for the sake of their children. Even in the United States, a highly "developed" country, a woman is beaten in her home every fifteen seconds. Domestic violence is the leading cause of injury to U.S. women. And the cycle of violence tends to perpetuate itself, affecting the lives of subsequent generations.[40] Women have also been sexually abused, raped, and tortured by dictatorial regimes and military juntas in order to instill fear and subjugate the people. In war-torn regions, large numbers of women and children are often displaced from their homelands and are vulnerable to all kinds of physical dangers. During the war in Kosovo, for instance, the Serbs systematically raped many Albanian women who were forced to leave their homes.

Engendering liberation theology means that we revisit its anthropological underpinnings and social analyses to spell out more clearly its implications for gender and sexuality. From such an investigation come new ways of speaking about God and images of the divine that are not limited by the masculinist imagination. Some of this work has already been done by feminist liberation theologians and womanist theologians who have imagined Christ in many different ways. Christ is no more imagined only as the black man or a poor peasant from Latin America. For Kelly Brown Douglas, "Christ can be seen in the face of a Sojourner Truth, a Harriet Tubman, or a Fannie Lou Hamer."[41] For Indian feminist theologian Stella Baltazar, the transcended Christ can be imagined as the embodiment of the feminine principle, the *Shakti*, the energizer and vitalizer of life.[42] Such new images require fresh theological formulations of the life and work of Christ in radical ways.

An engendered liberation theology will also need to think about the ministry of the church in a pluralistic world. When liberation theology began in Latin America, the argument was that the poor were already in the church, and the church needed to become a church of the poor and to stand in solidarity with the oppressed. Today, we have become sensitive to the fact that the majority of the world's poor are outside the church, and many do not want to join its ranks for good reasons. And within both the Christian and non-Christian poor are women and men whose issues differ from each other's. A church that is socially and politically radical but sexually oppressive has opted to stand in solidarity with half of the poor, while leaving the other half outside the door. While claiming to stand in solidarity with the Christian poor (meaning men), the church may even perpetuate androcentric ideologies and structures in Christianity that are oppressive to women, both Christian and non-Christian.

Liberation theology has captured the imagination of a generation of theologians who have sought to make Christian faith relevant to the concerns of our time. As theologians, we have been called to respond honestly to Gutiérrez's questions: "How can we make faith in the God who 'has a fresh and living memory of the smallest and most forgotten' the inspiration of our lives? How can we transform this time of dissipation and death into a time of calling and grace?"[43] The vision of the forerunners still provides helpful guides, but that vision needs to be continually broadened as we discern the density of the present.

NOTES

1. Gustavo Gutiérrez, *The Density of the Present: Selected Writings* (Maryknoll, N.Y.: Orbis, 1999), 120.

2. Larry Rasmussen, " 'Give Us Word of Humankind We Left to Thee': Globalization and Its Wake," *EDS Occasional Papers* 4 (1999): 13.

3. Pablo Richard, "Liberation Theology Today: Crisis or Challenge?" *Envío* 11, no. 133 (August 1992): 26.

4. Samuel P. Huntington, *The Clash of Civilization and the Remaking of World Order* (New York: Simon & Schuster, 1996), 38–39.

5. Scholars held diverse views on the relationship between liberation theology and postmodernity. See *Liberation Theologies, Postmodernity, and the Americas*, ed.

David B. Batstone, Eduardo Mendieta, Lois Ann Lorentzen, and Dwight N. Hopkins (New York: Routledge, 1997).

6. Jean-François Lyotard, *The Postmodern Condition: A Report on Knowledge* (Minneapolis: University of Minnesota Press, 1984).

7. G. de Schrijver, "Paradigm Shift in Third World Theologies of Liberation: From Socio-Economic Analysis to Cultural Analysis," in *Liberation Theologies on Shifting Grounds: A Clash of Socio-Economic and Cultural Paradigms*, ed. G. de Schrijver (Leuven: Leuven University Press, 1998), 3–83.

8. Fernando F. Segovia, "In the World but Not of It: Exile as Locus for a Theology of the Diaspora," in *Hispanic/Latino Theology: Challenge and Promise*, ed. Ada María Isasi-Díaz and Fernando F. Segovia (Minneapolis: Fortress, 1996), 198.

9. Ibid., 201.

10. Marcella Althaus-Reid, *Indecent Theology: Theological Perversions in Sex, Gender, and Politics* (New York: Routledge, 2001), 91.

11. Ibid., 30.

12. Gerald Boodoo, "Paradigm Shift?" in *Liberation Theologies on Shifting Grounds: A Clash of Socio-Economic and Cultural Paradigms*, ed. G. de Schrijver (Leuven: Leuven University Press, 1998), 353–54.

13. Elisabeth Schüssler Fiorenza, *Sharing Her Word: Feminist Biblical Interpretation in Context* (Boston: Beacon, 1998), 21.

14. Ibid., 18–19.

15. Roberto S. Goizueta, *Caminemos con Jesús: Toward a Hispanic/Latino Theology of Accompaniment* (Maryknoll, N.Y.: Orbis, 1995), 147.

16. Aloysius Pieris, *An Asian Theology of Liberation* (Maryknoll, N.Y.: Orbis, 1988), 87.

17. Donald S. Lopez Jr., *Curators of the Buddha: The Study of Buddhism under Colonialism* (Chicago: University of Chicago Press, 1995); Richard King, *Orientalism and Religion: Postcolonial Theory, India and "the Mythic East"* (New York: Routledge, 1999).

18. Wendy Doniger writes that "the academic world . . . suffers from a post-postcolonial backlash" in her discussion of how the study of myth responds to the challenges of postcolonial and postmodern critique of comparison. See her *Implied Spider: Politics and Theology in Myth* (New York: Columbia University Press, 1998), 66.

19. Edward W. Said, *Orientalism* (New York: Vintage, 1978).

20. King, *Orientalism and Religion*, 37.

21. Lopez, *Curators of the Buddha*.

22. Uma Narayan, *Dislocating Cultures: Identities, Traditions, and Third World Feminism* (New York: Routledge, 1997); David L. Haberman, "On Trial: The Love of the Sixteen Thousand Gopees," *History of Religions* 33.1 (1993): 44–70; Rachel Fell McDermott, "The Western Kali," in *Devi: Goddesses of India*, ed. John Stratton Hawley and Donna M. Wulff (Berkeley: University of California Press, 1996), 281–313.

23. Leila Ahmed, *Women and Gender in Islam: Historical Roots of a Modern Debate* (New Haven: Yale University Press, 1992), 144–68; Miriam Cooke, "Multiple Critique: Islamic Feminist Rhetorical Strategies," in *Postcolonialism, Feminism, and Religious Discourse*, ed. Laura E. Donaldson and Kwok Pui-lan (forthcoming).

24. David Chidester, *Savage Systems: Colonialism and Comparative Religion in*

Southern Africa (Charlottesville: University Press of Virginia, 1996); Lee D. Baker, *From Savage to Negro: Anthropology and the Construction of Race, 1896–1954* (Berkeley: University of California Press, 1998).

25. R. S. Sugirtharajah, ed., *The Postcolonial Bible* (Sheffield: Sheffield Academic Press, 1998), 18.

26. Jon L. Berquist, "Postcolonialism and Imperial Motives for Canonization," *Semeia* 75 (1996): 15–35; Richard A. Horsley, "Subjugated Biblical Histories and Imperial Biblical Studies," in *The Postcolonial Bible*, ed. R. S. Sugirtharajah (Sheffield: Sheffield Academic Press, 1998), 152–73; Musa W. Dube, *Postcolonial Feminist Interpretation of the Bible* (St. Louis: Chalice, 2000).

27. R. S. Sugirtharajah, *Asian Biblical Hermeneutics and Postcolonialism: Contesting the Interpretations* (Maryknoll, N.Y.: Orbis, 1998).

28. Fernando F. Segovia, "Biblical Criticism and Postcolonial Studies: Toward a Postcolonial Optic," in *The Postcolonial Bible*, ed. R. S. Sugirtharajah (Sheffield: Sheffield Academic Press, 1998), 49–65; Hector Avalos, "The Gospel of Lucas Gavilán as Postcolonial Biblical Exegesis," *Semeia* 75 (1996): 87–105; Randall C. Bailey, "The Danger of Ignoring One's Own Cultural Bias in Interpreting the Text," in *The Postcolonial Bible*, ed. R. S. Sugirtharajah (Sheffield: Sheffield Academic Press, 1998), 66–90; Jace Weaver, "From I-Hermeneutics to We-Hermeneutics: Native Americans and the Post-Colonial," *Semeia* 75 (1996): 153–76.

29. Mercy Amba Oduyoye, *Daughters of Anowa: African Women and Patriarchy* (Maryknoll, N.Y.: Orbis, 1995).

30. Kwok Pui-lan, *Introducing Asian Feminist Theology* (Sheffield: Sheffield Academic Press, 2000).

31. Ivone Gebara and Maria Clara Bingemer, *Mary: Mother of God, Mother of the Poor* (Maryknoll, N.Y.: Orbis, 1989).

32. Virginia Fabella, *Beyond Bonding: A Third World Women's Theological Journey* (Manila: Ecumenical Association of Third World Theologians, 1993), 93.

33. Frantz Fanon, *Black Skin, White Masks* (New York: Grove, 1967).

34. Althaus-Reid, *Indecent Theology*, 7.

35. Musimbi Kanyoro, "Cultural Hermeneutics: An African Contribution," in *Women's Visions: Theological Reflection, Celebration, Action*, ed. Ofelia Ortega (Geneva: WCC, 1996), 18–28.

36. Elsa Tamez, "Cultural Violence against Women in Latin America," in *Women Resisting Violence: Spirituality for Life*, ed. Mary John Mananzan et al. (Maryknoll, N.Y.: Orbis, 1996), 18–19.

37. Vandana Shiva, *Staying Alive: Women, Ecology, and Development* (London: Zed, 1989).

38. Thanh-dam Truong, *Sex, Money, and Morality: Prostitution and Tourism in South-East Asia* (London: Zed, 1990).

39. Rita Nakashima Brock and Susan Brooks Thistlethwaite, *Casting Stones: Prostitution and Liberation in Asia and the United States* (Minneapolis: Fortress, 1996), 236.

40. Elisabeth Schüssler Fiorenza, "Ties That Bind: Domestic Violence against Women," in *Women Resisting Violence: Spirituality for Life*, ed. Mary John Mananzan et al. (Maryknoll, N.Y.: Orbis, 1996), 40.

41. Kelly Brown Douglas, *The Black Christ* (Maryknoll, N.Y.: Orbis, 1994), 108.

42. Stella Baltazar, "Domestic Violence in Indian Perspective," in *Women Resisting Violence: Spirituality for Life*, ed. Mary John Mananzan et al. (Maryknoll, N.Y.: Orbis, 1996), 64.

43. Gustavo Gutiérrez, *Las Casas: In Search of the Poor of Jesus Christ* (Maryknoll, N.Y.: Orbis, 1993), 459.

4

The Situation and Tasks of Liberation Theology Today

Gustavo Gutiérrez
(Translated by James B. Nickoloff)

The question which has been put to me concerns the future of liberation theology. Two clarifications are necessary before beginning to make several points on this subject.

Efforts to understand faith, which we call theologies, are closely linked to questions which come from life and from the challenges which the Christian community faces in bearing witness to the reign of God. Thus theology is connected to the historical moment and cultural world in which these questions arise (thus to say that a theology is "contextual" is, strictly speaking, tautological; in one way or another every theology is contextual). This is one of the elements which establish theology as an ecclesial duty. Obviously, there are permanent elements in theologies which come from the Christian message, which is their focus; theologies help us to see these elements in a new light. But a theology's relevance depends in large part on its capacity to interpret the form in which faith is lived in a particular time and circumstances. The consequence is clear: on their mutable side theologies are born in a precise framework and contribute (or should contribute) to the faith-life of believers and to the evangelizing task of the church, but the accents, categories, terms, and focal points lose their "bite" to the extent that the situation which gave rise to them is no longer the same. What I am saying about the historicity of every theology, including those which perdured longest in the course of Christianity's history, is obviously true for an endeavor such as that of liberation theology. Theology always sinks its roots in the historical density of the gospel message.[1]

This leads me to a second observation which complements the

preceding one. What matters more than wondering about the future of a the-ology as such is to ask about the relevance and consequences of the great themes of Christian revelation which that theology has been able to revitalize and fix in the consciousness of believers. In the case of a faith-understanding reached through the lens of liberation, this would involve such points as the liberation process (with all the dimensions which this implies) of the poor in Latin America, the presence of the gospel and of Christians on this journey, and, in a very special way, the preferential option for the poor put forward and developed in this kind of theological reflection. These are situations and themes in continuous evolution. This is what really counts.

Perhaps a good way to consider the future of a theological perspective would be to set it over against other theological orientations of today, to submit its aim and its central axes to a new examination in relation to the present moment, and then to take a look at the tasks which it faces. In fact, the future does not simply arrive; we build it. We make it with our hands and hopes, our failures and plans, our stubbornness and our sensitivity to what is new. This is what I propose to present schematically in three steps in the pages which follow.

Three Great Contemporary Challenges to Faith

In convoking the Second Vatican Council John XXIII asked us—and himself—how to say today what Christians pray for daily, namely, that "your kingdom come." In seeking an answer to this prayer, he recovered an important biblical theme: the need to know how to discern the signs of the times. This means being attentive to the movement of history and, more broadly, to the world in which we live out our faith. It means being sensitive to the questions that the world raises, questions which challenge us and enrich us at the same time. Thus it also means being far from fears, from condemnations at all costs, and from the narrow-mindedness of those whom the same pope called "prophets of doom"—an attitude so relished by those who set themselves up as saviors from all the evils of the age.

In this order of ideas we could say, without making any exhaustive claim and leaving aside important nuances, that Christian faith and the proclamation of the gospel today face three great challenges: (1) the modern world and what is called postmodernity, (2) the poverty of so many, and (3) religious pluralism and the interreligious dialogue it requires. The three make far-reaching de-mands on Christian life and on the church's work. At the same time all three furnish elements and categories which allow us to take new paths in under-standing and deepening the Christian message. It is essential to take these two facets of a single reality into account. Theological work will consist of confront-ing, face-to-face, these challenges which stand before it as signs of the times.

At the same time, we must discern in them—in the light of faith—the new hermeneutical field which they offer us for reflecting on our faith and for speaking about a God who talks to the people of our time.

I would like to dedicate the greater part of these pages to the second of these challenges. Let us, then, examine the first and third more briefly.

The Modern (and Postmodern) World

With roots in the fifteenth and sixteenth centuries, the mentality which would come to be called "modern" had an effect on the life of the Christian churches from the eighteenth century on. It is characterized by (a) the affirmation of the individual as the starting point for economic activity, social life, and human knowledge; (b) critical reason, which accepts only what has been subjected to the examination and judgment of reason itself; and (c) the right to freedom in various spheres. It is what Kant called humanity's coming of age. This is what gives rise to the modern spirit's distrust of authority, on both the social and the religious plane. Christian faith, close to superstition and of an authoritarian bent—according to this line of thought—was destined to disappear or at best to be confined to the private sphere. In this way society would enter a rapid process of secularization and would make Christian faith lose the social weight and influence over people that it had in other times.[2] The forms this conflict took, for European Christians in a particular way, are well known. Also well known are the steps taken, and the steps not taken, in the responses provoked by these different disputes with the church. And this is to say nothing of the uncertainty, fear, effrontery, and suffering which people lived through for these reasons.

Vatican II distanced itself from those who saw nothing more in the modern world than a bad period destined to pass and who thought the only thing to do was to steadfastly resist until the storm dissipated. The council searched for and succeeded in finding answers to many of these questions (though not without difficulties and misunderstandings at the beginning, of course). There is still an enormous amount of work to do in relation to the situation created by modernity. It is clear that in this matter we face a long process.[3]

The task has become more complicated in recent years because of what has come to be called, for convenience, the postmodern era.[4] The postmodern outlook presents itself as a sharp criticism of modernity, which it accuses, among other things, of drifting into totalitarianism (fascism, Nazism, and Stalinism), thus contradicting its fervent assertion of liberty and of confining itself to a narrow and purely instrumental view of reason. Postmodernity sharpens the individualism which characterizes the modern world. The result of all this has been a somewhat apathetic stance toward possibilities for changing what used to be seen as not functioning well in our societies. The same can be said of its distrust of solid convictions in any area of human action or knowledge;

thus there arises a skeptical stance which relativizes the knowledge of truth. According to this view, we all have our own truth and thus everything is valid. This stance is without doubt one of the reasons for the lack of interest in social and political reality which we see in our time. This mentality, of course, also makes important contributions: from now on we will have to pay attention, for example, to what our assessment of cultural or ethnic diversity (with all its political ambivalences) might mean.

Whether postmodernity is a rejection of modernity or a more refined prolongation of it does not change the essence of what concerns me here. Taken as a whole, postmodernity constitutes a great challenge to Christian consciousness. The passage of time, it is true, has brought about valuable theological works which have taken the bull by the horns. Far from being a repudiation inspired by fear, they have not only faced the questions posed by the modern world and its repercussions with evangelical freedom and fidelity to the message of Jesus; these works have also pointed out what the modern world itself could contribute so that the significance of faith might be revealed to those to whom we had not been sensitive in the past or who, for one reason or another, had been eclipsed in the course of history.

Religious Pluralism

The great number of religions is, as we know, a very ancient fact of the human race. While both the great and well-known religions, as well as the less widespread ones, were not created yesterday, the contemporary problematic in this regard has reached theological consciousness only in recent years. In the past, religious pluralism raised certain practical problems and led to a consideration of the salvific potential of the missionary task of Christian churches, but in recent decades its presence has become a question of great magnitude for Christian faith. All those who study this topic agree that a theology of world religions, such as we find it today, is very recent and is moving along a path strewn with difficulties. Today we see a great debate about this taking place in the church. The question is, of course, delicate, and important texts from the magisterium, as well as inspiring theological studies, have been devoted to it.[5] As in the case of the modern world, but for different reasons, the existence of billions of human beings who find in these religions their relationship to God or to an Absolute or to the deepest meaning of their lives raises questions about fundamental points of Christian theology. At the same time, as also happens in the case of modernity, this fact furnishes elements and possibilities for theology to take another look at itself and to examine the meaning and significance today of salvation in Jesus Christ.

This is new and demanding territory.[6] Here there is a great temptation to withdraw and stick to positions considered safe. For this reason bold gestures such as those of John Paul II are particularly welcome; I am thinking of the invitation he issued a few years ago to representatives of the great religions of humanity to meet in Assisi to pray for the peace of the world. In fact, a theology of world religions cannot be constructed apart from the practice of interreligious dialogue, a dialogue which up to now has barely begun. Theology is always a second act. Many people are involved in this effort, and here too, and perhaps with greater urgency than in the previous challenge, there is an enormous amount of work to be done.

The modern mentality is the fruit of important changes in the field of human knowledge and in social life. These changes took place primarily in Western Europe when it had already begun its march to a standard of living which would distance it from the rest of the planet's countries. By contrast, those who bring questions arising from religious pluralism are found among the poorest nations of humanity. Perhaps this is one of the reasons why, as I noted, awareness of the questions they pose has only very recently arisen in the Christian churches, precisely at the time when these peoples were starting to make their voices heard in different regions of the world. This means that the response to the questions coming from Asia above all, but also from Africa and to a lesser degree from Latin America, must not separate religious matters from the situation of poverty. This twofold reality has many consequences for the faith-discourse coming from these regions.[7]

This last observation leads me to take up the challenge which comes from poverty. I will treat it at greater length, as it is a matter which is of particular concern to me.

An Inhuman and Antievangelical Poverty

The challenges to Christian faith which come from religious pluralism and from poverty were born outside the North Atlantic world. Those who bear them on their shoulders are the poor peoples of humanity, as I just said in regard to the world religions, and this is obviously the case with poverty. This final challenge to theological reflection was first raised with intensity in Latin America, a continent whose population is simultaneously *poor and believing*, as we have been saying for decades in the framework of liberation theology. I am referring to those who live out their faith in the midst of poverty, which means that each of these characteristics leaves its mark on the other; to live out and think through Christian faith cannot therefore be accomplished apart from an awareness of the situation of exploitation and marginalization in which such persons find themselves.

Rereading the Message

The Latin American bishops' meetings held in Medellín (1968) and Puebla (1979) denounced the continent's poverty as "inhuman" and "antievangelical."

But unfortunately we know that this is a worldwide phenomenon. Little by little the poor of the world were gaining a clearer awareness of their situation. A series of historical events in the 1950s and 1960s (decolonization, new nations, popular movements, a better understanding of the causes of poverty, etc.) made *present* around the globe those who had always been *absent* from the history of humanity or, to be more exact, invisible to those who limit history to the deeds of one part of it—the Western world—which is made to appear as the winner in every field. The historical fact which has been called the "irruption of the poor" is not, of course, an event which is finished; it is still in full swing and continues to raise new and pertinent questions. In Latin America and in the Caribbean this event was, and is, of particular significance for theological reflection.

Poverty is, like the religious pluralism of humanity, a situation which has existed for a long time. In the past it certainly led to admirable demonstrations of service to the poor and abandoned. But today knowledge of its crushing extent, the ever wider and deeper gap between the rich and the poor in contemporary society, and the way we have of conceiving it have meant that only in the second half of the century just ended has it really been seen as a challenge to our understanding of faith. Even now this is not true everywhere because there are still those for whom poverty remains only a problem of the social and economic order. This is not the biblical meaning of poverty, nor was it John XXIII's view when, on the eve of the council, he placed the church face-to-face with the poverty of the world ("the underdeveloped countries") and affirmed that it had to be "the church of all and especially the church of the poor." He thus proposed a demanding way of conceiving the church and its task in the world.

The message of Pope John was heard and later deepened in Latin America and the Caribbean; being a continent which is both poor and at the same time Christian, as I mentioned above, made us particularly sensitive to the theological depth of the challenge raised by poverty. This is a perspective which, in the different circumstances of the sixteenth century, figures such as Bartolomé de Las Casas and Peruvian Indian Guaman Poma pioneered in these lands in their defense of the indigenous population of the continent. Even today it is still far from being understood by everyone. This is why we still have problems trying to make clear the meaning of the basic affirmations of liberation theology and of the bishops' conference of Medellín, both of which, taking into account the present context, have a bearing precisely on our approach.

Despite this, the church of Latin America and the Caribbean and, soon after, the churches of other poor continents made clear just how far the demands go which arise from the situation of poverty and the marginalization of so many human beings. This issue is still pushing forward amid certain obstacles, so that it can be seen in its true depth as a problem for Christian life and theological reflection. It is important to note that this happens less with the challenge concerning the role of the world religions in the saving plan of the God of Christian revelation. In the case of religious pluralism, although there are those who refuse to go along, the theological character of the problem is seen, of course, more quickly. To underline the theological character of the questions which poverty brings does not in any way mean to dodge the unavoidable and constitutive socioeconomic dimension which poverty and social injustice have. This is obviously the case. But the attention which should be given to poverty and social injustice does not come merely from a concern with social and political problems. Poverty as it is known to us today hurls a radical and all-encompassing question at the human conscience and at the way we perceive Christian faith. It constitutes a hermeneutical field which leads us to a rereading of the biblical message and of the path we should take as disciples of Jesus. This is something which should be stressed if we want to understand the meaning of a theology such as the theology of liberation.

An Axis of Christian Life

What I have just said is captured quite clearly in the well-known expression *preferential option for the poor*. The term arose in the Christian communities and in the theological reflections of Latin America in the time between Medellín and Puebla. The latter conference took it up and made it known far and wide. Its roots lie in the experiences of solidarity with the poor and in the corresponding understanding of the biblical meaning of poverty, which had their beginnings early in the 1960s and which had already been expressed— at least the heart of the matter—at Medellín. This expression is very common today in the teachings of John Paul II and of different episcopal conferences of the universal church, as well as in the documents of various Christian denominations. The preferential option for the poor person is a fundamental axis in the proclamation of the gospel, which we commonly call (using the well-known biblical metaphor) the pastoral task. It is also a fundamental axis in the field of spirituality, that is, in the following of Jesus. Thus is it likewise an axis in our attempt to make sense of the faith, which is done by beginning with these two dimensions of the Christian life. Taken as a whole, this threefold character is what gives it strength and scope.

I have just traced the short history of a perception which is expressed in the formula noted: nevertheless, it is clear that at its core this formula is intended to help us see how in this age we approach a central datum of biblical revelation which in one way or another has always been part of the Christian universe. I am referring to God's love for every person and particularly for those who are most abandoned. But it happens that today we are in a position to be able to point out with all the clarity one could wish that the poverty, injustice, and marginalization of persons and of groups of persons are not irrevocable facts, but they have human and social causes. Furthermore, we are shocked by the immensity of this reality and by the growing distance, from this point of view, between the nations of the world and between persons within each country. This changes our approach to poverty and forces us to examine personal and social responsibilities in a new light. In this way it gives us new perspectives for knowing how to discover—continuously—the face of the Lord in those of other persons, in particular those of the poor and the mistreated. And it allows us to go directly to what, theologically speaking, is decisive: positioning ourselves in the heart of the proclamation of the reign of God, the expression of the gratuitous love of the God of Jesus Christ.

The vision evident in the formula *preferential option for the poor* is the most substantial part of the contribution to the universal church made by the life of the Latin American church and by liberation theology. The question posed at the beginning of these pages about the future of liberation theology must take into account its factual and contemporary connection to everything that option signifies. This perspective is obviously not something which belongs to liberation theology alone; the Christian message itself requires, and reveals the meaning of, a response to the poor in which God's gift of the reign is accepted. It is always a matter of a discourse on faith which simply allows us to recall and reread in today's context (with all of the newness that context reveals to us) something which, in one way or another, has always been present—ceaselessly but not without interruptions—throughout the march of the people of God in history. It is good to stress this, not in order to diminish the contribution of liberation theology, whose destiny is tied to the biblical meaning of solidarity with the poor. Rather, we must outline correctly the degree to which this theology both stands in continuity and parts ways with previous theologies—and above all, with earlier Christian experiences and routes taken to witness to God's reign.

As in the two cases treated above, I am concerned here with making it clear that the very challenge arising from poverty also opens up perspectives which allow us to go on bringing forth "the new and the old" from the treasure of the Christian message. Faith discernment must be lucid in this regard. But to assure this, we must overcome the obstinacy of seeing the world's poverty today as *only* a social problem. This would amount to disregarding what this painful sign of the times might have to say to us. All of this is summed up in the conviction that we must look at history from its underside, that is, from the side of its victims. The cross of Christ illuminates this vision and makes us understand it as a step toward the definitive victory of life in the Risen One.

Current Tasks

Let me indicate some areas in which certain tasks await the kind of theological reflection which concerns me. Naturally there would be many more things to say and clarifications to make, but this cannot be done in these few pages. I hope to treat them in greater detail in a single, longer work which is already begun.[8]

The Complexity of the World of the Poor

From the beginning, liberation theology took into account the different dimensions of poverty. To put it in other words—as in the Bible—care was taken not to reduce poverty to its economic aspect, though of course this is important.[9] This led to the claim that the poor person is "insignificant," a person who is considered a "nonperson," someone whose full rights as a human being are not recognized. We are talking about persons without social or individual weight, who count little in society or in the church. This is how they are seen or, more precisely, not seen, because they are in fact invisible insofar as they are excluded in today's world. The reasons for this are diverse: lacking material goods, of course, but also having a certain skin color, being a woman, belonging to a culture held in contempt (or considered important only because it is exotic, which, when all is said and done, amounts to the same thing). Poverty is, in fact, a complex and multifaceted reality. In speaking for decades about the rights of the poor (see, for example, the Medellín statement on peace), we were referring to the multidimensionality of poverty.

A second perspective, equally present from the very beginning, was seeing the poor as the others of a society constructed without regard for, or even over against, their most basic rights, far from their way of life and values. This is so true that when history is read from the vantage point of the outsider (a woman, for example), it becomes a different history. Nevertheless, to reread history could seem to be a purely intellectual exercise if we failed to understand that this also involves remaking it. Within this framework of ideas, the conviction remains firm—despite all the limitations and obstacles of which I am well aware, especially today—that the poor themselves must take charge of their own destiny. In this regard, taking up again the trajectory of these concerns in the field of history, ever since a person and theologian like Las Casas first attempted to view things "as if he were an Indian," remains a rich vein yet to be exploited. The first person to do so from firsthand experience was Guaman Poma. Only when we free ourselves from staring inertly, making prejudgments, and accepting certain categories uncritically will we be able to discover the other.

For this very reason, it is not enough to be aware of this complexity; we must deepen our awareness, enter into the details of the diversity, and notice its power to question us. But neither is it enough to notice the status of the poor person as other; this status must also be studied in greater detail and considered in its entire, challenging reality. This is the process in which we now find ourselves, thanks above all to the concrete commitments made in and from the world of poverty, stamped for the most part among us—as I have already noted—by some kind of experience of Christian faith. Theological reflection is nourished by this daily experience (which is already several decades old) and at the same time enriches it.

This concern has gone deeper in recent years. Valuable studies have made it possible to enter in a particularly fruitful way into several key aspects of this complexity. Indeed, along these lines today we find various efforts being made to conceptualize faith by beginning with the secular situation of marginalization and spoliation of the various indigenous peoples of our continent and of the black population, violently incorporated into our history centuries ago. In a variety of ways we have been witnesses during this period to the vigor and strength which the voice of these peoples has acquired, to the cultural and human richness they are ready to contribute, and to the facets of the Christian message which they allow us to see in all their starkness. To this we must add the dialogue with other religious conceptions which were able to survive the destruction of previous centuries. These are minority views today (though equally respectable because committed human beings hold them), but we must recognize, without trying to recreate them artificially, that they are present among us with their cultural and religious makeup.

The theological reflections which come from these universes are particularly demanding and new. The same is true of those which come from the inhuman, and therefore unacceptable, condition of women in our society, especially those who belong to the social and ethnic strata I have just recalled. In this area we are also witnessing rich and new theological perspectives carried forward above all by women, but which are important to and challenge everyone. One of the most fertile fields is that of reading the Bible from the perspective of the real situation of women. But of course there are many others which also enlarge our horizon for understanding the Christian faith. This is the time to note as well how much we can hope that a consideration of the feminine and masculine dimensions of the human being—and a dialogue between the two—will deepen our faith.

It may be opportune to note that this is not a matter of defending ancient cultures fixed in time or of proposing out-of-date projects which the historical process has gone beyond, as some tend to think. Culture is an endless creation, elaborated every day. We see this in very different ways in our cities. They are a crucible of races and cultures at their most popular; at the same time, however, they are cruel places where distances between the different social sectors which inhabit them are increasing. Both things are experienced in the cities of a continent undergoing rapid urbanization. This universe-in-process, which to a great degree carries with it and transforms the values of traditional cultures, conditions the lived experience of faith and the proclamation of the reign of God; it is, therefore, a historical starting point for reflection of the theological kind.

Nevertheless, the tone which a faith-discourse legitimately takes on be-cause it privileges the world of the poor should not make us lose sight of the larger picture of what is called into question by the situation of all the poor. Nor should we neglect the common terrain from which our languages and reflections start and on which they discourse: that of the insignificant, of their integral liberation, and of the good news of Jesus directed preferentially to all of them. In fact, we must avoid at all costs letting necessary and urgent atten-tion to the sufferings and hopes of the poor give rise to the useless search for private theological preserves. These would be the source of exclusivities and mistrust which, since in essence these are converging and complementary perspectives, end up weakening the daily fight of the dispossessed for life, justice, and respect for their cultural and religious values. The same goes for their fight for the right to be equal at the same time as being different.

The complexity of the universe of the poor and of the perspective of the other, as I have recalled, is today better delineated with all their problems and conflicts, but at the same time with all their promise. I will not try to locate all the theological currents which have arisen from this situation under a single rubric, for the diversity here is equally important. However, the obvious his-torical bonds among them, as well as the horizon of the complex world of the poor which they share and in which they are located, allow us to see them as fruitful expressions of the present tasks of theological reflection when carried out from the perspective of the dispossessed of our continent. They represent open quarries.

Globalization and Poverty

We are not with the poor if we are not against poverty, said Paul Ricoeur many years ago—that is, if we do not reject the condition which overwhelms such a huge part of humanity. It is not a matter of a merely emotional rejection; we must come to know what it is that causes poverty on the social, economic, and cultural levels. This requires the analytical tools which are provided by the human sciences, but like all scientific thought they work with hypotheses which allow us to understand the reality they seek to explain. This is the same as saying that they are called upon to change in the face of new phenomena. This is what is happening today in the face of the dominance of neoliberalism, which has been carried to power on the shoulders of an economy more and more independent of politics (and even more of ethics). This autonomy is due to something we have come to know by the somewhat barbarous term *global-ization*.

As is well known, the reality designated by this term comes from the world of the media but has strong repercussions in the economic and social arena and in other fields of human activity. Nevertheless, the word is deceptive, be-cause it makes us think that we stand before a single world, when in fact, and at this point in time, it leads ineluctably to its opposite: the exclusion of a part of humanity from the economic loop and from the so-called benefits of contemporary civilization. What we have is a more and more pronounced asymmetry. Millions of people are converted in this way into useless objects or into disposable objects which are thrown away after use. We are talking about those who remain outside the sphere of knowledge, the decisive element in the economy of our time and the most important axis of capital accumulation. It is worth noting that this polarization is the result of the way globalization is being carried out today. Globalization itself constitutes a fact which does not necessarily have to take its present course toward growing inequality. And, as we know, without equality there is no justice. We know this, but in our time the problem is becoming more urgent.[10]

Economic neoliberalism postulates a market without restrictions, expected to regulate itself by its own means, and subjects all social solidarity in this field to a harsh critique, accusing it not only of being ineffective in ending poverty but even of being one of the causes of poverty. That there have been cases of abuse in this regard is clear and widely recognized, but here we have a rejection in principle which leaves society's most fragile members out in the cold. One of the consequences of this kind of thinking—and among the most painful and severe—is the foreign debt which has left poor nations shackled and beaten down. This is a debt which grew spectacularly thanks to, among other things, the interest rates set by the very creditors themselves. Cancellation of this debt was one of the most concrete and important points of the convocation called by John Paul II to celebrate a Jubilee Year, in the biblical sense of the term, in the year 2000.

This dehumanization of the economy, begun quite a while ago, which tends to convert everything, including persons, into merchandise, has been condemned by a theology which exposes the idolatrous nature (in the biblical sense of the term) of this development. However, the situation today not only makes it increasingly urgent to point this out, but also provides new elements which allow us to make a deeper theological analysis. On the other hand, we are currently witnessing a strange effort to justify economic neoliberalism theologically by comparing, for example, multinational corporations with the Servant of Yahweh, attacked and vilified by all, but from which justice and salvation will nevertheless come. And this is to say nothing of the so-called theology of prosperity, which has very close links, of course, with the position I just mentioned. This has sometimes led people to postulate a certain parallelism between Christianity and neoliberal doctrines. Without denying these impressions, we might wonder how far such an effort can go when it reminds us of the attempt—at the opposite extreme—to refute Marxism by taking it as a kind of religion which supposedly paralleled, element for element, the Christian message (original sin and private property, the need for a redeemer and the proletariat, etc.). But of course this remark does not eliminate the need for a radical critique of the ideas prevailing today in the field of economics. Quite the contrary.

We cannot avoid doing theology by beginning with the poor, the favorites of God. This theology must take into account the autonomy proper to the discipline of economics and at the same time remain aware of its relation to the totality of the life of human beings. This requires, first of all, that we take up an ethical demand. For the same reason, while staying clear of the interplay among the positions I mentioned in the previous paragraph, we should not lose sight of the fact that the strongest rejection of neoliberal positions begins with the contradictions of an economy which cynically, and in the long run suicidally, forgets about the human being. In particular it forgets those who are defenseless in this field; today that means the majority of humankind. At issue is an ethical question, in the broadest sense of the term, which obliges us to look into the perverse mechanisms which distort from within that human activity which we call the economy. Valuable efforts at theological reflection along these lines are being made among us.

Within this problematic of globalization and poverty, we also need to situate the perspectives opened up by ecological concerns raised in the face of the destruction—equally suicidal—of the environment. These concerns have made us more sensitive to all the dimensions of the gift of life and have helped us to widen the horizon of social solidarity, which must include a respectful link to nature. This matter does not affect only the developed countries whose industries cause so much damage to the natural habitat of humanity; it affects everyone, including the poorest countries. It is not possible today to think theologically about poverty without taking into consideration these realities.

Deepening Spirituality

If the previous points were in one way or another already developed or intimated from the very beginning in liberation theology (which is not to deny, of course, what is new and creative in the work we have seen since then), the theme of spirituality was always a major concern. Not only is spirituality a matter of consequence to every Christian; the very fate of the kind of theology I have been proposing depends on it. Indeed, I have been deeply convinced for a long time—and am immensely indebted to the work of M. D. Chenu in this—that behind every faith-understanding is a way of following Jesus.[11] "Spirituality" is the word we use today to designate what is known in the Gospels as "following Jesus." This is what forms the backbone of faith discourse. This is what gives theology its deepest meaning and its breadth. This is one of the main points in construing theology as a reflection on practice, the very heart of discipleship. Its two great and interconnected dimensions—prayer and commitment in history—make up what the Gospel of Matthew calls "doing the Father's will" in contrast to simply saying "Lord, Lord" (7:21). Thus the claim that "our methodology is our spirituality" takes on meaning.[12] Both are paths to God, and we have to keep moving forward along them.

In recent years we have seen an abundance of publications along the lines of a liberation spirituality. The reason is simple: in the midst of a historical process which has known both successes and failures, the spiritual experience of the poor in Latin America has matured. Interest in spirituality in no way signifies a withdrawal from social commitments which for us remain totally in effect as expressions of solidarity with the poor and oppressed. Those who think otherwise seem innocent of the radicalness which comes from getting to the deepest level of things where love for God and love for the neighbor are united every day. Spirituality is located at this depth. Far from being an evasion of the challenges of the present, it provides steadfastness and durability to the commitments to which I just alluded. Rilke was right when he said that God is found in our roots. And we never finish deepening them.

In the very nucleus of the preferential option for the poor is a spiritual element: the experience of God's gratuitous love. The rejection of injustice and of the oppression it implies is anchored in our faith in the God of life. It is not surprising, therefore, that this option has been signed and sealed with the blood of those who, as Archbishop Romero used to say, have died with the "mark of a martyr." Besides the case of the archbishop of San Salvador himself, this is the reality suffered by numerous Christians on a continent which at the same time claims to be Christian. We cannot leave aside this cruel paradox in considering the spirituality of Latin America. The truth is that in many ways the experience of the cross marks the daily life of Latin American and Peruvian Christians.[13]

What is fundamental within this framework of ideas is the spiritual journey of people who live out their faith and maintain their hope in the midst of a daily lot of poverty and marginalization but also of plans and a greater awareness of their rights. The poor of Latin America have embarked upon the road of affirming their human dignity and their status as daughters and sons of God. On this journey there is an encounter with the Lord, crucified and risen. To be attentive to this spiritual experience and to gather up the oral accounts and writings which narrate it become an indispensable task of theological reflection done by Latin Americans. "Drinking from their own well": that is what I once called this moment, using an expression from Bernard of Clairvaux. Their own waters show us the degree to which Christian faith has been inculturated in those peoples who are poor but also possess a culture and a historical trajectory different from those we find in the North Atlantic world.

What I have just said follows from what was noted above, namely that Latin Americans are, for the most part, both poor and believing. At the heart of a situation which excludes and mistreats them and from which they seek to liberate themselves, the poor believe in the God of life. As our friends Victor (now deceased) and Irene Chero said to John Paul II in the name of the poor of Peru—more than a million of whom were present for the occasion—during the pope's 1985 visit to our country, "With our hearts broken by suffering, we see our wives pregnant while ill with tuberculosis, our babies dying, our children growing up weak and without a future." And they added, "But despite all of this, we believe in the God of life." This is a context, or rather a living reality, which reflection on faith cannot avoid. On the contrary, such reflection must be nourished by it—unceasingly.

Let me say a few words by way of conclusion. If, as might be expected, I have emphasized the challenge which comes from the world of poverty, I in no way think that the other two questions do not affect us in Latin America and the Caribbean. Theological reflection in the Christian world must face all three of the aforementioned challenges and also clarify their interrelationships. I have barely touched on them in these pages, but I am convinced of the importance and fruitfulness of establishing their interconnection.

To do this we will have to avoid the temptation of pigeonholing by assigning these challenges to the different continents: the challenge of modernity to the Western world, that of poverty to Latin America and Africa, and that of religious pluralism to Asia. This would be a simplistic solution which overlooks the interactions and points of contact among different peoples and cultures today. It also ignores the speed of communications, which we are now witnessing and which gives rise to a sense of closeness felt by people who are geographically far apart.

Naturally there are emphases proper to the diverse regions of humanity. But they are only that—accents. At the present we are called to a theological task which takes new routes and maintains with a firm hand both the particularity and the universality of the reality we are experiencing. This mission cannot be carried out apart from a great sensitivity to the diverse challenges I have recalled or without a respectful and open dialogue which takes as its historical starting point all aspects of the conditions in which human beings are living, as well as the condition of their dignity. This holds in a special way for the poor and the excluded who, for Christians, reveal the presence of the God of Jesus Christ among us.

We stand before a stimulating and promising mission in which there remains much for liberation theology to do and, above all, to learn.

NOTES

1. This is why—curiously enough—those who wonder if liberation theology remains valid after the events symbolized by the fall of the Berlin Wall (certainly an event of enormous importance on the international stage) need to be reminded that the historical starting point for this theology was not the situation of the Eastern European countries. It was, and certainly continues to be, the inhuman poverty of Latin America and the interpretation we make of it in the light of faith. What we have,

then, are a state of things and a theology which, at their core, have little to do with the collapse of real socialism.

2. One of the important factors in this process was, as we know, scientific thought. The matter has acquired a new urgency with the development of aspects of science (biogenetics, for example) which raise serious questions for the Christian view of life.

3. See in this regard the important work *Historia del Concilio Vatican II* in process of publication in various languages, directed by Giuseppe Alberigo.

4. See Gustavo Gutiérrez, "¿Dónde dormirán los pobres?" in *El rostro de Dios en la historia* (Lima: Universidad Católica, Instituto Bartolomé de Las Casas, CEP, 1996), 9–69.

5. See, for example, Jacques Dupuis, *Vers une théologie chrétienne du pluralisme religieux* (Paris: Cerf, 1997).

6. For a brief overview the reader may consult M. Fédou, *Les religions selon la foi chrétienne* (Paris: Cerf, 1996).

7. This is a point on which Sri Lankan theologian Aloysius Pieris rightly insists. See, for example, *An Asian Theology of Liberation* (Maryknoll, N.Y.: Orbis, 1988).

8. This will allow me to provide bibliographical references on these subjects which I am removing for now. Nevertheless, cf. those which are found in "¿Dónde dormirán los pobres?"

9. This is expressed in formulas found in the first works of liberation theology. In reference to the poor, I spoke repeatedly of "peoples, races, and social classes" (*A Theology of Liberation: History, Politics, and Salvation*, rev. ed., trans. Caridad Inda and John Eagleson [Maryknoll, N.Y.: Orbis, 1988], 103; see also 116, 118) and of "exploited popular classes, oppressed cultures, and races discriminated against" (see the 1973 essay "Liberation Praxis and Christian Faith" published in my *Power of the Poor in History* [Maryknoll, N.Y.: Orbis, 1979], 37; see also 51, 60, 62, 64, and 70). Similar expressions are found in my 1976 essay "God's Revelation and Proclamation in History" (in *Power of the Poor*, 18, 20–21, 22). Likewise, it was affirmed that "women from these sectors are doubly exploited, marginalized, and scorned" (found in my 1977 essay "Theology from the Underside of History" in *Power of the Poor*, 218 n. 54; and in my 1978 essay "The Historical Power of the Poor," in *Power of the Poor*, 102). See as well Gustavo Gutiérrez, "La mujer: Lo último de lo último," *Mujer y Sociedad* 44 (1991): 14–15.

10. Cf. in this regard the penetrating studies of Norberto Bobbio, *Destra e sinistra: Ragioni e significati di una distinzione politica* (Rome: Donzelli, 1994).

11. Cf. his famous *Une école de théologie: Le Saulchoir* (Paris: Cerf, 1985; originally published in 1937).

12. Gustavo Gutiérrez, "The Historical Power of the Poor" (1978), in *Power of the Poor in History*, 103–4.

13. See the excellent works of Jon Sobrino on these themes.

5

The Option for the Poor and the Exclusion of Women: The Challenges of Postmodernism and Feminism to Liberation Theology

Elina Vuola

In this essay, I start from the personally held conviction that what
we call postmodernism is an ambiguous legacy which should not
uncritically be either rejected or appropriated by scholars who see
themselves as speaking from such politically and socially critical intellectual spaces as liberation theology, feminism, and postcolonialism. I will argue for the importance of a dialogue between liberation
theology and selected variants of postmodernism, which would entail a critical look at how the option for the poor—as the crucial
epistemological claim in liberation theology—also has excluded
some voices. The postmodern challenge at its best asks to look at
the relativity of different subject positions with the critical eyes of
"yet another other." This characteristic of postmodernism is what
makes it important and relevant for any critical theory and practice,
without separating, let us say, feminism, liberation theology, and
postcolonial theories from each other. I also consider myself working inside the liberation-theological paradigm, if understood widely
in both a conceptual and a geographical sense. An ongoing dialogue
between different currents of liberation theology is necessary if we
want to develop some of its great insights further and take them seriously also in the contemporary global situation. In this essay, by
the phrase *liberation theology* I mean mainly Latin American liberation theology. Most feminist theologians I quote would see them-

selves doing liberation theology as well. My critique of some aspects of liberation theology rises from an empathetic expectation that the praxis starting point and the option for the poor be taken more seriously than has actually been done.

An option for something or somebody implies optionality. Ironically, the great liberation-theological insight of opting for the poor has also meant *not* opting for some others. This is probably most clear in how poor women *as women* have not been present in most of liberation theology. The bodily, subjective, intimate suffering of women, because of the denial of the church(es) and state(s) to take it seriously, is at the heart of the challenges that feminism and postmodernism pose for liberation theology. In Latin American studies and feminist theories, multiple interpretations of postmodernism have been offered, some of which could potentially serve as bridges in the faltering dialogue between important reinterpretations of the Latin American reality in contemporary world, such as postcolonial theories, liberation theology, and feminism. Liberation theology is certainly an important partner in this dialogue, but only insofar as its representatives are willing to look also at why and how the option for the poor has become excluding, based on a very narrow (Christian, Catholic) theological anthropology, on the one hand, and on an equally narrow class-based interpretation of praxis and of the poor, on the other hand.

Latin Americans at the Academic *Post* Office . . .

Among Latin American scholars and in the context of Latin American studies internationally, the challenges raised by postmodernism have been mainly debated in the fields of literary criticism, feminist studies, and philosophy—not theology. However, if we understand postmodernism so broadly that it would include all the discourses of the other and otherness, we could agree with Leonardo Boff when he says that "among Third World theologians, Latin Americans have engaged significantly with issues of postmodernity."[1] The ambiguous and even contradictory relationship of liberation theologians to postmodernism is expressed in the same quotation from Boff, where he goes on to say that issues of postmodernity "have influenced many intellectuals, particularly affluent young people with global connections."[2] As far as I know, most first-generation liberation theologians—maybe with the exception of Enrique Dussel, who would best be counted as a philosopher rather than a theologian—have *not* directly engaged the issues of postmodern debates. As I will show later, some scholars of a younger generation—not all necessarily Latin American—theorize postmodernism positively in the context of liberation theology.

There is also great confusion regarding what we in fact mean when we speak of postmodernism, but it cannot be analyzed here in depth. Sometimes postcolonial theories are seen as one expression or form of postmodernism, which again takes the definition in a different direction: "Third World theologies have, since their inception, already engaged themselves in a postcolonial task when they challenge the Western construction of Christianity and reformulate contextual theologies that aim to free themselves from being a tool of the colonial master."[3] My understanding is that postmodernism, in all its heterogeneity, is not only a project that belongs to or affects the West, nor is postcolonialism something that would have relevance only for colonial or Third World settings. There is a connection between the two, which several scholars also have tried to explicate. Unfortunately, liberation theologians by and large have not entered a substantial debate neither with postmodernism nor with postcolonialism.

There are understandable reasons for liberation theologians to reject postmodernism as the latest intellectual project of the West, if it is understood as a theory in which all attempts to interpret history and contemporary world from the margins are considered as partial, subjective, and without universal value or challenge. Extreme individualism, subjectivity, and "lightness," as well as the death of metanarratives, would thus be equated with postmodernism. However, there are more complex interpretations—mostly nontheological—of postmodernism in which it is seen as having both positive and negative impacts on critical thinking and political action.[4]

Among these, most notably, are different feminist theories, from both the North and the South, and postcolonial theories. Postmodernism can help the inclusion of a broader range of interests and positions that formerly have been allowed to participate in the public political sphere and, even if imperfectly, to create a critical self-consciousness of the present.[5] The latter could also be translated as a critical consciousness of the social location or position from which we speak and act, so important for both different liberation theologies and various branches of feminist theory. Even when the main currents of postmodernism have not been able to go beyond Eurocentrism, various critical thinkers from Latin America use postmodern theories for a *different* reading and critique of modernity, based on the experiences of colonialism and, especially in the case of Latin America, the conquest of America as an inherent part of European modernity.[6] Non-Eurocentric interpretations of modernity and its crisis can be found in different feminist theories, subaltern studies, and postcolonial studies. They share with postmodernism, even if critically, some important insights and owe an intellectual debt to several postmodern thinkers.[7] According to George Yúdice, "Rethinking democracy outside of the terms set by the *grand récit* of modernity is an enterprise many Latin American social movements see as necessary."[8] The debates on postmodernism are often about the possibilities for establishing a democratic culture in societies in which it is increasingly difficult to establish common meanings across the entire social terrain. This means that Euro-/North American interpretations of postmodernism need to be recreated in the Latin American contexts.[9] This, naturally, implies that they are neither rejected nor appropriated uncritically.

... And the Feminists

Similarly, the relationship between postmodernism and feminist theories is ambiguous, not only in a First World setting but in different Third World feminisms as well. Not even feminist theorists who would call themselves postmodern are one unified group—what they have in common is a critical attitude to the destabilization of traditional understandings of the "subject." Some feminists reject postmodern theories as unnecessary or even harmful for a feminist theory and political practice. However, questions of power, difference(s), subjectivity, marginalization, social location, and the contextual nature of knowledge are all issues that several postmodern thinkers share with both feminist and postcolonial theories.

As is well known, the postmodern feminist critique focuses on the very criteria by which claims to knowledge are legitimized. Postmodern feminist theory criticizes unitary notions of woman and gender and gender identity with plural and complexly constructed conceptions of social identity.[10] This is both a result of and a possibility for various non-Eurocentric women's voices and experiences becoming heard and taken seriously.

However, there are also those feminist theorists for whom postmodernism entails the danger of dissolving different subjects into "a perplexing plurality of differences, none of which can be theoretically or politically privileged over others." In the case of women, "*she* dissolves into *he*."[11] Postmodernism thus leads to ethical and epistemological relativism.[12] Here again, we can see how the conclusions we draw from postmodernism depend on how we comprehend the concept itself, resulting sometimes in not only ambiguous but also confusing discourses.

The contemporary emphasis on diversity in feminist theory is a result of both those postmodern views that reject modernity's claims to universal truth and criticisms made by women from the Third World, postcolonial feminism, and women of color. According to Deniz Kandiyoti:

> The critique of modernity, partly indebted to the poststructuralist turn in the social sciences, found echoes in a parallel body of feminist criticism which revealed the gender-biased and masculinist premises of universalist discourses about rights and citizenship in the West. An affinity thus developed between postcolonial scholar-

ship and feminist criticism in so far as they focus on processes of exclusion and domination implicit in the construction of the "universal" subject.[13]

Those voices in contemporary feminism which stress at least some aspects of a universal humanity and take that as the starting point for political activism usually have two things in common. First, they assume that culture (including religion and gender constructions) is not a transhistorical entity, homogeneous and immutable. Each culture is crisscrossed by internal divisions, including those of power. Each culture has changed and will change. Second, this perspective rises from concrete knowledge and analysis of various political practices and intellectual "counterdiscourses," including women's movements and feminisms. There is a practical knowledge of certain ideas that different women's movements (even those that do not call themselves feminist) have considered fundamental and unyielding in different cultures. The cornerstone of this is the recognition of the various forms of violence that women suffer all over the world as women, but also the richness and diversity of the forms of resistance to it. Postcolonial feminism "explores women's racialised and sexualised otherness by locating their marginality and oppression within a three-tiered structure of discrimination maintained by colonial and neocolonial indigenous patriarchies and the academic and cultural hegemony of Western feminism."[14] This, together with the postmodern claim that knowledge and power are integrally related and that knowledge is always partial, is but one of the things that brings this sort of an interpretation of postmodernism (and feminism) very close to the most original interests of any liberation theology. In fact, this link is explicitly made in different contexts.[15]

Many non-Western feminists stress *both* the universality of human and women's rights *and* remind that cultural differences must be taken seriously. This could maybe be called a pluralist position between the two extremes of a naïve universalism and cultural relativism. These persons are also extremely cautious about such a feminism that keeps silent about serious human-rights violations in another culture, just in order not to be labeled as ethnocentric or imperialist.

In Latin America, the disappointment of many women with both the institutional Catholic Church and the *iglesia de los pobres* alike, as well as with various revolutionary vanguard movements, which, in Jean Franco's words, "allowed them equality only in death,"[16] makes issues of gender construction(s) and gender relations especially important for a possible overlapping dialogue between liberation theology, postmodernism, and feminism, without forgetting that this dialogue should take place in a context for the demand of radical democracy (implying that gender and race are central in the construction of democracy) in Latin American societies.

The Theological *Post*

By stressing the ambiguous legacy of postmodernism on feminist and post-colonial theories, I am most concerned to point out that it would be important to find some sort of a critical space that takes seriously different forms of oppression and suffering, on the one hand, while also simultaneously looking critically at the different attempts to interpret them, on the other. These attempts include liberation theologies. This means, among other things, that there might be unexpected allies for theorists and political activists who seek alternatives to the present chaos—for example, secular feminists for liberation theologians, liberation theologians for postmodernists. In reality, liberation theologians are sometimes found siding with the Vatican (in issues of sexual ethics and reproduction, as well as in the critique of neoliberal economics) and mostly at odds with any sort of feminist discourse and practice, especially those which wish to look at all the aforementioned issues together: the effects of neoliberal policies on already impoverished women and their lack of power in their reproductive role.

I would argue that a more nuanced and clear analysis of postmodernism in the context of Latin American liberation theology could make some of its claims about representing or speaking for or opting for the poor clearer and, more importantly, politically more radical. This means entering into a more serious dialogue with such nontheological theories as postcolonialism (post-occidentalism according to Walter Mignolo)[17] and feminist studies in the Latin American context.[18] The traditional multidisciplinarity and use of social sciences in liberation theology would mean today taking into account these new ways of theorizing and interpreting suffering, marginalization, and colonialism in the Latin American context.

That task has been taken up by a new generation of Latin American(ist) scholars, influenced not only by liberation theology and the social scientific and philosophical theories behind it, but by feminist and postcolonial theories and postmodernism as well. These scholars are not self-evidently located in the geographical Latin America but are physically and intellectually scattered around the world. It is a generation which speaks from a "global context" in which it is not as easy as before to define one's intellectual, political, and social location. Even though possibly trivial, I could take myself as an example. I am writing this essay on the Arctic Circle in Finnish Lapland, aiming at participating, as a feminist, in a discussion that has to do with Latin America but principally for a U.S. audience. My wish to take seriously postmodernism, feminism, and liberation theology—all three—is shaped by my political and intellectual interest in different attempts of human liberation, in the midst of so much evidence of the opposite. An emancipatory interest, in the terms of Jürgen Habermas, can be found in all those three attempts to interpret the contemporary world. This does not mean, however, that it is to be found in them without critical interpretation. The most fruitful location may be found at the intersection and dialogue of the three, but this again is not guaranteed by simplistic notions of location, subjectivity, and experience.

These Latin American(ist) scholars, who are trying to realize this kind of a dialogue, recognize the theoretical and political importance and impact of liberation theology, but they also raise issues that are either foreign or new for most first-generation liberation theologians. The impact of postmodern thinking on them takes the issues of social location, context, subjectivity, and power in a new and different direction. It is by and large these scholars with whom I agree when they claim that

> its many-sided grounding and method of decentering one domi-
> nating voice put liberation theology in natural dialogue with post-
> modern analyses. Postmodern thinking also concerns itself with the
> limitations and underside of rationality and of subjectivity. It is a
> "decanonization" of conventional authorities, since it assumes that
> no thinking is free from time, place, or interest. Much like postmod-
> ernity, liberation theology situates itself as a way and language of
> the "outposts," a delegitimizing of the center of knowledge and of
> power.[19]

The *locus* of liberation theology, the poor of the marginalized Latin American continent, "the South," has meant from the very beginning a new critical subject position of the intellectual, in this case the theologian. Thus, what takes most liberation theologies close to postmodern and feminist theories is their claim for a different voice, a different identity, a different *locus* from which to speak and act—the *desde donde* of Latin American liberation theology. However, identity hardly is about only national, geographical, cultural, or religious identity. It is also about gender, sexuality, ethnicity, education, age, and the overlapping of these. It is the latter constructions of identity which have been lacking in much of liberation theology, designed and defined primarily around macrolevel questions such as nation, class, and (anti)imperialism. The neglect of the individual subject in liberation theology has not necessarily meant re-jecting "Western individualism" as sometimes is claimed, but it has also meant closing one's eyes to a suffering which has some most devastating effects on the individual level, such as sexual or racial violence.

According to Mignolo, a radical liberation theology or philosophy would question the basic assumptions of occidental rationality from the perspective of local histories and colonized or subaltern knowledges—a project which by definition is pluri-topic and not mono-topic, di- or pluri-versal rather than uni-versal.[20] It is easy to see how this project has been present in liberation theology since its beginning ("thinking from the underside of history," "thinking from the margins," etc.)—however, it is less clear how liberation theologians have been able to conceptualize and differentiate that *from where*. The postmodern insight on the relativity of different subject positions is relevant here. This does not mean an absolute relativity of all positions; instead, it means that one should always be willing to look at one's own truth-claims and positions with the critical eyes of others.

The poor in Latin American liberation theology form a similar category to women in feminist theory, or especially in feminist theology.[21] In much of feminist thinking, the term *woman* has been deconstructed and revealed to be a much too vague and homogenous concept to include the multiple forms of oppression that women experience. This has happened mainly because of a simultaneous influence of postmodern theories on feminist theory and the critique from Third World and postcolonial feminists of the impossibility of a hegemonic feminist theory to include the experiences of women outside the Western academic world. However, a similar deconstruction of the poor has not happened in most of mainstream liberation theology, in spite of the now-common claim that the poor do not suffer only because of their material poverty but also—and even more—as women, indigenous, black, and so on. In liberation theology, this recognition of the multiple forms of poverty and the heterogeneous experiences of the poor has happened mostly at the level of inclusion of new subjects within the more general and homogenous poor. However, there has not been a sufficiently critical look at the presuppositions of what *de facto* forms the praxis and the option for the poor in liberation theology and what are the results of giving primacy to a praxis which not only includes but also excludes.

This is an extremely complicated and large issue and cannot be worked out in detail in this limited context. I will look at this problematic from one angle, that of the impoverished and marginalized women in Latin America and the silence that surrounds their life conditions and basic rights. However, let us first take a short look at how the option for the poor has been understood in liberation theology.

The Option for the Poor: Who Opts for Whom?

Since the 1968 Medellín conference, the preferential option for the poor has been *the* option of the Latin American Catholic Church, at least formally. It is a concept created by liberation theologians and introduced into official church documents. According to Julio Lois, "The option for the poor consists, first of all, of a voluntary decision that leads to an incarnation in the world of the poor, to assume with historical realism their cause for integral liberation."[22] The option must be realized both at a personal-individual level and at a communitarian-ecclesiastical level. Individual believers, Christian groups and communities, different ecclesiastical sectors, and the church in its entirety are all responsible for the realization of the option.[23]

According to Lois, there are four fundamental elements in the option for poor:

1. rupture (*ruptura*) with one's own social, cultural, and political status
2. incarnation or identification with the poor that expresses itself in the encounter with the poor; entering the world of the poor and assuming it as one's own
3. active solidarity with the poor and the defense of their rights; this equates to the historical praxis of liberation
4. assuming the destiny of the poor as one's own; often this means persecution and martyrdom; this is the final criterion for the verification of the authenticity of the second element[24]

Naturally, all this is quite different for those who are poor and for those who are not poor themselves.

For Boff, the option for the poor is threefold: (1) a political option, (2) an ethical option (since the situation is not accepted as it is), and (3) an evangelical option (because the poor were the first addressees of Jesus' message).[25] For Gustavo Gutiérrez, the term *preferential* rejects all kinds of exclusion and refers to the universality of God's love, giving preference to those who must be the first. The word *option* refers to the free and committing character of a decision. In the ultimate instance, the option for the poor means an option for God: it is a theocentric and prophetic option.[26] The Christian message is universal, but universality can be affirmed and realized only from particularity (the poor).[27]

According to one of the think tanks of liberation theology, Departamento Ecuménico de Investigaciones (DEI) in San José, Costa Rica, the option for the poor today translates into an option for the excluded. In an inclusive society (*una sociedad donde quepan todo/as*, a term borrowed from the Mexican Zapatista movement) the option for the poor also means defending the absolute character and value of human life, which is a concrete reality. The option for the poor in the contemporary system of globalization thus means affirming life as an absolute (*la afirmación de la vida como un absoluto*) and as the central ethical criterion.[28] The option for the poor today also means, according to the research team of DEI, a radically anti-idolatrous option toward a postcapitalist alternative society. Human life and the human body become the sources for a globalization of solidarity.[29] I will come back to this at the end of the essay; for now, it suffices to show how there are also new interpretations in liberation theology of what the option for the poor means.

Especially at the dawn of liberation theology, academic liberation theologians preferred to understand themselves as "organic intellectuals" in the

Gramscian way. According to Juan Luis Segundo, liberation theologians accepted being organic intellectuals, seeing as their tasks the representation of the community, the articulation of a foundation for their intra- and extracommunal demands, and the providing for them of the fundamentals of a conscientization that is appropriate to their possibilities of knowledge and analysis of reality.[30] According to him, "There is no doubt that liberation theology, in its simplest and most basic forms, plays an important and, in some extraordinary cases, decisive role in satisfying these needs." He himself "translates" this role of a theologian into "teaching to analyze reality." This, according to some, is a crucial shift in the role of the intellectual (theologian) from individual scholarly authority to reflective community advocate.[31] Even if true, it also entails problems which have to do with the question of who represents whom and speaks for whom, opts for whom, and in what way.

It is, however, the issue of representativeness that has changed the role of a "radical" intellectual. According to Horacio Cerutti Guldberg, the theoretical problems and difficulties included in the option for the poor have generally been obscured. If most liberation theologians' claim that "only the exploited and those who side with them can see the perversity of the system" (José María Vigil) is true, how can one change the position or place (lugar), asks Cerutti Guldberg. He criticizes the option for the poor in most of liberation theology as some kind of guarantee of orthodoxy and orthopraxis, which is not far from "the unsustainable uncriticality of a proletarian science."[32] Thus, it is the question about the epistemological status of one's truth-claims, rising partly from postmodern theories, that has had an impact on thinkers who neither want to give up critical thinking nor the political implications of their role as intellectuals—in other words, who want to combine scholarship with some sort of social and political transformation. This combination may and probably does look different from the "organic intellectual" of the 1970s.

According to Santiago Castro-Gómez, referring to Gayatri Chakravorty Spivak, the role of the critic of colonialism is not to represent "the wretched of the earth" as did the earlier anticolonialist narratives.[33] He places liberation theology among these anticolonialist discourses which use the language of otherness and frame their discourse in binary opposites (oppressors—oppressed, the powerful—the powerless, the center—the periphery, etc.).[34]

Very much the same could be said of the sort of feminist discourse which tended to see the world only in terms of male-female opposition, being unable to theorize those women who do not experience oppression only as gender oppression. It is important to remember that the differentiation of the very term woman and the acknowledgement of the interrelatedness of different sorts of oppression came to feminist theory largely due to the critique from Third World feminists and economically or racially disadvantaged women in the First World setting. Thus, it is not only—or even mainly—an abstract postmodern discourse which brought these questions to the fore; it is also the other way round: the acceptance of the multiplicity of subject positions and voices, which cannot be subsumed in any one big narrative of oppression, came to post-modernism through the political struggles of feminists, antiracist movements, and anticolonialist movements.

According to Castro-Gómez, what the postcolonial discourses do is a critique of modernity, similar to postmodernism, not from inside Europe or North America but from the perspective of the former colonies.[35] The representation of others becomes impossible; instead, the intellectual (liberation theologian, feminist, postcolonial critic, etc.) takes a consciously political position in the multiple spaces of oppression, one of them being the academy, both in the North and the South.

In the words of Mignolo, speaking of a philosophy of liberation, which can be applied to theology as well: "As long as forms of domination are multiple, there cannot be a single principle of social transformation, and a grand theory is no longer possible. . . . Liberation philosophy cannot be monotopic and universal discourse 'speaking' the liberation of diverse constituencies of civil society that can be identified as 'oppressed.' "[36]

This, in a sense, is a postmodern way to say that the role of the intellectual, including the liberation theologian, is not to speak for or represent anybody. It is also about the question of the thinking and acting subject: who is he (usually he) who speaks for others but not for or about himself? This is where feminist theorists, including theologians, have brought in the bodily, gendered, individual subject who not only sees and interprets suffering but who experiences it in her own being. It does not mean stressing the isolated individual at the cost of the community. It is often the voice of the individual whose experiences of suffering have been silenced in the name of the community, which does not take seriously those personal experiences. This is the experience of many women in progressive social movements and revolutionary processes, of which contemporary Latin America offers us several examples.

Obviously, the option for the poor and its theological, epistemological, spiritual, and political consequences can be seen as the major innovations of liberation theology. But a radical and critical question about the subject of theology goes further. Liberation theologians have consciously taken "the dominated and dependent Latin America" as their starting point, but they have not been as critical of other "places" that define their theologizing, such as race and gender. This is why we should be critical of idealizing statements such as this, by Spanish theologian Juan José Tamayo-Acosta:

> The theologies developed in the First World are "theologies of
> (de)" while Latin America is the cradle of "theologies from (desde)."
> This means that the liberation theologians are conscious of the lim-

its and conditionings of their theologizing. . . . This is something of capital importance, since these conditionings constitute "an indispensable hermeneutical factor."[37]

If "limits and conditionings" reflect only economic, political, and overall social factors, then this statement certainly is true, especially when comparing liberation theology with most of European and North American theology. But surely there are other limits and conditionings, of which Latin American liberation theologians are not much more conscious—or are even less so—than their European or North American colleagues.

The supposed collective subject (the poor, the other) of liberation theology certainly has changed the role of an academic intellectual. Nevertheless, the majority of the most prominent liberation theologians are clerics (with a special meaning in the Catholic Church where women's ordination is out of the question and priests do not marry), highly educated, male, and *mestizo*, that is, "white" in the eyes of the black and indigenous population.[38]

From a feminist perspective, there are serious aspects of poverty that liberation theology has said nothing about or, worse, on which they tend to agree with or come close to the official Vatican teaching. This is clearest in issues of sexuality and reproduction and how they are related to high incidences of both maternal and infant mortality in the context of poverty, women's overall lack of power over their reproductive capabilities, and the everyday violence experienced by them. The option for the poor has not been translated as the option for the poor woman, in spite of the presence of feminist liberation theology in Latin America and elsewhere, which has made this point explicitly since at least the mid-1980s.[39] In María Pilar Aquino's words, "The struggle against the sin of sexism is *not optional* for Third World liberation theologians, feminist or non-feminist."[40] The reality, however, is that still today much of liberation theology considers sexism as either an issue of and for women or as something that would take them to such a conflicting position with the official church(es) that it is best avoided: the option for the poor woman has been optional for liberation theology.

Opting for Women and Their Reproductive Rights

When it comes to reproductive rights and issues of sexuality, it is obvious that the Catholic Church is one of the most important power factors—if not the most important—in these issues in Latin America. As a scholar of religion, I would say that the Catholic monopoly in sexual ethics and values concerning that ethics must be met and challenged by adequate tools of analysis. Neither secular feminist movements nor Catholic women without any formal education (especially in theology) meet this need. Very much the same can be said of the most prominent liberation theologians, both male and female, who keep silent about issues of sexuality and reproduction.[41]

It is the silence, along with cultural taboos, around issues of sexuality that creates the strange situation where women simultaneously consider themselves as good Catholics, embrace the Catholic teaching on contraception and abortion, but in reality use contraception and abort when necessary. The amount of shame and inner conflict for a woman after an illegal abortion (when it did not kill her) is, of course, a direct result of a sexual ethic that is not based on women's everyday concrete experiences and needs, but it may be intensified by a kind of feminist discourse which does not understand and take into account the importance of the Catholic tradition for women. Many women are in a situation where nobody understands them fully. Sometimes the persons who come closest to understanding them are Catholic, feminist-oriented nuns. It is no wonder, then, that the first person in Latin America to speak openly on the need for decriminalization of abortion from within the church and liberation theology has been Ivone Gebara, a Catholic nun working with poor women in northeastern Brazil.[42] However, even an open political stance for the decriminalization of abortion has not led liberation theologians to rework the theological underpinnings of traditional sexual ethics, which could be seen as a more urgent thing to do, considering the silence that surrounds issues of sexuality and sexual ethics in Latin America and the weight of Catholic teaching about them.

(Secular) feminist interpretations too easily see Catholic women as passive recipients of religiously founded images of selfhood and sexuality. Polarized explanations too easily omit the practices of agency and the experiences of conflicting images of selfhood in women, both individually and collectively. This may lead to scholars seeing women as a homogeneous group of "poor Third World women," passive victims of colonialism, misogynist religions, and sexism.[43] If (feminist) scholars see established religion only as oppressive or backward, they are operating within the same polarized framework characterizing the most conservative sectors of different religious traditions. There is no space for a critical dialogue, because the other side (feminists by the fundamentalist elites and *vice versa*) is seen as inherently dangerous, wrong, or perverted.[44]

In other words, I am arguing for a nuanced, critical, comprehensive understanding of the interplay of women's lives and religious traditions. A feminist perspective should include not only feminist (re)interpretations of those religious traditions, done by adequate tools of analysis (a large group of feminist scholars from different religious backgrounds is realizing that task). A feminist perspective should also be careful not to judge religion as per se oppressive for women, without listening to the different voices of real women all over the world who are balancing their identities as women and their places in religious communities.

In the case of Christianity, this means that there must be a simultaneous effort of well-based critique of its important role in women's subordination throughout the centuries and an openness to the possibilities of feminist reinterpretations of Christianity, even if we would not agree on the need for or the possible consequences of this kind of feminist scholarship. Even if there would be no need for feminists to "save" different religious traditions for women, it is important to be able to analyze critically the social and political role that religious institutions and traditions have in the contemporary world. In Latin America, the Catholic Church is far from being a marginal institution, even though it has lost its colonial power. In some countries, conservative Catholics and politically powerful elites are forming new alliances—as a kind of modern continuation of the colonial *patronato* system—between the church and the state. Nowhere is this clearer than in the activities of the Catholic Church in issues of sexual ethics.

Liberation theology was an important interlocutor in grassroots social movements in Latin America in the 1970s. Thirty years later, the new social movements, including the feminist movement, have not had the same impact on and closeness with liberation theology. One reason for this is the understanding of women's political organizing mainly in terms of the *movimientos de mujeres* type of day-to-day survival strategies of poor women, theoretically and practically tied to the Latin American left, including the progressive wing of the Catholic Church and the base communities, as well as various human rights organizations. However, according to Tessa Cubitt and Helen Greenslade,

> The considerable body of research that shows a more complex picture of modern social settings than the dichotomized separate spheres [of the public and private] model has important implications for understanding women's political action and consciousness. The material which indicates growing empowerment suggests women's awareness of gender subordination is gained through participation in social movements.[45]

If this is true, it means that at the level of the contemporary array of social movements in Latin America, issues considered "feminist" are being addressed and reinterpreted not only in the narrowly understood feminist movement, but in any other movements in which an adequate analysis of the political sphere cannot afford excluding an analysis of gender dynamics, issues of sexuality and sexual identities, and the relationship of these to issues of power, authority, repression, and political change. Liberation theology frequently mentions these new social movements, but just as frequently without any critical analysis of the role of religion, theology, and the church in the formation of repressive sexualities and the issues of life and death tied to that. The lack of interaction between liberation theology (including feminist liberation theology) and feminist movements in Latin America has led to an absence of concrete political demands in a theology which twenty years ago was seen as the vanguard of political struggle. Most feminist—even several nonfeminist— women's movements and groups in Latin America work on issues of violence against women and reproductive rights and health. They are seen as the most urgent issues for women, especially the poorest and most marginalized of them; in fact, they are issues of life and death.

People working in these movements and organizations know very well what to expect and not to expect from the churches and theologians: "Even the progressive wing of the church holds conservative views in matters that directly challenge the church's own authority over personal lives: sexuality, reproduction, women's rights."[46] The same is expressed in different words by anthropologist Nancy Scheper-Hughes, who did extensive field work on mothering and infant death in rural Brazil: "Despite its radical praxis, liberation theology has still failed to respond to *the useless suffering of mothers and infants,* two social groups abandoned by the rhetoric of empowerment and by the 'good news' of the social gospel of Jesus. On questions of sexuality and reproduction, it is the new church that is mute."[47] This is because even the "newness" of liberation theology has not been able to overcome the traditional hostility toward female sexuality and reproduction and, as a result, remains mute on the theological sources of gender oppression.[48]

If issues of sexual identity and sexuality are understood only in terms of a stereotypical postmodern individualistic influence of the West on the Latin American societies, as often is the case, it means that there is a superficial understanding of both postmodern debates and the importance of sexuality and gender for social change. However, I would argue that liberation theology could be the privileged space or context for addressing these issues in the Latin American context. To be able to do so, liberation theology today should take seriously the critique posed by both postmodernism and feminism and engage itself with women's political movements in the continent. The critical edge of liberation theology in interpreting these discourses could be the same as ever: the perspective of the poor, with a deeper and more serious understanding of the poor also as gendered, sexual, and reproductive beings, and a critical analysis of the "Vatican roulette" played especially with poor women's lives.

Religion and Reproductive Rights in Latin America: Not *Post* Yet

The Catholic Church has officially adopted some of the language of dissident Latin American liberation theologians (and feminism, as well) in its discourse on sexual ethics. When speaking of "demographic imperialism" (*imperialismo demográfico* or *imperialismo anticonceptivo*), a term coined by Latin American

Catholic bishops in their meeting in Santo Domingo in 1992, and condemning coercive birth control practices in the Third World—including dangerous contraceptives and forced or unconsulted sterilizations[49]—the Vatican joins many Third World intellectuals and activists who have good grounds for their suspicion of the motives behind global population policies. Nevertheless, in condemning both artificial contraception and abortion and in adopting the absolute "right-to-life" position only in the context of reproductive issues, the Vatican is a long way from the concerns of the women's movement. According to Betsy Hartmann,

> The population control and antiabortion philosophies, although diametrically opposed, share one thing in common: They are both antiwoman. Population control advocates impose contraception and sterilization on women; the so-called Right to Life movement denies women the basic right of access to abortion and birth control. Neither takes the interests and rights of the individual woman as their starting point. Both approaches attempt to control women, instead of letting women control their bodies themselves.[50]

It is fairly common that a fundamentalist interpretation of women's rights is justified by cultural differences (so called cultural relativism). Human rights, especially women's rights, are seen as a form of Western imperialism which pretends to legitimize the cultural superiority of the West. This is especially true in some Muslim countries, but more and more one can hear this sort of arguments being expressed in Latin American Catholic countries as well. Thus, it is not only about Christianity as the religion of the West and Islam as the religion of the East, but also about the growing gap between the North and the South. The church of the West, the Catholic Church, is thus seen as defending and representing the South inside Latin America,[51] emphasizing its cultural differences with the church in Europe. The secularized North, with its moral decline and lack of values, is seen as controlling the South, where values concerning the family and the patriarchal social order are considered so central that without them the entire culture is in danger of collapsing. This explains partly why feminism—both the one born in the industrialized countries and a more indigenous feminism—is experienced as such a threat and even the principal sign of social degradation.[52]

This is also the context in which the activity and collaboration of certain Muslim governments and the Vatican become more understandable. Especially during the tenure of the current pope, John Paul II, the Vatican has become a strange mixture of one of the most Eurocentric (or rather "Vaticancentric") institutions in strictly church-related issues in which all the orders come from above, from Europe (e.g., the nomination of conservative bishops against the preference of the local churches in Latin America, the silencing or expulsion of liberation theologians, direct and open political pressure on national governments, especially in issues of sexual ethics), and of an institution which pretends to represent the weak, the poor, the South, in the larger society, both nationally and internationally. This observation is also made by Margaret E. Keck and Kathryn Sikkink, in the context of the U.N. Conference on Population and Development, held in Cairo in 1994: "The Vatican also invoked the counterclaim of cultural imperialism, charging that Westerners were attempting to impose immoral and inappropriate ideologies."[53]

These complex and often contradictory roles of the Catholic Church in Latin America have not been analyzed by liberation theologians. If such an analysis were undertaken, it would become clear how difficult it is to speak in an undifferentiated way of Latin America or the poor. The Latin American Catholic Church is, even formally as an institution, a critic of neoliberal economic policies on the poor and thus sides with liberation theology, but it is also one of the powerful institutions which stubbornly refuse to look at the statistics on maternal and infant mortality or to revise its teaching on sexuality, gender roles, and reproduction. The poorer the women we are talking about, the deadlier the combination of traditional Catholic teaching and the gendered violence of their everyday lives is for them. It would help liberation theologians to give the option for the poor new depth and meaning if they would take seriously the postmodern *and* feminist claim that there is no one "essential" way of being a woman or poor or even Latin American. For example, it is not women per se, but poor women, who die of reasons directly related to reproduction, maternity, and their lack of power to decide over them. If liberation theology takes up this challenge, including a serious dialogue with both feminism and the church hierarchy, it will not only be faithful to and deepen the epistemological and practical (ethical, political) meaning of the option for the poor, but possibly will also offer an interesting example of a positive synergy between liberation theology, feminism, and postmodernism in a Third World setting.

Taking up this challenge would also make it necessary for liberation theologians to look at their use of concepts such as life, defense of life, or liberation theology as a theology of life (*teología de la vida*). To defend the life of poor women means defending their right for reproductive choice, derived from a sexual ethics which would be able to start from the practical and concrete life conditions of these women. What we see, instead, is a discourse of life which excludes women and even makes allusions to an absolutist Vatican type of sexual ethics.[54] As long as women are not fully seen as moral agents, who by and large are also in a privileged but silenced position to define what we mean when we speak of life, the defense of life, and the right to life, liberation theology will not be able to have a say in today's struggles to combat poverty and needless death in poor countries.

*Post*script

Much of what I have said in this essay about the understanding of the poor and the option for them in liberation theology could be read as a standard postmodern critique against any "essentializations," whether of the poor or of women. However, my point is that women—and other "others"—are in fact being excluded from the concept, if they are only added to an endless list of the oppressed but their real differentiated life situations and problems, starting from primarily bodily realities such as sexuality, reproduction, and race, are not being dealt with critically. The concept of option for the poor, in all its novelty and continuing relevance, has been both too general and too narrow to include the multiplicity of situations in which the poor live. My critique is not derived from a faddish postmodern attack of essences, whether in liberation theology or feminist theory, but arises out of the option for concrete women in terms of the liberation-theological option for the poor.

A critical feminist perspective takes the option for the poor to a direction in which it is impossible to stay mute in front of the "useless suffering" of women in societies, which sees them either primarily as mothers and reproducers or refuses to see what motherhood and reproduction mean and imply for them. The traditional Christian, in Latin America especially the Catholic, teaching on women, sexuality, and reproduction, is one of the primary sources and legitimizers of this suffering. If liberation theology takes this seriously, it would not only be faithful to its option for the poor, but it would also critique the abstract but tight understanding of (gender) difference of the traditional Catholic theological anthropology from an understanding of difference not derived from abstract essentials but from people's real life conditions. All this is already present in a liberation-theological discourse which talks of the human body and life as the source and criteria of ethics and of theology as theology of life. However, this discourse and language need to be concretized. Postmodern insights on the relativity of subject positions and difference(s) can enrich this task, when appropriated critically. As long as liberation theology is not willing to question the traditional sexual ethical teaching of the church, it is not able to plausibly speak of the realities of the poor. And, as long as liberation theology does not speak of the poor also as gendered, reproductive beings and does not take seriously the effects of both poverty and sexist religion on women, it will not be able to create a theology or ethics which would be plausible in contemporary Latin America.

NOTES

1. Leonardo Boff, "Modernity/Postmodernity," in *Dictionary of Third World Theologies*, ed. Virginia Fabella and R. S. Sugirtharajah (Maryknoll, N.Y.: Orbis, 2000), 146.

2. Ibid.

3. Wong Wai Ching, "Postcolonialism," in *Dictionary of Third World Theologies*, ed. Virginia Fabella and R. S. Sugirtharajah (Maryknoll, N.Y.: Orbis, 2000), 169–70. He is critical of Third World theologies "freezing themselves within a category of difference designed by the West." However, it is debatable, first, whether the category of difference that is being used in, let's say, Latin America, was designed by the West (if Latin America is not considered as part of the West) and, second, whether the category has been taken seriously enough in Third World liberation theologies. The cases in point are women and racial and ethnic minorities who may think that their difference was neither designed in the West nor taken seriously by liberation theologians.

4. Edgardo Lander, "Eurocentrism and Colonialism in Latin American Social Thought," *Nepantla: Views from South* 1.3 (2000): 523.

5. Patricia Seed, "More Colonial and Postcolonial Discourses," *Latin American Research Review* 28.3 (1993): 151–52.

6. See, e.g., the various articles in *Nepantla: Views from South* 1.3 (2000); George Yúdice, "Postmodernity and Transnational Capitalism in Latin America," in *On Edge: The Crisis of Contemporary Latin American Culture*, ed. George Yúdice, Jean Franco, and Juan Flores (Minneapolis: University of Minnesota Press, 1992), 4–5.

7. Lander, "Eurocentrism and Colonialism," 525.

8. Yúdice, "Postmodernity and Transnational Capitalism," 7.

9. Ibid., 8–9.

10. Nancy Fraser and Linda J. Nicholson, "Social Criticism without Philosophy: An Encounter between Feminism and Postmodernism," in *Feminism/Postmodernism*, ed. Linda J. Nicholson (New York: Routledge, 1990), 34–35.

11. Christine Di Stefano, "Dilemmas of Difference: Feminism, Modernity, and Postmodernism," in *Feminism/Postmodernism*, ed. Linda J. Nicholson (New York: Routledge, 1990), 77.

12. Seyla Benhabib, "Epistemologies of Postmodernism: A Rejoinder to Jean-Francois Lyotard," in *Feminism/Postmodernism*, ed. Linda J. Nicholson (New York: Routledge, 1990), 107–30.

13. Deniz Kandiyoti, "Reflections on the Politics of Gender in Muslim Societies: From Nairobi to Beijing," in *Faith and Freedom: Women's Human Rights in the Muslim World*, ed. Mahnaz Afkhami (Syracuse: Syracuse University Press, 1995), 19–20.

14. Brinda J. Mehta, "Postcolonial Feminism," in *Encyclopedia of Feminist Theories*, ed. Lorraine Code (New York: Routledge, 2000), 395.

15. For example, Wong Wai Ching writes concerning postcolonialism in the *Dictionary of Third World Theologies*: "The term 'postcolonialism' has come to mean not only a simple periodization after Western countries dominated militarily, but also a methodological revisionism that enables a wholesale critique of Western structures of knowledge and power since the Enlightenment" (169).

16. Jean Franco, "Going Public: Reinhabiting the Private," in *On Edge: The Crisis of Contemporary Latin American Culture*, ed. George Yúdice, Jean Franco, and Juan Flores (Minneapolis: University of Minnesota Press, 1992), 77.

17. Walter D. Mignolo, "Posoccidentalismo: El argumento desde América Latina," in *Teorías sin disciplina: Latinoamericanismo, poscolonialidad y globalización en de-*

bate, ed. Santiago Castro-Gómez and Eduardo Mendieta (Mexico City: Porrúa & University of San Francisco, 1998), 31–58.

18. See, e.g., various articles in David Batstone, Eduardo Mendieta, Lois Ann Lorentzen, and Dwight N. Hopkins, eds., *Liberation Theologies, Postmodernity, and the Americas* (New York: Routledge, 1997); in Castro-Gómez and Mendieta, *Teorías sin disciplina;* and in Linda Martín Alcoff and Eduardo Mendieta, eds., *Thinking from the Underside of History: Enrique Dussel's Philosophy of Liberation* (New York: Rowman & Littlefield, 2000).

19. David Batstone, Eduardo Mendieta, Lois Lorentzen, and Dwight N. Hopkins, "Introduction," in *Liberation Theologies, Postmodernity, and the Americas* (New York: Routledge, 1997), 1.

20. Walter D. Mignolo, "Dussel's Philosophy of Liberation: Ethics and the Geopolitics of Knowledge," in *Thinking from the Underside of History: Enrique Dussel's Philosophy of Liberation*, ed. Linda Martín Alcoff and Eduardo Mendieta (New York: Rowman & Littlefield, 2000), 45–46.

21. I present this argument in detail in Elina Vuola, *Limits of Liberation: Feminist Theology and the Ethics of Poverty and Reproduction* (Sheffield: Sheffield Academic Press, 2002); Spanish edition *La ética sexual y los límites de la praxis: Conversaciones críticas entre la teología feminista y la teología de la liberación* (Quito: Editorial Abya-Yala, 2001).

22. Julio Lois, *Teología de la liberación: Opción por los pobres* (San José: Editorial DEI, 1988), 195.

23. Ibid., 196.

24. Julio Lois, "Opción por los pobres: Síntesis doctrinal," in *La opción por los pobres*, ed. José M. Vigil (Santander: Editorial Sal Terrae, 1991), 11–12.

25. Leonardo Boff, *La fe en la periferia del mundo: El caminar de la iglesia con los oprimidos*, trans. Jesús García-Abril (Santander: Editorial Sal Terrae, 1981), 74–75.

26. Gustavo Gutiérrez, *Teología de la liberación: Perspectivas*, 14th ed. (Salamanca: Ediciones Sígueme, 1990), 28–30.

27. Lois, *Teología de la liberación*, 199, quoting the Puebla document.

28. "Justicia y mercado: La sociedad en la que quepan todos," *Pasos* 95 (2001): 7.

29. Ibid., 8–9.

30. Juan Luis Segundo, *Theology and the Church: A Response to Cardinal Ratzinger and a Warning to the Whole Church*, trans. John W. Diercksmeier (Minneapolis: Winston, 1985), 150. On the theologian as an "organic intellectual," see also Leonardo Boff, . . . *Y la iglesia se hizo pueblo: "Eclesiogénesis": La iglesia que nace de la fe del pueblo*, trans. Jesús García-Abril (Santander: Editorial Sal Terrae, 1986), 137–42, 227–52.

31. Mary Potter Engel and Susan Brooks Thistlethwaite, "Introduction: Making the Connections among Liberation Theologies around the World," in *Lift Every Voice: Constructing Christian Theologies from the Underside*, ed. Susan Brooks Thistlethwaite and Mary Potter Engel (San Francisco: Harper & Row, 1990), 2.

32. Horacio Cerutti Guldberg, "Pensamiento y compromiso social," unpublished manuscript (1996).

33. Santiago Castro-Gómez, "Epistemologías coloniales, saberes latinoamericanos: El proyecto teórico de los estudios subalternos," in *El debate de la postcolonialidad*

en latinoamérica: Una postmodernidad periférica o cambio de paradigma en el pensamiento Latinoamericano, ed. Alfonso de Toro and Fernando de Toro (Frankfurt am Main: Vervuert/Madrid: Iberoamericana, 1999), 81.

34. Ibid., 82.

35. Ibid., 87. It is not totally clear to me if he implies here that postmodernism is largely a North American and European phenomenon, which then would have a "parallel" phenomenon of postcolonial theorizing in the South. Since both large theories are produced and reproduced in both settings and also beyond the merely geographical location, I would assume that the relationship between postmodernism and postcolonialism is rather a two-way dialogue in a globalized world, where individual scholars also live and work in both First and Third World settings.

36. Mignolo, "Dussel's Philosophy of Liberation," 42.

37. Juan José Tamayo-Acosta, *Para comprender la teología de la liberación* (Estella: Editorial Verbo Divino, 1990), 68, quoting J. I. González Faus (emphasis original).

38. On the relationship of liberation theology to multiculturalism, syncretism, and black religiosity, see Josué A. Sathler and Amós Nascimento, "Black Masks on White Faces: Liberation Theology and the Quest for Syncretism in the Brazilian Context," in *Liberation Theologies, Postmodernity, and the Americas,* ed. David Batstone, Eduardo Mendieta, Lois Ann Lorentzen, and Dwight N. Hopkins (New York: Routledge, 1997), 95–122.

39. See Ivone Gebara, "La opción por el pobre como opción por la mujer pobre," *Concilium* 214 (1987): 463–72.

40. María Pilar Aquino, "Sexism," in *Dictionary of Third World Theologies,* ed. Virginia Fabella and R. S. Sugirtharajah (Maryknoll, N.Y.: Orbis, 2000), 183 (emphasis added).

41. See my *Limits of Liberation* (in English) and *La ética sexual y los límites de la praxis* (in Spanish) for a more comprehensive analysis of liberation theologians' relation to issues of sexuality, feminism, and reproduction.

42. Gebara was submitted to an ecclesiastical process of either retracting her statement on the legalization of abortion or facing dismissal from her religious order.

43. Chandra Talpade Mohanty, "Under Western Eyes: Feminist Scholarship and Colonial Discourses," in *Third World Women and the Politics of Feminism,* ed. Chandra Talpade Mohanty, Ann Russo, and Lourdes Torres (Bloomington: Indiana University Press, 1991), 51–80.

44. I am not arguing that there is no anthropological or sociological research on Latin American women that takes religion into account or analyzes it only in this stereotypical, polarized way. Scholars such as Carol Ann Drogus, John Burdick, Hannah Stewart-Gambino, and Elizabeth Brusco have been doing pioneering research in combining religion with both social sciences and gender studies. However, I still would claim that there is not enough knowledge of or communication between feminist scholarship in religion—including theology—and social scientific Latin American studies. See Elizabeth Brusco, *The Reformation of Machismo: Evangelical Conversion and Gender in Colombia* (Austin: University of Texas Press, 1995); John Burdick, *Looking for God in Brazil: The Progressive Catholic Church in Urban Brazil's Religious Arena* (Berkeley: University of California Press, 1993); idem, *Blessed Anastácia: Women, Race, and Popular Christianity in Brazil* (New York: Routledge, 1998); Carol Ann Drogus,

Women, Religion, and Social Change in Brazil's Popular Church (Notre Dame: University of Notre Dame Press, 1997).

45. Tessa Cubitt and Helen Greenslade, "Public and Private Spheres: The End of Dichotomy," in *Gender Politics in Latin America: Debates in Theory and Practice,* ed. Elizabeth Dore (New York: Monthly Review Press, 1997), 57.

46. Carmen Barroso and Cristina Bruschini, "Building Politics from Personal Lives: Discussions on Sexuality among Poor Women in Brazil," in *Third World Women and the Politics of Feminism,* ed. Chandra Talpade Mohanty, Ann Russo, and Lourdes Torres (Bloomington: Indiana University Press, 1991), 155.

47. Nancy Scheper-Hughes, *Death without Weeping: The Violence of Everyday Life in Brazil* (Berkeley: University of California Press, 1993), 528 (emphasis added).

48. Ibid., 529.

49. On Latin American examples of coercive sterilization operations, see Betsy Hartmann, *Reproductive Rights and Wrongs: The Global Politics of Population Control,* 2d ed. (Boston: South End Press, 1995), 247–51.

50. Ibid., xviii.

51. In this essay, I am not taking into account the growth of Protestantism in the region, since my primary interest is in the political role of Catholicism in reproductive issues.

52. See more on this in my article "Remaking Universals? Transnational Feminism(s) Challenging Fundamentalist Ecumenism," *Theory, Culture, and Society* 19.1–2 (2002): 1–21.

53. Margaret E. Keck and Kathryn Sikkink, *Activists beyond Borders: Advocacy Networks in International Politics* (Ithaca: Cornell University Press, 1998), 189.

54. I have written more extensively on this in "El derecho a la vida y el sujeto femenino," *Pasos* 88 (2000): 1–12.

6

More Than Ever: The Preferential Option for the Poor

Dwight N. Hopkins

My thesis is that the preferential option for the poor is needed today more than ever. Indeed, postmodernity intensifies the necessity for the preferential option for the poor. Unfortunately, some interpretations of the implications of postmodernity have had the tendency to obscure this fact. In contrast to these mistaken opinions, the demand for the preferential option for the poor in postmodernity is the central message of the work of Gustavo Gutiérrez. It is in his writings and life that we learn of the imperative to place the experiences and realities of the poor at the center of postmodern theological discussions. God prefers the poor because God opposes all forms of injustice which block the full humanity of the least in society. To prefer the poor is to call for a transformed individual self in service to the larger collective ownership of all of God's creation. As co-laborers with God in the struggle to realize the preferential option of the poor, we will begin to bring about the New Self and the New Commonwealth.

Postmodernity has raised issues about the lack of one singular way of analyzing reality, the fall of any grand narratives about human progress, the demise of the Union of Soviet Socialist Republics, the turn toward capitalism in the People's Republic of China, the transition from smokestack-industrial, monopoly-capitalist economies to increased information technology and service-based economies, the transformation of the clear existence of class formations into loosely formed social strata, the decline in the membership of mainline Protestant churches and the rapid expansion of fundamentalist and evangelical churches, the introduction of such language as

"political correctness" and "multiculturalism" in ways that obscure white supremacy and the changing of power dynamics among asymmetrical social relations, the move from one focus to many sites of oppression and resistance,
the celebration of particularity over universality, the fragmentation of voices in
opposition to the notion of a single voice of protest, the change from seizing
state power to integrating into and reforming the existing political and economic structures.

Moreover, postmodernity suggests an endless play of language, the lack
of a telos (i.e., an inevitable end where justice prevails), the call for fun and
frivolity, an end to any struggle against the ruling classes, the end to any foundation for objectivity and thus the importance of relativism (i.e., everyone is
right and no one is wrong), the irrelevancy of content and the rise of the
persuasiveness of the medium and not the message, the change from producing commodities for their use to marketing products that sell images and
status, the decline of the nation-state as a result of the globalization of finance
capital, the internationalization of monopoly capitalism's division of labor, an
accent on consumption rather than production, the denial of the possibility of
art and language reflecting or representing some objective beauty or truth, the
emphasis on imitations or copies over the originals, the move of former radi-
cals, progressives, and liberals to the center and the right of center.[1]

Given these issues raised by postmodernity about today's changes in ge-
ography, politics, race, political economy, culture, and the human condition,
shouldn't we abandon the idea of a preferential option for the poor? Isn't this
phrase an outdated longing of middle-aged academics for the high times of
the 1960s? Haven't today's special interests groups canceled out the reality of
a sector of society called the poor? To respond to these questions, we need to
understand what the preferential option for the poor meant and still means
for today.

The Preferential Option for the Poor

In the context of the United States, the phrase *preferential option for the poor*
received widespread and controversial exposure when the U.S. Roman Catholic
bishops published their pastoral letter "Economic Justice for All" in 1984.
Though the exact phrase may be from the twentieth century, the concept is
strongly rooted in the biblical tradition. The Bible uses very specific language
for poverty: the beggar, the weak one, the frail one, the rural worker, the bent-
over one, the humiliated one, the wretched, the one lacking the means to
subsist, and the one humble before God. We find many passages in the Bible
that tell us that the poor are made poor by the wicked. Amos 2:6–7 reveals that
the perpetrator sells "the innocent for silver and the destitute for a pair of shoes.
They grind the heads of the poor into the earth and thrust the humble out of

their way." People are poor because they are victims of others. Wicked people "make unjust laws," Isaiah writes in 10:1–2. And they "publish burdensome decrees, depriving the poor of justice, robbing the weakest of my people of their rights, despoiling the widow and plundering the orphan."[2]

The biblical stories not only clearly define poverty as the result of human sin; these same stories call on the human community to oppose poverty. Throughout all the messages of the prophets, we discover the recurring prophetic word against those who would trample over and exploit the least in society. Hosea, Micah, Jeremiah, Amos, and Ezekiel, as well as the Gospel of Luke and the Letter of James, clearly denounce those who create poverty and take advantage of the poor. In the Hebrew Scriptures, the main message of the God-human relation is that Yahweh chooses not to favor the rich and the ruling classes of ancient times. Instead, Yahweh makes a deliberate and calculated move to hear the cries of slaves, the poor, and working people. Yahweh colabors with them to remove them from systemic oppression into liberation—a place where they can be full human beings.

In the Christian Scriptures, we find two major texts. The first is in Luke 4:18ff. Here, from the Christian perspective, it is no accident that Jesus is handed Isaiah 61 to read. In this major public proclamation, Jesus describes how the divine Spirit has anointed him to side with the poor, the imprisoned, and the broken hearted and to proclaim the year of the Lord or the year of Jubilee for the poor. Similarly in Matthew 25:31ff., Jesus provides explicit criteria for those who have done his work. The tests entail helping the poor, the hungry, the thirsty, the homeless, and the least in society. Throughout the entire Bible, this is the only place where clear criteria are given for those on earth who want eventually to enter heaven. Unfortunately, the dominant mainstream Christian denominations have said that these two passages are simply spiritual stories and should not be read literally. Or they claim that Jesus is using metaphors or symbols. When it comes to changing economic and political structures harming the poor, those who control and benefit from these structures will always reward those Christians who oppose God's attempt to make the liberation of the poor a concrete, earthly spiritual formation. But God is concerned about the concrete identities and social locations of the poor. Divine spirit shows itself in the incarnation—in the flesh of the poor. Is this not exactly who Jesus was and what Jesus did?

Not only do we find this preferential option for the poor in the Bible, we also discover it in the tradition of black sacred life in the United States. In other words, we need the preferential option for the poor more than ever because of the biblical call to do so and because we stand within the justice tradition of poor black Americans. Two time periods will suffice for our purposes. The first is the sacred life experiences of enslaved African Americans. Black workers during this period held on to their own interpretation of the Bible. They knew that these stories had a special meaning for them. For instance, they could see themselves in the tales of the Hebrew slaves who were delivered from Egyptian bondage. They identified with the three little Hebrew boys forced into a fiery furnace, because black folk worked from sunup to sundown in the scorching heat of the South and in the agricultural and service industries in the slavery of the North.

If Yahweh heard the pitiful and lowly cries of pain and suffering from the slaves in Egypt, then most definitely the same God would hear the wailing and beseeching of similar slaves in America. That is why believers in the African American sacred tradition prayed for freedom when the material world seemed to be controlled completely by white Christian slaveholders. After slavery ended, a Mrs. Minnie Folkes could now tell the truth about the faith of formerly enslaved blacks. She states: "In dem back days chile, meetin's was carried on jes' like we do today some whatly. Only diffe'nce is de slaves dat knowed de mos' bout de Bible would tell an' explain what God told him in a vision . . . dat dis freedom would come to pass; an' den dey prayed for dis vision to come to pass."[3]

Enslaved black workers felt that the good news of the biblical passages was not denied by the changing events of earthly existence. Regardless of how classes, communities, or people changed, one thing was certain: "God don't like ugly." That is, the constant feature of black faith is a profound truth and a hoped-for reality that God does not like anyone harming those at the bottom of society. Black workers understood this by combining their everyday survival and freedom acts with their interpretation of the Bible. Their conclusion is that human beings might change, but God's love for the little ones of society and God's giving of God's self for the liberation of these little ones remain a constant throughout the ages. No amount of sophisticated analysis of social changes or new theological insights could alter this belief that the divine spirit is partial to working people and others who are suffering. God sides with the oppressed. Indeed, it is a faith tradition among the poor which gives them the preferential option in the eyes of God.

Here, the preferential option combines sacred love with the practice of freedom. Love from God is not an abstract, "touchy-feely" sensation of being warm and fuzzy. Love stands for taking steps to help people get out of poverty in order that they might practice freedom—a freedom where they are just as equal in wealth ownership and power control as all others, especially being equal in all respects to those who previously held privileges and wealth over them. Former enslaved worker Henry Baker confirms this point when he explains:

> We sut'only [certainly] wuz happy in dem days tuh hear dat we
> wuz free. . . . We served de Lawd sho nuff aftuh we wuz sot free
> cause we had sumpin tuh be thankful fer. . . . Ol' man Jesse Wallace
> wuz a preacher en he 'clared dat God luved his folks en he sent his

angels down tuh set his folks free en yuh shoulder seen de shou-
tin'.[4]

Divine love brings freedom for those who are not able to live in their God-
given right to be full human beings. It is this love for freedom which empowers
the black poor and gives them hope. Hope is in a future place where a person
can be able to be fully what God has made one to be. Ultimately, heaven
contains this new place and new time. One Negro spiritual (i.e., the songs
created by blacks during slavery) captures the sense of heaven as a location
where there are no obstacles stopping poor, black workers from fulfilling their
vocation from God:

1. Dere's no rain to wet you.
   O yes, I want to go home,
   Want to go home.
2. Dere's no sun to burn you,—O yes, etc.
3. Dere's no hard trials.
4. Dere's no whips a-crackin'.
5. Dere's no stormy weather.
6. No more slavery in de kingdom [heaven].
7. No evil-doers in de kingdom.
8. All is gladness in de kingdom.[5]

The preferential option for the poor is an ongoing and long-term process which
culminates in heaven, where the poor are no longer blocked from their true
selves and where they thereby find happiness.

Drawing on this radical tradition of enslaved black folk's experience of
Christianity, Martin Luther King Jr. is the second example of black sacred life
that focused on the poor. King also took the liberation theme from the Bible
and applied it to the structures of poverty in his day. Toward the end of his
life, he concentrated on two crucial projects—the black working-class strike in
Memphis, Tennessee, and a nationwide campaign to bring all of the country's
poor to shut down Washington, D.C. Never perceiving himself as a politician,
King based his solidarity with the oppressed on his Christian faith. Faith provided the guide for his social analysis. For instance, near the end of his life,
King raised serious questions about the overall political economy in the United
States from the perspective of the least in society:

As we talk about "Where do we go from here," . . . we must
honestly face the fact that the Movement must address itself to the
question of restructuring the whole of American society. There are
40 million poor people here. And one day we must ask the question, "Why are there 40 million poor people in America? And when
you begin to ask that question, you are raising questions about the

economic system, about a broader distribution of wealth. When you ask that question, you begin to question the capitalist economy."[6]

The movement of King from an ordained black Baptist theologian to an anticapitalist preacher shows us how, in the tradition of black sacred life, faith pushes a person to a class analysis. The preferential option for the poor in black belief does not begin with a social analysis which the community then applies to its situation. On the contrary, from the perspective of the Bible and the African American heritage (i.e., the traditions of enslaved black folk and of King), a community of believers follows God's preferential option for the poor into a radical political economy. In this instance, political economy includes a questioning of the capitalist system, the exploitation of all workers, and the oppression of black folk. The preferential option for the poor means beginning with belief and pursuing social change. It is not faith seeking understanding; rather it is faith engaged in a radical redistribution of power and wealth on behalf of those whose voices aren't taken seriously in society.

This faith was the foundation for the first generation of black theologians in North America during the 1960s. Combining their heritage from enslaved black beliefs, the revolutionary theology of King, and the freedom message in the Bible, black theologians applied the gospel of Jesus Christ to the survival and life-and-death conditions of the black marginalized in North America. When James H. Cone wrote the first two books on liberation theology in 1969 and 1970,[7] African American faith moved closer to integrating a racial social analysis with one confronting poverty. However, it wasn't until Cone's August 1977 lecture to the Black Theology Project of the Theology in the Americas conference did class analysis become an intentional component of a racial social analysis. Cone put forth the following points to his African American audience:

> I reject dogmatic Marxism that reduces every contradiction to class analysis and thus ignores racism as a legitimate point of departure in the process of liberation. There are racist Marxists as there are racist capitalists, and we must struggle against both. But we must be careful not to reject the Marxist's social analysis simply because we do not like the vessels that the message comes in. If we do that, then it is hard to explain how we can remain Christians in view of the white vessels in which the gospel was first introduced to black people.[8]

Consequently, from the black experience, to be a Christian in any time period is to practice a preferential option for the poor. Restated, a believer stands with the least in society and uses whatever class, racial, and gender analyses will help bring about the conditions for the full humanity of all.

But the concern about what comes before what—that is, the gospel mandate for the poor or a radical class interpretation—becomes more of a pressing issue because of some postmodern claims today. If, from the postmodern perspective, relativity means that there is no right and wrong, that social strata replace class consciousness, that the lack of a long-term human purpose substitutes for an ultimate goal of liberation, that particularity trumps universality, that the appearance of many voices overcomes an overarching master story, and that individualism cuts against the grain of obligation to a specific community—then it appears as if the idea of class is an outmoded concept which evaporated with the fall of Eastern Europe and Chairman Mao. And if we accept this theory, then the latest or most fashionable social analysis would make the preferential option for the poor unnecessary. The current usage of the term *postmodernity* would decide whether the preferential option for the poor is needed or not needed. On the contrary, as long as there exists the poor in society on earth, God opposes poverty and calls on all of humanity to live a sacred life of preference for the poor, in spite of postmodern analysis.

At the same time, we must be clear. There is nothing in and of itself sacred about being poor. God has chosen a preferential option for the poor because God does not like poverty. The key is liberation and the practice of freedom for all human beings. In other words, we respond to the calling for full humanity for all, free from individualism and private monopolization. In this sense, the vocation also challenges all persons who are poor and marginalized, as well as those who are victims of various structural discriminations in society. Just because people are poor doesn't mean that they will not strive to monopolize God's resources and abuse God's people.

Poverty Defined

Perhaps no one else has been as clear and sharp in defining the preferential option for the poor as Gustavo Gutiérrez, one of the world's leaders of liberation theology. With his usual sharp insight, Gutiérrez offers three parts to his definition of the poor. The first definition concerns the economically poor. In his ground-breaking 1971 text, *A Theology of Liberation*, he writes, "The term poverty designates in the first place material poverty, that is, the lack of economic goods necessary for a human life worthy of the name."[9] Poverty, in this sense, involves people who do not own wealth, people who work every day and can barely make ends meet, those who clean bathrooms and make up our beds, and workers in factories. Moreover, poverty includes the unemployed, the overworked, those permanently without jobs, those lacking health insurance, women who have to sell their bodies to feed their children, people who work double and triple shifts on one job, others who work two and three different jobs, those who were forced off welfare and now work jobs that put them in worse positions, working-class people who drive buses, cabs, and subway trains, secretaries and administrative assistants, flight attendants, technicians, nurses, railroad workers, construction laborers, and others who labor and are underpaid. Today, we still have a working class, working people, and the appearance of a new category of workers as a result of the rise of the technological, service, and information industries.

The second form of poverty is spiritual poverty. It means, as elaborated by Gutiérrez, being open to God and being willing to be used by God. Unfortunately, the dominating churches (i.e., the mainline churches) have a tendency to see spiritual poverty as including those who can both maintain their extraordinary wealth and income and still be poor in spirit. From this sinful belief and practice, those who exploit, oppress, and discriminate against others do not have to share their wealth and do not have to stop their evil ways. But they still can have a poor spirit. This false understanding of poverty is a highly spiritualized one; it is a hocus-pocus poverty which churches preach with the result of making Christianity an opiate of the people. In this view, which stands contrary to Gutiérrez, there really is nothing fundamentally different from a working-class family and a monopoly-capitalist family since they both suffer spiritual poverty. What makes us all humans, for this interpretation, is that God has given all people spirits which we have all equally damaged and, therefore, Jesus came for the poor in spirit, regardless if your family members work at McDonalds and the United Parcel Service or if your family members make millions from the stock market every year. One person heads a household and works a double shift every day. Another person heads a household and owns an island in the Caribbean or the Pacific Ocean. But they are both poor in spirit. However, a person cannot be open to God while giving allegiance to the private hoarding of God's resources.

Gutiérrez then elaborates a third understanding of poverty. He states the following: "In the Bible poverty is a scandalous condition inimical to human dignity and therefore contrary to the will of God." One who is wretched, bent over, or weak exists in conditions of poverty. Gutiérrez correctly reads the Bible differently. Jesus of the Christian Scriptures is one who came to help the poor have a quality daily existence and ultimately have liberation in order to reach their full potential (291–96). Gutiérrez challenges us to look at sacred writings with a new lens—with the spectacles of the voiceless in our society. If Jesus' entire existence and the complete purpose of the resurrected Christ is to work with the least in society, and if the entire story of the Hebrew Scriptures tells us about Yahweh's colaboring with slaves to move them out of oppressive structures in one space and time and into a new location of freedom, then surely our divine calling begins first with the poor (292–96).

Gutiérrez is one of the world's leaders of liberation theology. Yet, more importantly, it is his commitment to the gospel of Jesus Christ and his compassion for the poor that mark his way of being in the world. In his life,

Gutiérrez exemplifies this faith style by living and working with the poor in Lima, Peru. For it is not theory or new theologies that change the world. In the final prophetic words of A Theology of Liberation, he states (307–8):

> We must be careful not to fall into an intellectual self-satisfaction, into a kind of triumphalism of erudite and advanced "new" visions of Christianity. . . . All the political theologies, the theologies of hope, or revolution, and of liberation, are not worth one act of genuine solidarity with exploited social classes. They are not worth one act of faith, love, and hope, committed . . . in active participation to liberate [women and men] from everything that dehumanizes [them] and prevents [them] from living according to the will of [God].

Lessons from Gustavo Gutierrez

What can we learn from such a person as this?

First, Gutiérrez has taught us that true Christianity begins with sharing our humanity with those who have been made the underside of history, the wretched of the earth, and the marginalized in our communities, families, churches, and the world (288–91, 299–302). Unfortunately, today's mainline or mainstream churches argue that a true Christian is one who supports the system of capitalism and all of its forms of focusing on the individual. That is why in the United States, Christianity supports the economic and political system of this country. Based on this interpretation of the gospel of Jesus of Nazareth, one would think that Jesus Christ was an American citizen supporting the stars and stripes and singing "The Star Spangled Banner." Obviously, Gutiérrez does not read the Bible this way.

Second, Gutiérrez teaches us a new way of doing theology. Here theology is reflection on a prior commitment to the poor. Instead of assuming that correct theological ideas fall from the sky, Gutiérrez understands that talk about God arises from the poor. It comes from this social location because God is already present with the oppressed. It is, therefore, a theology from below. Not only does he present us with a new epistemology (i.e., he tells us where knowledge comes from), he also helps us to understand that true theology is a second step (11). We must first take a stand with the victims in our communities.

In contrast, the prevailing way of teaching and living out theology in the United States is to worship theological ancestors from Europe or white North American academics. In order to be successful in graduate schools of religion, one practices "true" theology; one starts with the systems of these thinkers, explains their systems, and then attempts to apply these systems to the North

American situation. In the status quo theology, one gains success by repeating ideas from whites, primarily from Europe but also from North America. However the norm for doing theology would be much richer if the rest of humanity (i.e., over 90% of the world's theoreticians and intellectuals from Africa, Asia, Latin America, the Pacific Islands, and Third World peoples within the United States) were taken seriously as sources for understanding the relation between humans and God.

Third, Gutiérrez brings theology back down to earth, the only place where it can be (6–8). Theology comes from two Greek words—*theos* and *logos*. Obviously *theos* deals with God, and *logos* means human beings reflecting on something. In mainline or mainstream theology, one gets the impression that God does theology and that theology is abstract, objective, universal truth. Dominant theology gives the impression that the divine being reflects on and talks about itself as God and, thus, does theology. But we must remember that theology is *logos* about *theos*. That is to say, human beings are doing theology, not God. God talk is not God talking, but humans talking about God. But if we know that humans do theology and not God, then a whole host of questions arise. Who are these theologians doing theology? What are their class backgrounds and class interests? What are their colors and ethnicities? What is their gender? What are their sexual identities? Do they support capitalism? Do they separate faith from the secular? What are they passionate about? Do they think that the United States is the best manifestation of what God wants human beings to do and be? How do they see the new society promised to us by Jesus?

Moreover, if we take seriously the lessons that theology is done by human beings and that we should therefore look at the people doing the God talk, we are confronted by the reality of the people who occupy positions of power in the institutions of religious studies. More specifically, why are 90% to 95% of the leadership positions in theological seminaries and graduate schools of religion occupied by white heterosexual men? Is it because God ordained this? Is it because they have a better intellect than everyone else? Is it because they are stronger and better at making administrative decisions? Is it because they are socialized to do this? Is it because they better represent the new society that Jesus lived and died for? I think not. I think this goes against the majority. The majority is constituted by brown, yellow, red, and black people and white women. Instead of institutions of religious studies reflecting the majority, they depict a minority population. The challenge becomes: how do we broaden a way of life from a minority reality to a democracy?

Fourth, Gutiérrez teaches us that churches must take sides. Too often the dominating communities of faith in North America believe that it is not their duty to side with the poor against those who create institutions and a culture that make and keep the poor poor. Is not the church the *ecclesia*, those called out, those set apart to do the will of liberation for those who do not yet have a voice in society (107–19, 255–58, 265–79)? It is understandable why North American churches do not seem to take a stand. Some churches do not know that not taking a stand is, in reality, actually taking a stand in support of a situation of conflict and injustice. Many churches have no idea how the unjust power dynamics on the national and international levels relate to the deepening of pain for people. For them, victims have become victims due to their own effort or lack of effort. This, of course, is the blame-the-victim syndrome. Other churches know in their hearts and in their conscious minds that there are very serious powerful families and institutions that dominate this country. Yet these same churches do not dare follow the gospel of Jesus Christ for fear of losing money, members, and privileges. Finally, some North American churches have some social analysis and realize that one cannot be a true Christian unless one takes a stand with the least in society. But these churches usually are willing only to give charity and not to work for systemic social justice and healing.

Fifth, Gutiérrez helps us to see that the new human being we are all longing for has to also have a profound transformation or *metanoia* on the spiritual level (90–92, 289–90). Deep within the souls of each of us, there lurk negative feelings, deep scars, and the wounded children within us. How can we move into a new heaven and new earth when we are burdened with the baggage of emotional and psychological mess? How can we raise up the sacred goodness that God has planted deep within us if it is battling with, spending energy on, and being distracted by the evil of negative emotions and wounds? We need spiritual healing as part of the definition of liberation theology.[10] But this has nothing to do with many of the contemporary North American spirituality movements. Some people prefer spirituality over churches because they have been injured by the hypocrisy of churches. At the same time, however, this spirituality is anchored in individualism, a thirst to feel good. I think that feeling good is a worthy goal in life. But how can one feel good as an individual when that me-focused spirituality does not make one accountable to the pain and suffering in American society? What type of spirituality can it be when one can feel good in one's spirit but still be a white racist, a sexist, a heterosexist, or an ignorer of the poor? Spirituality should make us feel so good that we cannot stand seeing the sins of the world. We would then be so filled with the Spirit that we would seek to change the world. Such spirituality would give us new eyes to see and new ears to hear. We would see the standards for a healthy economy and a quality everyday existence determined not by Wall Street but by the streets of those without wealth or massive incomes.

Sixth, Gutiérrez's life and writing teach us about the wisdom of the poor.[11] How many of us really think that poor people, folk at the bottom of North American society, actually are the ones who produce the knowledge of this world? This is a revolutionary idea. If this were true, it would raise questions about all of the institutions of learning in this country. Why are people leaving these institutions with all of this financial debt if the location of knowledge is outside these hallowed halls? If knowledge and wisdom begin from below, we would organize the life of educational institutions around the real lives of people who live day to day keeping their families together. These are the scholars who clean our bathrooms, cut our grass, cook our food, work in the factories, and carry out the secretarial and administrative assistance work. What would it mean to refocus the vision, resources, time, energy, and financial rewards on those who work with, learn from, and write about the bottom of society? Our knowledge base and wisdom storehouse would be much richer than it is now.

Finally, we learn from Gutiérrez the necessity of having a passionate love for people, especially those without voices. To love another is to recognize oneself in the face and life of another. To love someone is to immerse oneself in and to expose oneself to the context, conversation, and culture of another. Love is the ultimate risk of faith—a faith grounded in liberation of all humanity, a faith with a vision for a new heaven and a new earth where each person can achieve the fullest realization of her or his calling as it serves the greater collective whole. To have such a love, Gutiérrez instructs us, is to have a hope that comes from within and from on high. Through the ups and downs and apparent lack of progress, what is it that sustains us? Even when it looks like all the world is going to hell, this hope can carry a people through. Faith, hope, and love embody the theology of liberation. But more than that, it is what has kept and continues to keep poor and marginalized folk alive and seeking a better life for themselves, their children, and their grandchildren. If we are to honor Gustavo Gutiérrez, let us not only praise him. Let us also, in our practice, in the United States, imitate him.

The Contemporary Crisis

Indeed, we need the preferential option for the poor more than ever today because postmodernity includes an intensification of worker exploitation, racial oppression, discrimination against women, and sexual-identity exclusion. In the current conversation about postmodernity and in the latest theoretical discussions on class, culture, and the economy, we must not forget those who are the underside of history. For those of faith, we must stand first with the spirit of liberation that lives with the bottom of postmodernity. Being with this spirit of the underside causes us to fix our eyes on the poor. Likewise, it forces us to begin with the least in society as our starting point. Cornel West defines the contemporary crisis in the following manner:

> The exodus of stable industrial jobs from urban centers to
> cheaper labor markets here and abroad [among other factors] have

helped erode the tax base of American cities just as the federal government has cut its supports and programs. The result is unemployment, hunger, homelessness, and sickness for millions. And a pervasive spiritual impoverishment grows. The collapse of meaning in life . . . leads to the social deracination and cultural denudement of urban dwellers, especially children. . . . The result is lives of what we might call "random nows," of fortuitous and fleeting moments preoccupied with "getting over"—with acquiring pleasure, property, and power by any means necessary. [Rage against women and among young black men] is fueled by a political atmosphere in which images, not ideas, dominate, where politicians spend more time raising money than debating issues.[12]

The environment today reflects the intensification of a capitalist concentration of wealth and an addiction to the individual self. The ongoing mergers of monopoly-capitalist corporations point to an unchecked tendency of hoarding God's gifts of creation for all of humanity. For instance, the entertainment industry is divided into four major divisions:

1. General Electric (the biggest corporation in America), comprising the NBC network, numerous cable stations, and other properties.
2. Time Warner, comprising Time Warner Entertainment; Turner Broadcasting; CNN; Warner Brothers; HBO; numerous magazines, such as *Time, Fortune,* and *Life*; numerous publishing houses, such as Little, Brown and Time-Life; numerous other cable channels; numerous production services, such as World Championship Wrestling; and other properties.
3. Disney Corporation/Capital Cities, comprising the ABC network; several television stations in major urban areas that together reach 25% of American households; numerous cable stations, such as the Disney Channel, ESPN, and the Lifetime Network; numerous magazines; numerous newspapers, such as the *Kansas City Star* and the *Fort Worth Star-Telegram*; numerous retail stores; sports teams; theme parks; record companies; motion picture companies; and other properties.
4. Westinghouse Corporation (one of America's biggest defense contractors), comprising the CBS network; the CBS radio network; numerous cable stations, such as TNN and the Nashville Network; satellite distribution companies; and, of course, Westinghouse's nuclear power and nuclear engineering divisions.[13]

Such an example is the tip of the iceberg of concentrated power in the United States.

To Risk a Future

If we are to be faithful to the practice of the preferential option for the poor, then we must take the risk of envisioning what the future goal and ultimate society will look like. I think that the final end is a new beginning for all of humankind. This new time and new space is what I call the New Self and the New Commonwealth. Traditionally it is referred to as the kingdom of God. This new heaven and new earth follow the example of Jesus, who established a type of faith and practice for others; he conducted his life not for himself or his inner circle, but for the majority. He received internal strength in order to serve the larger human family. In a similar way, during the time of the New Self and New Commonwealth, each individual will be able to achieve the fullest potential that God has created her or him to be. No longer will there be obstacles to the full humanity of each person. Class exploitation, racial oppression, gender discrimination, and sexual-identity exclusion will end. Likewise, the negative feelings internal to each person's body will come to an end. When low self-esteem, negative anger, depression, and other harmful psychic and spiritual wounds are done away with, each person can use the maximum positive spirituality inside him or her to be all that God has called them to be.

However, this is not a vision for individualism, which is simply a form of capitalist emphasis on "me first." On the contrary, it reflects *individuality*. Individuality differs from individualism; individuality calls for accountability and obligation to the community. A person cannot live, think, and be alone, separate from the group. An individual cannot make decisions and take actions just for the self or even just for his or her family. This insight will require a new type of freedom where we are free to serve the collective interests. Indeed, in West African philosophy, without community, a person is less than an animal. Consequently, not only will there be a New Self, there will also be a New Commonwealth. Theologically, God created all things equal. In particular, God gave all of the earth's wealth to be shared by all of us as stewards. Human beings cannot own personally that which does not belong to them. No one, therefore, will have private ownership of wealth which belongs to God. Thus the final goal, the ultimate aim, is to share in common all that God has created. Instead of the central value being "I think therefore I am" or "I have a right to a profit or make money," the key to the definition of being a human being will be "I am because we are" and "I exist to share with the community."

The New Self and the New Commonwealth represent the final goal. Yahweh of the Hebrew Scriptures promised this time and place to the Hebrew workers who were enslaved in Egypt. Jesus walked this earth, delivered his first public speech, and laid out the criteria for entering this new time and place. The Book of Revelation speaks about this final goal. In the folk wisdom of black believers, it describes what they mean when they say they'll meet you on the other side of the Jordan, where there's no more pain or sorrow, only happiness. And Martin Luther King Jr. gave his life toward this end.

In addition, between the cutthroat reality of the now, on the one hand, and the period of the ultimate and final goal, on the other hand, we envision an intermediate period. Here the preferential option for the poor becomes even clearer. During the in-between time, we envision the poor, the least sectors of society, and the marginalized people among us owning and controlling the wealth of this land. A true majority of society will govern. With this condition in place, issues of universal healthcare, housing, employment, vacations, recreation, education, day care, and all of the issues that ensure the quality of daily life for those suffering from poverty will become easily attainable. The sole criterion during this interim period will be how we participate in the process of eliminating poverty and the host of related forms of brokenness in the human family.

It is through the majority of the society that the Spirit will lead and work with human beings to bring about a universal liberation and the practice of freedom for all of humanity. The sacred vocation is to empower the poor, to work with them on their own negative spirituality, and also to participate in releasing them from structures of oppression created by the small group of monopoly owners of the world's wealth. As a result, we, under the guidance of the divine, can aid in gradually recreating a new personality and new social relations which will liberate even the minority population of monopolizers. In the present moment, during the in-between time, and in the final ultimate, new divine reality, the anchor to our belief and practice is the preferential option for the poor. Upon this rock, we judge postmodernity.

NOTES

A similar text was given as a lecture at Perkins School of Theology (Dallas, Texas, May 18–19, 2000) at a symposium on the preferential option for the poor, postmodernity, and the work of Gustavo Gutiérrez. I would like to thank my research assistant, Kurt Buhring, for reorganizing the content of this essay.

1. Regarding postmodernism, see David Ashley, *History without a Subject: The Postmodern Condition* (Boulder, Colo.: Westview, 1997); David Harvey, *The Condition of Postmodernity* (Cambridge, Mass.: Blackwell, 1995); Hans Bertens, *The Idea of the Postmodern* (New York: Routledge, 1995); David R. Dickens and Andrea Fontana, eds., *Postmodernism and Social Inquiry* (New York: Guilford, 1994); Stephen Barker, ed., *Signs of Change: Premodern—Modern—Postmodern* (Albany: State University Press of New York, 1996); Thomas Docherty, ed., *Postmodernism: A Reader* (New York: Columbia University Press, 1993); Steven Seidman, ed., *The Postmodern Turn: New Perspectives on Social Theory* (New York: Cambridge University Press, 1994); Charles Jencks, ed., *The Post-Modern Reader* (New York: St. Martin's, 1992); and Jean Francois Lyotard, *The Postmodern Condition: A Report on Knowledge* (Minneapolis: University of Minnesota Press, 1984).

2. Gustavo Gutiérrez, *A Theology of Liberation: History, Politics and Salvation* (Maryknoll, N.Y.: Orbis, 1973), 292–93.

3. Charles L. Perdue Jr., Thomas E. Barden, and Robert K. Phillips, eds., *Weevils in the Wheat: Interviews with Virginia Ex-Slaves* (Charlottesville: University of Virginia Press, 1997), 94.

4. John W. Blassingame, ed., *Slave Testimony: Two Centuries of Letters, Speeches, Interviews, and Autobiographies* (Baton Rouge: Louisiana State University Press, 1977), 661.

5. Mark Miles Fisher, *Negro Slave Songs in the United States* (Secaucus, N.J.: Citadel, 1978), 121.

6. Martin Luther King Jr., "The President's Address to the Tenth Anniversary Convention of the Southern Christian Leadership Conference, Atlanta, Georgia, August 16, 1967," in *The Rhetoric of Black Power*, ed. Robert L. Scott and Wayne Brockriede (New York: Harper & Row, 1969), 161.

7. James H. Cone, *Black Theology and Black Power* (New York: Seabury, 1969) and *A Black Theology of Liberation* (New York: Seabury, 1970).

8. James H. Cone, "Black Theology and the Black Church: Where Do We Go from Here?" in *Black Theology: A Documentary History, 1966–1979*, ed. Gayraud S. Wilmore and James H. Cone (Maryknoll, N.Y.: Orbis, 1979), 358.

9. The following three-part definition of poverty can be found in Gutiérrez, *Theology of Liberation*, 288–99. Subsequent page references to *Theology of Liberation* are embedded in the text.

10. Gustavo Gutiérrez, *We Drink from Our Own Wells: The Spiritual Journey of a People* (Maryknoll, N.Y.: Orbis, 1984), 2.

11. Ibid., 30–32.

12. Cornel West, *Race Matters* (Boston: Beacon, 1993), 5–6.

13. Ashley, *History without a Subject*, 168.

7

Knowing the God of the Poor: The Preferential Option for the Poor

Roberto S. Goizueta

With each passing year in one's life, memories—and, therefore, history—increasingly become the sources of our continuing struggle and hope for the future. If the ardor of youth impels us into a future that, at times, rejects its past, the growing awareness of our mortality that comes with age prompts us also to glance toward the past every once in awhile. Age has a way of teaching us that, in the words of William Faulkner, "the past is not dead; it is not even past."

As a theologian and, especially, as a Christian, as I look back upon the last third of the twentieth century, the theological insight that has had the greatest impact on my life and—dare I say—on the life of the church is the notion that the God of Jesus Christ is revealed in a privileged, preferential way among the poor and marginalized peoples of our world—a notion at the very heart of the gospel itself. There is not a single corner of the Christian world today that has not been impacted by the renewed attention to that claim, whether as an impetus for conversion and transformation or as a challenge to established theological and ecclesial practices. Today, one cannot do Christian theology, or even think theologically, without in some way confronting the claims implicit in the preferential option for the poor.

A Privileged Criterion of Christian Orthodoxy

Indeed, if leading figures in the theological movement that came to be known as "liberation theology" no longer make the front pages of our newspapers, the reason is not that the issues that movement addresses have either disappeared or decreased in significance. On the contrary, global poverty, injustice, and exploitation remain as intransigent as ever and their consequences as devastating. If the public visibility of liberation theology has diminished, this is, in large part, because the fundamental questions raised by liberation theologians—once so novel and controversial—are today unavoidable in any theological conversation that demands to be taken seriously by either the churches or the academy. And foremost among those questions is the one which Gustavo Gutiérrez locates at the very heart of the theological enterprise:

> Our task here is to find the words with which to talk about God in the midst of the starvation of millions, the humiliation of races regarded as inferior, discrimination against women, especially women who are poor, systematic social injustice, a persistent high rate of infant mortality, those who simply "disappear" or are deprived of their freedom, the sufferings of peoples who are struggling for their right to live, the exiles and the refugees, terrorism of every kind, and the corpse-filled common graves of Ayacucho [a scene of civil strife in Peru].[1]

In the wake of the bloodiest century in the history of humanity, and given the fact that much of that blood will be found on the hands of self-proclaimed Christians, the victims of that history are today the theologian's principal interlocutors. And, thus, God's preferential solidarity with those victims is an inescapable challenge—*the* inescapable challenge—for Christian theology at the dawn of the twenty-first century. More specifically, the claim that, in the person of the crucified and risen Christ, God is preferentially identified with the victims of history transforms the preferential option for the poor from an ethical imperative into the privileged *locus theologicus* of *all* Christian theology. After such a claim has been explicitly made, no Christian theology can avoid it, even if only to dismiss it.

When I suggest that the preferential option for the poor represents a claim that the God of Jesus Christ is revealed in a privileged, preferential way among the poor and marginalized, I mean to argue, therefore, that the option for the poor makes not only an ethical but also epistemological and theological claims. That is, the preferential option for the poor is not only a privileged criterion of Christian orthopraxis (correct practice), calling us to live our faith; it is, more fundamentally, a privileged criterion of orthodoxy itself (correct worship, or *doxa*), calling us to believe in and worship a God who is revealed on the cross, among the crucified peoples of history. Unless we place ourselves alongside the poor, unless we look at reality through their eyes, we are unable to see, recognize, or worship the God who walks with the poor. Conversely, if we lack such a practical solidarity with the poor, the "god" in whom we believe and whom we worship will necessarily be a false god, an idol of our own making.

Thus the question posed to us by the crucified peoples of history is not only, "Are you a good, loving, just Christian?" but, more fundamentally, "Are you a Christian *at all?*"

This, it seems to me, has been the real source of so much resistance to the preferential option for the poor, not only as a challenge to Christian theology but, especially, as a challenge to Christian faith itself. That is, the notion that a Christian should love the poor—even love the poor in a preferential way—can be and has been affirmed by many First World Christians. Such an assertion carries relatively little risk of confrontation: if one wants to be a good Christian, one should have a special concern for the poor.

Yet while Gutiérrez and other liberation theologians have certainly been saying that, they have also been saying something that, I think, goes much deeper, right to the heart of the act of faith itself. If the God of the Scriptures is preferentially present among the marginalized peoples of our societies and if religious faith is, by definition, a knowledge of God, then we *cannot* know the God of the Scriptures unless and until we *place ourselves* in the presence of that God. If the God of Jesus Christ is preferentially identified with the poor, then, if we are to be identified with God, we must identify ourselves preferentially with the poor. If the margins of society are the privileged locus of God's revelation in history, then we *will not and cannot see or know* that God unless we also make that our own privileged locus. In short, the option for the poor is not merely a consequence or even a concomitant of Christian faith; it is, at bottom, a condition of the possibility of Christian faith. And *that* is the assertion which, whether implicit or explicit, so many First World Christians find threatening.

The most significant and ground-breaking theological insight of Latin American liberation theologians has been precisely this transposition of the Christian commitment to social justice from the realm of ethics (i.e., "social ethics") to the realm of theology and, indeed, to Christian belief itself. As long as the imperative to "do justice" is conceived as fundamentally an *ethical* imperative *derived from* or *consequent upon* Christian belief, Christian faith can be effectively immunized from that imperative.

At the same time, I think we misread Gutiérrez's understanding of the option for the poor if we interpret it as *reducing* Christian faith to such a practical option. Throughout his writings, Gutiérrez is quite clear that the warrants for a preferential option for the poor are, above all, *theocentric*: "The ultimate basis for the privileged position of the poor is not in the poor themselves but in God, in the gratuitousness and universality of God's *agapeic love*."[2] Our praxis of solidarity with the poor is not *itself* the foundation of Christian faith; rather, that praxis is a *response* to God's own initiative, a response to God's own gratuitous revelation in our world and in our own lives. " 'God first loved us' (1 John 4:19)," writes Gutiérrez; "everything starts from there. The gift of God's love is the source of our being and puts its impress on our lives. . . . The other is our way for reaching God, but our relationship with God is a precondition for encounter and true communion with the other."³ Before we can "opt for" God or others, God has already opted for us; we can opt for the poor in a preferential way *because* God has already opted for the poor preferentially. And because the God who has chosen and loved us gratuitously is revealed in Scripture, in tradition, and in history as a God who has chosen and loved the poor preferentially, we are compelled and empowered to love the poor preferentially. "The ultimate basis of God's preference for the poor," avers Gutiérrez, "is to be found in God's own goodness and not in any analysis of society or in human compassion, however pertinent these reasons may be."⁴

Indeed, the Peruvian theologian warns against such distorted interpretations of the option for the poor:

> A hasty and simplistic interpretation of the liberationist perspec-
> tive has led some to affirm that its dominant, if not exclusive,
> themes are commitment, the social dimension of faith, the denunci-
> ation of injustices, and others of a similar nature. It is said that the
> liberationist impulse leaves little room for grasping the necessity of
> personal conversion as a condition for Christian life. . . . Such an in-
> terpretation and criticism are simply caricatures. One need only
> have contact with the Christians in question to appreciate the com-
> plexity of their approach and the depth of their spiritual experience.⁵

What defines and makes Christian faith possible is not praxis as such but praxis *as encountered by God's Word*. And it is precisely a supreme confidence in God's gratuitous love for us, as that love is revealed in our lives and in God's Word, that above all characterizes the faith of the poor themselves.

Gutiérrez's understanding of the preferential option for the poor presents us with an epistemological paradox: the more profoundly we accompany the poor, the more profoundly we identify with the Christian praxis of the poor and reflect critically on that praxis in the light of God's Word, the more we are confronted with a lived faith that takes as its starting point, not human praxis per se (since there is no such thing as human praxis independent of God's own prevenient activity in our lives), but the gratuitous Word of God, Jesus Christ himself as the foundation of our liberative praxis. The more we direct our gaze to the poor, the more they remind us of what God has done and continues to do for the poor in history: "The gratuitousness of God's love is the framework within which the requirement of practicing justice is to be located."⁶ The poor understand, argues Gutiérrez, that, before we can choose God or others, God has already chosen us. Christian praxis is, at its most fundamental level, an action of reception and response. We become historical agents in the process of receiving and responding to God's liberating grace and therefore becoming living mediators of that grace in history. Hence, insofar as theology is *Christian* theology, it can never be simply a "critical reflection on praxis" per se; rather, as Gutiérrez avers in his now-classic definition, Christian theology must be a "critical reflection on Christian praxis in the light of the Word."[7]

A Participation in Theopraxis

An authentically human praxis is always, by definition, a participation in a *theo*praxis, God's own praxis in history. Our ability to act as historical agents, our freedom, our very identity are themselves given us by the God who loved us first, the God who is fully revealed in the wounded body of the crucified and risen Christ. Echoing Gutiérrez's words, Jon Sobrino observes:

> To be encountered by the Lord is the experience of the love of God. Indeed it is the experience of the fact that love is the reality that discloses to us, and makes us able to be, what we are. It is God's coming to meet us, simply because God loves us, that renders us capable of defining our very selves as who we are, in order, in our turn, to go forth to meet others. . . . Without a true encounter with God, there can be no true encounter with the poor. . . . To have genuine love for our sisters and brothers, we must have an experience of the God who first loved us.[8]

The grounds for the preferential option for the poor, then, are ultimately theological: "Gutiérrez insists on commitment to the poor and on the epistemological privilege of their vantage point on *theological* grounds, namely, the special care of the God of the Bible for the poor and God's choice of the oppressed as the favored instrument for the accomplishment of the divine will in history."[9] The call to enter into solidarity with the marginalized is a call that, when acted upon, reveals to us not only who the poor are, not only who we ourselves are, but above all who God is.[10] Our ability to recognize, receive, and embrace, in the crucified and risen Christ, God's gratuitous love as the source of our very identity is inseparable from the ability to embody that love in our social praxis; these are two inseparable dimensions of liberation.

Though Gutiérrez has written extensively on the option for the poor and is currently writing what will be the definitive work on the subject, his most powerful and inspiring treatment of this topic thus far has been—in my opinion—his book on the great Spanish Dominican missionary Bartolomé de Las Casas. Though not explicitly a work on the option for the poor, this book provides a vivid portrait of Las Casas, a Christian whose life embodied as few others the option for the poor and whose prophetic theological arguments represent a sophisticated defense of the evangelical principles underlying what later came to be known as the preferential option for the poor. In my opinion, no published work of Gutiérrez's better articulates the specifically epistemological and theological grounds (as opposed to the ethical implications) of the option for the poor.

Gutiérrez's poignant description of the conversion of Bartolomé de Las Casas retrieves what is one of the great historical examples of a "Christian's" conversion from idol-worship, even when that idol is a nominally Christian deity, to the worship of the God of Jesus Christ. The intrinsic connection between orthodoxy and orthopraxis has never been exemplified as clearly as in the Dominican's conversion while he was preparing to celebrate the eucharistic liturgy. Reflecting on the Scripture readings for the day, he came upon the following words in the Book of Sirach (34:18–22):

> Tainted his gifts who offers in sacrifice ill-gotten goods!
>   Mock presents from the lawless win not God's favor.
> The Most High approves not the gifts of the godless,
>   nor for their many sacrifices does he forgive their sins.
> Like the man who slays a son in his father's presence
>   is he who offers sacrifice from the possessions of the poor.
> The bread of charity is life itself for the needy;
>   he who withholds it is a person of blood.
> He slays his neighbor who deprives him of his living;
>   he sheds blood who denies the laborer his wages.[11]

As he read them, Las Casas saw himself mirrored in and challenged by those words: he was preparing to offer to God bread and wine produced by his own Indian slaves. What was thus ostensibly an act of Christian worship was, in fact, an act of idolatry; he was purporting to worship the God of Jesus Christ while, in reality, worshiping a god of violence and destruction, a god who accepted the fruit of exploited human labor. While condemning the Amerindians for their practice of human sacrifice, he himself—along with the rest of the Spaniards—had been sacrificing human blood, sweat, and tears in the form of bread and wine. As Las Casas insisted repeatedly in the wake of his conversion, that *metanoia* implied not only a different way of living but, in so doing, it also implied belief in and worship of a radically different God from the "god" to whom he had previously been offering the mass. Conversely, any worship conducted in the absence of a solidarity with the poor can only be idolatry.

As I have suggested, the intrinsic connection between the option for the poor, on the one hand, and authentic Christian belief and worship, on the other, is the most challenging—and threatening—aspect of the preferential option for the poor. This, despite the fact that, of course, such a connection is explicitly made repeatedly throughout the Scriptures, especially in the prophetic writings and the Gospels.

Indeed, as liberation theologians and other Third World theologians have attempted to articulate the principle of the preferential option for the poor, they have called attention to this very connection insofar as they are giving increased attention to the place of popular religion, or what Orlando Espín has called the "faith of the people," within the liberation struggle and, therefore, within the preferential option for the poor. Popular religion is at once theocentric and sociopolitical: it is theocentric in that its foundation is an unvanquished faith in God's solidarity with the poor, and it is sociopolitical in that that solidarity is encountered first on the margins of society, among the outcasts and victims of sociopolitical and economic power.

An Option for the Faith of the Poor

At the very heart of what Gutiérrez has called the "culture of the poor" one finds the religious practices, symbols, and narratives which embody a lived faith: "From gratuitousness also comes the language of symbols. . . . In their religious celebrations, whether at especially important moments or in the circumstances of everyday life, the poor turn to the Lord with the trustfulness and spontaneity of a child who speaks to its father and tells him of its suffering and hopes."[12] This fact reveals an important dimension of the preferential option for the poor, one which Gutiérrez himself underscores, but one too often missed by critics of liberation theologies: the option for the poor necessarily implies an option for the *lived faith* of the poor, an option for the *spirituality* of the poor. To opt for the poor is necessarily to pray as the poor pray and to pray to the God to whom the poor pray. If, as Gutiérrez avers, at the center of the worldview of the poor is an unshakeable belief that "God first loved us" and that "everything starts from" that belief, then all human praxis becomes, at bottom, an act of worship, an act of prayer—and every act of prayer becomes a sociopolitical act. In the absence of such a practical spirituality, which is lived in response to God's love for us, any putative option for the poor cannot engender the solidarity or empathy necessary if that option is to define not only an ethics but also an epistemology and, especially, a theology. "It is not possible to do theology in Latin America," writes Gutiérrez, "without taking into account the situation of the most downtrodden of history; this means in turn that at some point the theologian must cry out, as Jesus did, 'My God, my God, why hast thou forsaken me?'"[13]

However, such an understanding of the preferential option for the poor— as an act of response to God's loving action in history—becomes incomprehensible within both modern and postmodern worldviews. Modern Western notions of praxis emphasize the character of human praxis as autonomous agency, which itself is understood instrumentally. (I have elsewhere argued that even the postmodern deconstruction of the agent-subject presupposes what it claims to reject.)[14] Such understanding of praxis, however, fails to locate human praxis within the broader ambit of God's own praxis in history.

For the lived faith of the poor is precisely a faith lived in the light of the Word which, as such, demands a theological reflection itself illumined by that light. These are a faith and a theology for which historical praxis, context, and experience are always themselves incorporated into a divine praxis: orthopraxis presupposes a theopraxis and, more specifically, a Christopraxis. Thus, the praxis on which theology is based is itself derived from and in-formed by the Word who is received as grace, as gift. For Gutiérrez, "the light of the Word" forms our theology and praxis, which, in turn, must themselves—precisely as *Christian* theology and praxis—con-form to the Word. Paradoxically, we can become truly autonomous only to the extent that we are receptive to God's gratuitous love and, in our historical action, are conformed to that love.

This affirmation of the *reality* of God's universal love as foundational points to a further obstacle which the option for the poor must confront in our contemporary society. At least at the level of popular U.S. culture, the post-modern deconstruction of the subject and the rejection of all so-called meta-narratives have often resulted in a denial of the possibility of any truth-claims per se. Quite simply, the question of truth is reduced to a question of either meaning or usefulness: Is faith meaningful or useful *for me*? Is the faith of the poor meaningful or useful for them? Does it work for them? Does it liberate?

However, if Christian faith presupposes a preferential option for the poor—*as the privileged criterion of that faith's credibility*—then the possibility of affirming normative, universal truths is itself essential to and a presupposition of the cause of liberation. Otherwise, we are ultimately incapable of even dis-tinguishing between oppression and liberation. Any notion of pluralism or diversity that precludes, *a priori*, such a possibility will only contribute to the marginalization of the poor.

A tolerance of diversity or difference without preference can never be the foundation of freedom and justice. The appeal to tolerance as sufficient for ensuring inclusiveness and diversity effectively neutralizes the voices of the poor. Whatever the outward appearances, the logic of such an appeal reinforces marginalization insofar as (1) ethical judgments are reduced to mere matters of personal experience, personal taste, or personal opinion that are, as such, immune to public critique; (2) the radical relativism resulting from the priva-tization of ethical judgments precludes the possibility of adjudicating between competing ethical claims (since to do so would require some normative criteria against which to evaluate those claims); (3) the impossibility of adjudicating between competing claims precludes, in turn, the possibility of making a *pref-erential* option for the poor; and (4) thus, the voice of the marginalized person is "heard" as simply one among many others, unable to make any normative claims, for example, in the name of justice.

Truth Claims and the Possibility of Preference

Against both a Rawlsian "tolerance" and a nihilistic relativism, the preferential option for the poor presupposes that the good of the whole cannot be achieved unless and until preference is given to a *particular* good, namely, the good of the marginalized. A prerequisite for justice is a preferential option for the poor, the marginalized. Far from promoting conflict or divisiveness, such a preference is a precondition for an authentic, pluralistic community which affirms the dignity of all peoples. The failure of the "appeal to tolerance" that characterizes popular modern and postmodern notions of freedom is that it defines all preference as *ipso facto in*tolerable and unjust. A call for justice can be dismissed as one opinion among many others, to be "heard" and tolerated but, at the same time, precluded *a priori* from making any claim on the others— for to do so would be to assert that the perspective of the poor reveals a reality or truth that transcends that perspective. In short, where diversity and inclusivity are defined by mere tolerance, marginalization (i.e., intolerance) will be reinforced even as existing inequalities are hidden beneath an appearance of pluralism. The *possibility* of preferring some points of view over others or of making normative truth-claims is not a threat to pluralism but its very precondition. The possibility—indeed, the necessity—of affirming a normative, universal truth is presupposed in the preferential option for the poor, even though this can never be a merely abstract, conceptual truth.

In my own work in the Latino community over the years, I have been reminded over and over again that, for the poor, the fundamental question is, quite simply, "is it *true?*"—not in an abstract, propositional sense, but in the sense of a reality that makes ultimate claims on our whole lives, a reality that defines us, gives us our identity and mission. When we are encountered by Christ, contends Gutiérrez, "we discover where the Lord lives and what the mission is that has been entrusted to us."[15] Thus, for the poor, liberation depends precisely on the truth, the reality, of the body of Christ and its claims. And, to the extent that postmodern culture absolutizes difference, otherness, and the particular over against the universal, such normative, universal claims are difficult if not impossible to make.

Far from denying the unbiased universality of God's love, the preferential option for the poor is the guarantee of that universality; it is the guarantee of faith in a God who loves all people gratuitously and equally. As Gutiérrez has insisted, to say that God's love is universal is not to say that it is neutral; indeed, universality and neutrality are mutually contradictory terms. An authentically Christian notion of universality is not opposed to particular preference, rather the universal is mediated in and through the particular: God's universal love is mediated in and through the particular person, Jesus of Nazareth, the crucified. Both modernity and postmodernity presuppose an inherent contradiction between the universal and the particular, between normative truth and personal meaning; Christianity, on the other hand, claims that the universal and normative is made present in and through the particular and personal form of the crucified and risen Christ. If that claim is true, if Jesus Christ was crucified and raised from the dead, then we can dare to hope in the future and to work for liberation. On the other hand, if that claim is merely one among other equally valid claims (e.g., that the God of the Scriptures is apolitical or politically neutral), then we will become paralyzed in the face of that future.

The Truth of the Cross

For the marginalized in society (and, I would argue, for the majority of people outside modern Western culture), the most fundamental question is not "will it liberate?" or "do I find it meaningful?" but "is it true?" "is it real?" (though not in a modern conceptualist way that contrasts the symbolic and the real). And yet this is the very question which, in the dominant U.S. culture, we are reluctant to ask or, perhaps, are incapable of asking. "Be the problems of the 'truth' of Christ what they may," writes Sobrino, "his credibility is assured as far as the poor are concerned, for he maintained his nearness to them to the end. In this sense the cross of Jesus is seen as the paramount symbol of Jesus' approach to the poor, and, hence, the guarantee of his indisputable credibility."[16] Because Jesus accompanies us, he is real; and because he is real, he liberates. And the cross is the guarantee that he does, in fact, remain with us, that he does, in fact, walk with us even today. Sobrino continues:

> A vague, undifferentiated faith in God is not enough to generate hope. Not even the admission that God is mighty, or that God has made promises, will do this. Something else besides the generic or abstract attributes of the divinity is necessary in order to generate hope. This distinct element—which, furthermore, is the fundamental characteristic of the Christian God—is something the poor have discovered viscerally, and in reality itself: the nearness of God. God instills hope because God is credible, and God is credible because God is close to the poor. . . . Therefore when the poor hear and understand that God delivers up the Son, and that God is crucified— something that to the mind of the nonpoor will always be either a scandal or a pure anthropomorphism—then, paradoxically, their hope becomes real. The poor have no problems with God. The classic question of theodicy—the "problem of God," the atheism of protest—so reasonably posed by the nonpoor, is no problem at all for the poor (who in good logic ought of course to be the ones to pose it).[17]

The cross, which for the nonpoor is a sign of God's absence, is, for the poor, the assurance of God's presence—not just any god, not just a "vague" or "generic" god, but the God of Jesus Christ, the God who accompanies us today.

This is a faith that—contrary to all modern (and, I would argue, postmodern) theologies—does not take the autonomous, self-constituting human subject per se as its starting point at all but rather affirms, at great personal cost, a transcendent reality to which the human subject *responds* and in which he/she *participates* in the act of faith or praxis of faith. "To profess 'this Jesus,' to acknowledge 'Jesus the Christ,' " argues Gutiérrez, "is to express a conviction. It is not simply putting a name and a title together; it is an authentic confession of faith. It is the assertion of an identity: the Jesus of history, the son of Mary, the carpenter of Nazareth, the preacher of Galilee, the crucified, *is* the Only Begotten of God, the Christ, the Son of God."[18] "If we believe in Jesus as the Son," avers Sobrino, "it is because in him the truth and love of the mystery of God have been shown in an unrepeatable form, and been shown in a way that is totally convincing to a crucified people who have no problem in accepting Jesus' unrepeatable relationship with God so that they can confess him to be in truth the Son of God."[19]

If our praxis is liberating, it is so only because it affirms something that is real or true. As Sobrino insists:

> The resurrection of the one who was crucified is *true*. Let it be foolishness, as it was for the Corinthians. But without this foolishness, because it is true—or without this truth, because it is foolish—the resurrection of Jesus will only be one more symbol of hope in survival after death that human beings have designed in their religions or philosophies. It will not be the Christian symbol of hope.[20]

For the poor, the resurrection is not merely the assurance of life *after* death; it is, above all, the assurance of life *before* death.[21] Because Jesus lives, we can dare to live.

The preferential option for the poor forces us to confront the question of truth. To the hungry person, the truth of Christ's claims about himself is much more than an academic issue, to be debated and deconstructed by exegetes and theologians. If I take that hungry person seriously, then, so too must I be willing to render a verdict on those claims. Am I willing to stake my own life on those truth-claims?

The faith of the poor demands from us that we stake our own existence on a reality, a truth that irrupts in our world in the form of the cross, thereby subverting and overturning our own conceptions of love, justice, and freedom. It demands, moreover, that we understand the *act* of receiving a gift, or giving thanks, as indeed an *act*, as *praxis*. Such a contemplative faith-stance becomes increasingly difficult, however, in a society in which we are taught from childhood that to be fully human we must be able and willing to grab, to grasp, to acquire; to receive is to be passive, and to be passive is to be less than human. To be free, therefore, is to "go for the gusto," to "grasp the brass ring," to grab all you can while you can.

Yet this fully reflects the understanding of freedom embodied in the lived faith of the poor that Gutiérrez has defined so poignantly, especially in his books *On Job* and *We Drink from Our Own Wells*, where freedom presupposes the capacity for receptivity, a capacity for responding to an other. The ability to receive is precisely what empowers one to act, to "grasp" freedom. *Because* we are indeed accompanied by the crucified and risen Christ, we have the courage to go on. Thus, for the poor themselves, the question of truth is essential. For the poor, whether or not Jesus Christ was truly raised from the dead is not an issue of secondary importance; though, of course, that is true. But it is true *because* Jesus Christ was raised from the dead.

As Gutiérrez reminds us, Jesus asks his disciples and asks us: "Who do *you* say that I am? You; not the others. . . . what is asked refers to an objective reality, something exterior to the disciples. . . . The question pulls us out of our subjective world and, 'turning us inside out,' locates the point of reference of our faith, and of our life, beyond ourselves, in the person of Jesus."[22] And the question "who do you say that I am?" demands not a theoretical answer but a practical answer, a lived answer.[23]

Ultimately, then, the preferential option for the poor represents a call to conversion. To make an option for the poor is to allow ourselves to be transformed by the same God who accompanies the poor. "It is not the same thing merely to treat things scientifically and doctrinally," observes Sobrino, "as really to shed light on them. It is not the same thing to speak of many things as to allow things to speak for themselves."[24]

If taken seriously, then, the preferential option for the faith of the poor overturns contemporary assumptions about the possibility of preferring one truth-claim, one option over others. With Sobrino, the faith of the people challenges us to ask:

> Is there anything that is ultimate and incapable of being manipulated, anything that makes an ultimate demand on human beings in the form of promise and fulfillment? Is there anything that will prevent us from relativizing everything, reducing everything to a lowest common denominator in terms of value, although perhaps without our knowing why we should not make such a reduction? Is there anything that makes a total demand on us—anything to remind us that despite the ideals of a consumer society, despite the growing preoccupation with material security and a life of self-centeredness, as we find for example in many places in the First World, there is after all a "something else," and a "someone else," and not just as a factual datum, but as a "something" and a "some-

one" in terms of which we either succeed or fail in our own self-fulfillment.[25]

The faith of the poor will eventually force us all to take a stand, to declare: "*This* I believe; on *this* I am willing to stake my life." Then and only then will we be liberated, freed to commit ourselves wholeheartedly to struggle alongside the God who stays with the victims of history, the God whose nearness inspires in us a hope against hope. Insofar as our own praxis is conformed to God's cruciform praxis in history, we can become participants in the historical struggle for liberation.

As the foundation of the Christian theological enterprise, the preferential option for the poor thus offers an antidote to the postmodern woman's or man's reluctance to make particular commitments. Rooted in a praxis of compassion wherein we walk alongside Christ in his passion and, therefore, alongside the crucified poor in their historical suffering, the option for the poor becomes an option for tolerance in the deepest sense of this word. Authentic tolerance is not that of the abstract, dehistoricized, or unsituated self standing outside all particular commitments or the selfless self so radically particular that it is incapable of making judgments of any reality beyond its particular social location. Denying either the intrinsically social character of the person, in the former case, or the intrinsically self-transcending character of the person, in the latter, both alternatives are silent accomplices of the status quo. Rather, authentic tolerance presupposes and is grounded in a preferential option for those persons and groups whose ongoing crucifixion, like that of Christ, *must not* be tolerated. The most credible arbiters of tolerance are precisely those persons whom society continues to deem intolerable: the hungry, the naked, the homeless. If the ground-breaking insights of Gustavo Gutiérrez, as developed especially in his writings on the option for the poor, challenged modernity to embrace those whom it had excluded, those same insights today challenge postmodernity to make that embrace itself the starting point for constructing a truly tolerant, truly pluralistic society.

NOTES

1. Gustavo Gutiérrez, *Essential Writings*, ed. James B. Nickoloff (Maryknoll, N.Y.: Orbis, 1996), 318.

2. Gustavo Gutiérrez, *On Job: God-Talk and the Suffering of the Innocent* (Maryknoll, N.Y.: Orbis, 1987), 94.

3. Gustavo Gutiérrez, *We Drink from Our Own Wells: The Spiritual Journey of a People* (Maryknoll, N.Y.: Orbis, 1984), 109–12.

4. Gutiérrez, *On Job*, xiii.

5. Gutiérrez, *We Drink from Our Own Wells*, 96.

6. Gutiérrez, *On Job*, 89.

7. Gustavo Gutiérrez, *A Theology of Liberation: History, Politics, and Salvation* (Maryknoll, N.Y.: Orbis, 1988), 11.

8. Jon Sobrino, *Spirituality of Liberation: Toward Political Holiness* (Maryknoll, N.Y.: Orbis, 1988), 56–58.

9. James B. Nickoloff, "Introduction" to Gutiérrez, *Essential Writings*, 18.

10. Gutiérrez, *On Job*, xiii.

11. Quotation from New American Bible; cited in Gustavo Gutiérrez, *Las Casas: In Search of the Poor of Jesus Christ* (Maryknoll, N.Y.: Orbis, 1993), 47.

12. Gutiérrez, *We Drink from Our Own Wells*, 111–12.

13. Gutiérrez, *Las Casas*, 101.

14. Roberto S. Goizueta, *Caminemos con Jesús: Toward a Hispanic/Latino Theology of Accompaniment* (Maryknoll, N.Y.: Orbis, 1995).

15. Gutiérrez, *We Drink from Our Own Wells*, 38.

16. Sobrino, *Spirituality of Liberation*, 171.

17. Ibid., 166–67.

18. Gutiérrez, *We Drink from Our Own Wells*, 46.

19. Jon Sobrino, *Jesus in Latin America* (Maryknoll, N.Y.: Orbis, 1987), 165.

20. Ibid., 158 (emphasis original).

21. I am indebted to Professor Otto Maduro for this insight.

22. Gutiérrez, *We Drink from Our Own Wells*, 48.

23. Ibid., 51.

24. Sobrino, *Spirituality of Liberation*, 70.

25. Ibid., 105.

8

The Work of Love: Feminist Politics and the Injunction to Love

M. Gail Hamner

Love works as a force that can straddle two seemingly incommensu-
rate discourses: identity politics and postmodernity. Love incites a
feeling that can respond to how identity is constructed by difference,
being simultaneously affirmed and disavowed *within* the strictures
of both institutionalized power and diffuse commonsense. Consider
this (true) story.

I enter into a church's small classroom for the first meeting of
the "Dialogue on Race and Racism," feeling distinct trepidation
about the ivory-tower elitism that marks my speech and manners (I
think too quickly, I am told; I use big words). In the room sit two
facilitators and six other participants, four of whom are African
American Americorps volunteers. I enter with an extensive book-
knowledge about race theory and life experiences as a white girl
from the South and white professor in the North. I have come to
"dialogue" about race but know clearly, instinctively, that the more
fundamental divide in the room is class or, more precisely, the particular constellation of race and class in U.S. culture. The six two-
hour sessions in which we talk together proves my instinct correct.
Week after week I listen to the stories of these bourgeois European
Americans and working-class—or, sadly, not even *that* economically
stable—African Americans and feel the words as an incarnation of
the demographic and statistical generalizations that fill the literature
I know so well. I speak less, feeling that my thoughts and questions
are too remote and irrelevant, too intellectual. I wonder repeatedly
why I am there. Didn't I know at the outset that this "dialogue"
would not have the room for the questions I want to ask, much less

time for the answers? I feel trapped in my ivory-tower construction, reduced within this dialogue on race by my formation as "intellectual," reduced to the limited options of talking about race with these persons as if they were students or subjects of some idiosyncratic ethnography. I like them very much, and I enjoy the coffee talk and premeeting chitchat, but I feel no connection to them with regard to discussing race.

At the final meeting—one I seriously consider skipping in light of my previous boredom and frustration—one young African American woman interrupts me saying, "Girl, you should run for president!" I laugh, "No one would vote for me," and begin to complete the simple (I hope) point I'd been offering about the workbook's final statements. She taps her hands on the table and declares, "Well, I would. Where you teach? Hmmph. I wish I was a student of yours." It is only at this point that it dawns on me that the effectiveness of this "dialogue" lies not in the discussion of race and racism, but precisely in the coffee talk and premeeting chitchat. In a sense this young woman articulates bravely and clearly what I have been feeling, though I felt it as failure and disappointment: that she doesn't know how to talk to me and wouldn't claim to understand me, but she respects me and loves me. Unlike the bond formed within identity politics, the love between us was not around our identities as women or as white and black or as rich and poor, but came about through discussions of school and children and grandparents, more than through the "dialogue work" on how our identities have been formed through our unique experiences within a (partially) shared culture. Unlike many postmodern theories of the self, we did not celebrate our difference or find anything playful in it; more, we felt that our differences, as well as our connection, are charged with political consequence, though I perhaps had more words for that feeling than did she. This politics of love, this political work of love, forms the thematic focus of my essay.

Love is positioned as the central force of the feminist politics of Donna Haraway, Kaja Silverman, and Luce Irigaray. But what viability or feasibility can love offer as a political strategy? What is this work of love? I contend that these feminists deploy love as a Christian-inflected option for the marginalized. Love ignites the program by which these feminists attempt to stand with and advocate for those without power or voice. In this feminist and political work, love operates religiously, even Christianly, in that social redemption and human salvation are envisioned as possible only through the indirect, uncontrollable, and yet necessary work of love. Although in my eyes each project fails to accomplish what it attempts, the noteworthy point remains the very desire to deploy (Christian) love toward political ends.

The religious connotations of the term *love* are as apparent as its emotional nuances; it calls up a range of injunctions in a variety of religious traditions about a believer's or follower's dispositions toward neighbor, foreigner, marginalized, and the divine itself. Of the three theorists only Irigaray makes this nuance overt, but I see the religiosity of love critical to all three projects. I could say I see Christianity instead of religiosity in each project, but these feminists are quite distant from any stance within the circle of Christian discourse, much less Christian belief. Of the three, only Irigaray explicitly draws upon and *re-stages* Christian images of God and woman, and she juxtaposes these Christian gestures with images of the Buddha and of Hindu chakras that carry just as much if not more argumentative weight for her. Haraway sometimes uses Christian semantics, but Silverman's deployment of love, while using terms with Christian connotations, skirts any direct appropriation of Christianity. Still, in light of the uncontested fact that Christianity remains the hegemonic understanding of "religion" in the United States, it does not seem impudent to suggest that these two West-coast theorists are affected (infected?) by this hegemonic force, despite their overt rejection of some of Christianity's legacies. More specifically, their use of love draws from its Christian associations a tone and timbre that combines passion and respect, engagement of the other and an awe-filled letting-be.

The political appeals to love are clear. Haraway opens her treatise *Primate Visions* with the question: "How are love, power, and science intertwined in the constructions of nature in the late twentieth century?" Evoking Judaic/ Christian Scripture, the epigraph above her opening sentence reads, "For thus all things must begin, with an act of love."[1] Silverman acknowledges love as a central thematic of *Threshold of the Visible World*, saying that the book examines "visual representation as the domain within which . . . we can be enabled to see in a way that is narrowly determined neither by the self, nor by normative values—to affirm 'otherness.' In this sense, then, *Threshold* is in fact a book about love."[2] For Silverman the possibility of feminist politics relies on the possibility of love, and, therefore, feminist struggle must be articulated in terms of transcendence, otherness, and gift—all terms with religious purchase. Irigaray ends the first essay of her book *I Love to You* with a call to politicize and deprivatize our notion of love: "Love between us, women and men of this world, is what may still save us. . . . We are the ones who have to make this word ['companions'] designate a loving relationship, ranging from the most private aspects of our lives to a political ethics that refuses to sacrifice desire for death, power, or money."[3] Repeatedly, Irigaray explicitly conjoins feminist politics with salvation through her philosophy of love.

Each of these theorists clearly calls on love to bear the active burden of her feminist movement. Indeed in all three, love is the material substance of a feminist politics. But love hardly seems an apt concept around which to build a political program. The word is vague and too familiar, with too little traction and too much sentimentality. Feminist theorists, especially, might be suspicious of an appeal to love since it risks falling prey to wearying stereotypes such as women's "inability to control emotions" and our "incapacity for precise and logical thought." And yet even as these feminist theorists combat these stereotypes, they do make appeals for a politics of love. Why? As suggested above, I see love working as the third option between the perceived necessities of identity politics and the acknowledged critique of those politics by poststructuralist theory. If identity politics is crucial to feminists because of its ability to organize women around a common political cause, it also is problematic in requiring some kind of common (essential) subjectivity; this is the poststructuralist critique. On the other hand, many feminists perceive the postmodern "celebration" of difference, play, and undecidability as cynically rendering political action impotent if not impossible. Love, then, can be seen as a tactical line of escape from the theoretical aporia of identity politics and postmodern cynicism, an escape that refuses either choice by accepting parts of both. The political appeal to love recognizes the need for coalition politics *and* nonessentializing conceptions of subjectivity. More, the appeal shows how the divine has found a new incarnation in secular thought: the work of love betrays an explicit, albeit quiet, insertion of Christianity into late twentieth century's leftist feminist politics. To me, these feminists grasp the symptom of our times, the unthought of global capitalism,[4] namely, the fact that thousands live the "victory" of global capitalism as a punishment, torture, and/or enslavement.[5]

I discuss these feminist projects chronologically, but I can impose another logic that elicits the stakes involved in their appeals to love. Haraway advocates for poststructuralist theory and yet recognizes its failure to account for affect. In her project she demonstrates skillfully how the voiceless animals of scientific research can be mapped onto the structured inequities of gender, race, ethnicity, and nationality. Instead of simply repeating Foucault's famous assertion that "power is knowledge," Haraway mirrors that insight with her own that "love is power." Around this insight she constructs a powerful method of storytelling that clearly, but indirectly, advocates a politics of love. Silverman's politics of love can be seen as the inverse of Haraway's. Instead of a wide-ranging map of power relations, Silverman articulates and critiques the psychic mechanisms that support a coherent and stable sense of self. To her, the homeless are metonymic of the abject that always threatens coherent identity, and she posits love as the other-directed mechanism by which the abject can be kept at bay without resorting to the "incorporative" logic that usually structures subjectivity. Irigaray, by this imposed logic, is a Hegelian synthesis of Haraway and Silverman. She joins Haraway's macrocosmic focus on power relations with Silverman's microcosmic focus on subjectivity in a project that evokes a new vision and new economy for global society. She speaks toward an impossible "place" in which love saves us from a state and civil society structured phallocentrically as "one." Calling herself a "political militant for the impossible," Irigaray advocates a currently impossible society and economy in which justice, law, responsibility, and obligation are rescripted entirely according to an indirect love—a "love *to* you"—that is as private and personal as it is public and social.

Haraway, Silverman, and Irigaray have constructed projects that they frame with political hope for a new and better society and with the methodological necessity of indirection in either articulating or achieving it. Put differently, these theorists are politically grounded but struggling with how to be politically effective. Their appeals to love seem to me beautifully desperate. Like the religious (in its multitudinous understandings), love is something we cannot control; like Christian love for God, love elicits hope in the power of something we have no power to control. In the writings of Haraway, Silverman, and Irigaray, love forms an affirmation of life and possibility spoken through an indirection that resonates strongly with Christian love.

Donna Haraway

Throughout *Primate Visions* Donna Haraway reiterates the triplet "love, power, and knowledge." Her addition of love to the familiar Foucauldian pairing of power and knowledge is jolting. Moreover, she never overtly explains its presence, but keeps her use of love methodologically vague. She writes, "In the border zones, love and knowledge are richly ambiguous and productive of meanings in which many people have a stake."[6] The border zones implied are those between humans and primates, but many other contested spaces are at play in Haraway's text, including those between nature and culture, reason and passion, sexuality and gender, woman and man, and the "white West" and the "dark colonies" (Africa and Asia). In each contested space I read love as Haraway's medium for affiliating the privileged (those with education, money, and position) with the powerless and marginalized, while rejecting the presumptions of essentialized identity. Love is her political tool that combines passion and respect; it enables speaking for (in place of and on behalf of) those without voice (education, money, or position) by those whose own rich voices are trapped by the gazes of structured power.

Haraway asserts love as "ambiguous," but also "productive of meanings." Instead of delineating logical arguments about these meanings, her text tells dense and overlapping stories that both exemplify love and incarnate a mandate to love. Haraway constructs her stories and offers her commitment to love in direct opposition to science's realist aesthetic and political commitment to progress (4). To her, natural scientists hide their loves behind masks of neutrality that wreak personal, political, and economic havoc in the name of truth and progress. Haraway counters with a politics of explicit passion wrought through overlapping stories that reject theories of truth as representation and politics of progress that depend on univocity, linearity, and clarity. She sees such theories and politics supporting the money machines of corporate-sponsored, and, hence, willfully capitalist, scientific research. Thus Haraway's storytelling opposes "realism" to a postmodern confusion of boundaries. In place of a realist narrative that captures axes of existence like a snapshot, she offers an aesthetics akin to cinematic montage, full of jump cuts and dissolves that proliferate stories within stories, relativize boundaries, and leave the perceptual apparatus desperate for coherence. Precisely within this confusion a space opens up, like the moving emptiness of a vortex; out of this confusion-created vortex, love fuels the utopian possibility that a new mode of seeing and being will break forth.

Love is both the engine of Haraway's storytelling aesthetic and the injunction that follows from it. The love she herself feels for the voiceless in the multiple border zones pushes her to create a storytelling aesthetic that is necessarily—respectfully—ambiguous. Haraway presents formally scientific, coherent, and richly detailed stories, but the content of these stories confuses the meanings of science, coherence, and empirical detail by disturbing the boundaries between sexuality and gender, gender and race, race and culture, culture and nationality, nationality and science, science and what is accepted as objective truth. Instead of arguing for her aesthetics and politics of love, she incarnates them through a methodology and subject matter that refract each other infinitely. Haraway cannot argue for her politics of love, but aesthetically she can tell a story about them by telling stories that tell a story about them.

To exemplify this textual practice I offer a reading of a short, dense chapter titled "Metaphors into Hardware: Harry Harlow and the Technology of Love." Haraway opens the chapter with a sentence that introduces the comparative psychologist as "the recipient of the highest awards and public acclaim that his science could offer." The approbation should legitimate the subsequent accounts of Harlow's work, but the words framing it prevent the formula from working. Directly above the opening words, the section is titled "Father Knows Best." Over that parodic frame Haraway places three epigraphs. First is Harlow's description of the birth of the research tool that made and sustained his fame: "The cloth surrogate mother was literally born, or perhaps we should say baptized, in 1957 in the belly of a Boeing stratocruiser high over Detroit during a Northwest Airlines champagne flight. Whether or not it was an immaculate conception, it was a virginal birth." The third epigraph balances Harlow's initial rapture over this false virgin with his stated desire not to "go down in history as the father of the cloth mother." These allusions to Christian accounts of miraculous birth and Harlow's own attribution of himself as "father" amplify the connotations of father in "Father Knows Best" and complicate the professional accolade that follows it. The second epigraph, inserted between the words of this "father," is a short line from film theorist Laura Mulvey: "Sadism demands a story" (231).[7]

These multiple frames imply that the chapter will use Harlow to tell a story about sadism. But Haraway is not calling Harlow a sadist; the claim is more general and consequential. To Haraway, human efforts to forge coherence out of the chaos of our surroundings necessarily induces a stratification or categorization of perceived reality, and this need for coherence and consistency is "sadistic" in that it reduces the other to a mirror of the self; it fetishizes the self and denies any substantial assertion of difference except that of the powerful on the bodies of the powerless. Following Mulvey, Haraway asserts that sadism operates through "pleasure in vision"; but if this is so, how do we stand enough outside the pleasure of the gaze to condemn it?

Haraway's implicit answer, I suggest, is that we cannot *stand* anywhere, but through stories of love, we can *feel* our way to a condemnation of the sadism we cannot avoid. Haraway's rhetoric about Harlow resists a simple denunciation of him by telling stories that reveal a complex pattern of training, publishing, and public recognition which together weave a tight legitimizing blanket around this respected scientist. The form of her stories (as in their parodic framings) implies that while Haraway does hold Harlow responsible, she also casts the net of responsibility wider than his bodily frame. In that net she catches the rules of scientific discourse, the system of scientific training, the structure of grant-giving bodies, and the cultural capital of institutions such as Stanford. Haraway's stories tease out the constructed, contingent character of the boundaries that Harlow (and others) took for granted. "Sadism," Haraway writes, "is about the structure of scientific vision, in which the body becomes a rhetoric, a persuasive language linked to social practice. The final cause, or telos, of that practice is the production of the unmarked abstract universal, man" (233). Scientific discourse functions sadistically by fetishizing "white, capitalist, abstract man" as the single, ideal subject. Haraway's storytelling responds to this sadism by attempting to decenter the enunciative self in delaying easy submission to a "scientific" rhetoric that forces the visible world into a reality made by and for us. Her love attempts, then, to combine passionate engagement with respect gained through the indirection of epistemological disruption.

The false mothers who sprang fully formed from Harlow's head while he cruised the heavens "were a series of variations of cloth-covered or wire mesh, milk-dispensing or dry, rocking or stationary, endowed with head and face or only a trunk, 'mothers' to which otherwise isolated baby monkeys had access." Harlow then created gruesome versions of the cloth mother designed to repel the baby and create mental pathology. These "evil mothers" had ice packs instead of heat, compressed air bursts, motors that produced vigorous shaking, springs that would catapult the infants away, or brass spikes that would appear randomly when the baby clung to it (238). Haraway wryly notes that none of these evil mothers modeled *human* psychopathology to any degree, "though they might, obviously, be said to provide good models of psychopathology among experimenters" (239). One of Harlow's published conclusions regarding these evil mothers states, "There is only one social affliction worse than an ice-cold wife, and that is an ice-cold mother" (240). That telling "joke" is not the punch line. The children "raised" by these evil mothers were uninterested in sex, and since Harlow was bent on discovering what kind of mothers the female children of these "evil mothers" would be, he developed something he called, in print, the "rape rack," whereby a female child of an evil mother was immobilized on a rack and then artificially inseminated.

For my questions about love I draw two conclusions from Haraway's story about Harlow. First, I find it important that she condemns Harlow's misogyny not by commenting on his attitudes about wives or rape, but by pondering the fact that such statements (accepted by the editorial boards of peer-reviewed scientific journals) are embedded in jokes. The point is not Harlow's reprehensible judgment, but the strategy of joking: it is the only way Haraway can "stay in the story"; otherwise it is too "profoundly painful" to follow (242). Her story thus rejects a strategy of rational, or evidence-driven condemnation, for our judgment can fall neither on Harlow's sexism nor on the psychology of joking nor on the tacit approval of science journal editorial boards, but somehow implicates all of these. Haraway's "profound pain" arises in part because there is *not* one person to blame, because the legitimizing blanket is thick and heavy and seemingly impenetrable. Her love for monkeys drives her to tell ever-widening circles of stories of how their pain could have been approved, funded, and supported by entrenched misogyny. The hope of her storytelling lies in planting seeds of skepticism or awareness or simply confusion in her readers; she hopes that we, too, will find our loves offended.

Second, Haraway's love for monkeys conjoins her love for mothers and thus her love for women and commitment to a vision of society not structured around misogyny. Haraway moves from the conclusions of Harlow's research—children's need for a warm body, for comfort and security, for social interaction—to how they bred anxieties for women entering the work force in the 1950s. Harlow spoke directly to what he thought was the threat of women "taking over" the workplace, especially in light of the crisis that coup would initiate for child rearing. His heated wooden posts covered with rubber and cloth indicated—but unpleasantly—that any warm body would be sufficient to prevent major pathologies and, hence, suggested—but, again, with reservations—that men could just as easily stay home and provide the infant with all it needed. Haraway's storytelling forces readers to ask not only how scientific questions are pursued, but what leads *those* questions to be funded and what effect they have on the bodies of voiceless monkeys and economically dependent (and, hence, relatively powerless) women. Again without condemnation, but certainly with a wry sense of irony, Haraway maps the effects of Harlow's "neutral research" onto the gendered plane of economic relations: men produce, and women produce the next generation of workers—a balance upset by women's growing entry into the workforce.[8] The effect of Haraway's story about Father Harlow gestures to many loves: the love of creation, the love of children, and the love that (sometimes) produces children. Indirectly, Har-

THE WORK OF LOVE 165

away's readers hold these loves up to our own loves in such a way that her aesthetics of storytelling becomes a virtual politics of love.

Haraway does connect her interest in sadism with her project of love in one small footnote to an earlier chapter (385):

> Visual communion, a form of erotic fusion in themes of heroic action, especially death, infuses modern scientific ideologies. Its role in masculinist epistemology in science, with its politics of rebirth, is fundamental. Feminist theory so far has paid more attention to gendered subject/object splitting and not enough to love in specular domination's construction of nature and her sisters.[9]

I read this as arguing that feminists should not restrict analysis to the ways in which gender is split across the border zones of race, class, nationality, and sexuality or to the "traffic" between nature and culture or between woman and man. Instead feminist analysis should turn to love and consider how love works with (within) sadism ("specular domination") to construct the objectified images that gender analysis has been in the business to name. Naming the misogyny is not sufficient. Deconstructing women or Woman detours us from understanding what enables their rapid reconstruction. Instead, Haraway meticulously maps the linguistic, cultural, and political forces that function collaboratively and dissonantly to construct subjectivity: love with knowledge and power; gender with race and science; research universities with corporate grants and field research in colonized (or formerly colonized) countries.

Love, here, works politically, but vaguely. But if love is necessarily vague, is it also ineffable? If so, what use is it as a political tool? In another text Haraway writes, "Life is a window of vulnerability. It seems a mistake to close it."[10] I contend that Haraway's aesthetics of decentered storytelling is for the reader the precognitive level at which we grasp this "window of vulnerability." Like the moving emptiness of a vortex, storytelling presents immediate impact without immediate sense. Immediate impact resolves sensation into response and then into conduct or habitual, reasoned action. If love is the engine of storytelling, its direction and efficacy, then our love is the sensation that responds and, in time, forms new dispositions. If we grasp storytelling as a pre- or unconscious sensing of potentiality, then love is the disciplined process of directing that potential. Still, love remains vague. The most that Haraway's readers can garner is that love "should" extend human thought and being toward the marginalized and powerless in life's militarized border zones. This seems a Protestant religiosity, in which conversion is intimate and personal, albeit pregnant with social and political consequences. To me, the material effect of Haraway's appeal to love is to heighten awareness of the boundaries and lines of power that map my own passionate investments and constitute the sadism of my gaze. The moral? To get me to ponder not how to break down the boundaries and obliterate the sadism, but to understand how they continue to persist despite our best deconstructive efforts. We live in a world that always limits and taints our love, and yet still we love. Put differently, that we are born into sin does not exculpate us from striving against it.

Kaja Silverman

Love is anything but elusive in Kaja Silverman's *Threshold of the Visible World*: "Most of this book was written in Berlin, which is for me the city of love," she writes.[11] She thus asserts the personal "urgency" of theorizing love and tells how the book arose out of a seminar that took up the question of a psycho-analytic theory of love: "All that emerged with absolute clarity from the pages of Freud's writings," she concludes, "was that love is intimately bound up with the function of idealization" (1). Idealization is the psychological mechanism by which we assimilate and try to attain what is valuable to us.

Idealization is not always tied to love, however, and a quick scan through *Threshold of the Visible World* might indicate that the book's greater interest is in the former than the latter. In fact, one can easily imagine Silverman writing these passages without mentioning love, despite its avowed importance. Even in the first few chapters—in which she asserts love as a "central category" (2)—Silverman writes more extensively on the mirror stage and ego formation. She discusses the emergence of the subject in the field of vision with respect to the cultural screen and gaze, those social symbolic mechanisms that dictate unconsciously both who and what will be idealized and the relation of the self to normative cultural ideals. Aside from this formal displacement of love, Silverman also indicates that love is anti-intellectual, kitschy, and potentially dominating over the other (2). What fruitful work, then, can love do for feminist theory?

At first her project seems recuperative. She argues that Freud and Lacan too easily dismiss the link between idealization and love. Freud declared the impossibility of a nonnarcissistic love, but Silverman counters that idealization, "that psychic activity at the heart of love," might be put to new, radical, and politically liberating uses. Indeed, she calls idealization a "crucial political tool, which can give us access to a whole range of new psychic relations" (2). Reading Freud against the grain, Silverman pursues what Lacan calls "the active gift of love" as a political strategy. Resonant with Haraway, she envisions this work of love through an aesthetic medium, this time the storytelling of film; it is the images of film that conjure idealization. Silverman argues that through a proliferation of antinormative, filmic texts and through this "active gift of love," we can learn to "confer ideality upon socially devalued bodies" and, in the end, find a way to "ethically love ourselves" (4). Antinormative images, then, resist hegemonically devalued bodies by teaching us to love them. Like Haraway's border zones, Silverman's "socially devalued bodies" become the subjects and objects of love that fuel her feminist politics.

Silverman makes the personally amorous conditions of writing *Threshold of the Visible World* clear. She loves a man who lives in Berlin, where she wrote her book. "He put the bliss in Blisse Strasse," she tells us (1). While this seems a rude intrusion of idiosyncratic detail, the claim is consistent with the feminist insight that the personal is political. Clearly, Silverman does *use* her love of Harun Farocki: she turns her love for him into a theoretical quest to understand love, and this quest articulates a political program designed to love the unlovable. The program hinges on loving the other in her/his otherness— which she claims is possible only through a proliferation of antinormative visual texts. To compare this to Haraway, for whom love was the political force of an aesthetic medium (storytelling), Silverman's love is a psychological force that she politicizes through the aesthetic medium of film.

Instead of a complex map of social and global power relations, however, Silverman's theoretical axis is subjectivity. Before love gripped her as a "central category" for *Threshold of the Visible World*, Silverman imagined the project as one that would challenge the notion of a "ceaselessly mobile" subject. She thus held reservations about a postmodern, fluid subjectivity and planned to articulate her hesitations in terms of inevitable limits to that fluidity. In fact the book's title, *Threshold of the Visible World*, is a Lacanian phrase referring to how "the subject's corporeal reflection constitutes the limit or boundary within which identification may occur" (11). The threshold of the visible body constructs the self-same body, an image of coherence. But Silverman's plan of critiquing a fluid subjectivity crumbles in the face of what she comes to see as the dangers of the very boundaries she set out to assert. *Threshold of the Visible World* critiques the self-same body for its ruthlessly "incorporative" logic, a logic that mandates either ingesting the other (assimilating it to oneself) or utterly repudiating it. Coherent identity is a delusion that keeps us from genuine love precisely by not respecting the difference of the other.

According to Silverman (and Lacan) a sense of self requires identification with some subset of cultural ideals, and, eventually, subjects come to idealize (value, love) certain images over others according to the logic of this cultural screen. Cornel West once spoke of walking down an empty urban street late at night; hearing footsteps behind him, he glanced back and was relieved to see a white man—only to then be horrified by his relief! In terms of Silverman's argument, West's experience narrates his idealization of the cultural norm of whiteness and the devaluing of blackness. The horror arises as these idealizations—which pose little or no paradox for white subjects—are felt as "external impositions" by devalued bodies. Silverman offers examples similar to West's that exemplify the devaluation of blackness from Fanon and that of the female from Freud. She then shares her own experiences of having to walk daily past a group of homeless persons on her way to work. To me, her encounter with *economic* abjection stands as a crucial second confession, a mirror image of the confession of love but one with greater social import and truth than she indicates.

Silverman's heightened anxiety among the homeless was caused by her feelings of helplessness in the face of their abject loss and pain. Like a good liberal, she reasoned that she required a logical plan of when and how to give (economic) assistance. Soon recognizing the impossibility of such a rational plan, she continued to wonder why the homeless rendered her so anxious. Instead of reflecting on the structural causes of this anxiety, Silverman maintains her psychological focus on individual subjectivity: the homeless symbolize the abject against which the subject constructs a mask of coherent selfhood. Silverman then notes that to imagine herself in the place of the homeless was to abolish herself. The *imagined* failure of the incorporative logic that protects coherent subjectivity conjoins the devaluation of homeless persons by/in our cultural screen and gaze and results in the impossibility of a loving relationship to these abject others.

To Silverman the failure of imagination that results in a failure of the self evidences the "colonization of idealization by the [cultural] screen," a fact that explains why idealization has been trenchantly criticized. But, Silverman insists, life without idealization would be "unendurable," primarily because she claims that idealization is the only psychic function that makes possible a genuine relation to the other. Thus Silverman urges a theoretical and political program that will show how to "idealize oppositionally and provisionally." Her politics will be actualized through films that will jump-start a *better* imagination: "Visual texts which activate in us the capacity to idealize bodies which diverge as widely as possible both from ourselves and from the cultural norm" (37). The political consequence of these visual texts will not be a new set of cultural ideas, but a new understanding of the body, one that "would not so much incarnate ideality as wear it, like a removable cloak" (37). The divinity of love, then, moves salvation from material incarnation to material performance, a lethal difference to her project, as we shall see.

Silverman posits the possibility for this oppositional idealization through a rarely used Lacanian concept called either "the gift of love" or "the active gift of love." Lacan equates the gift of love with sublimation and Silverman argues that sublimation works to idealize at a distance from the self and separate from the ego-ideal. As such, the gift of love is a benign idealization: it limits the self without denying either self or other. Because, in Silverman's reading, the object of sublimation (idealization-at-a-distance) remains stubbornly other than the ego, she argues that sublimation works "to the 'credit' or enrichment of the object rather than the ego" (75). Thus, the gift of love *gives otherness* to the object of love. Through the active gift of love, we can learn to position our egos in a way to value bodies we have been taught to abhor, such as the homeless or persons with dark skin.

In theory this sounds enticing enough. But when Silverman turns to the question of how we actually *confer* this gift of love, she seems to recognize defeat. To be active, the gift of love must be conscious, and yet the cultural, ideological work of idealization operates unconsciously. We cannot *confer* the gift of love, but can only be in an active relation to it *after the fact*. But how can we alter the unconscious, the place of idealization, the seat of the gift of love? Silverman answers: Only through "ceaseless textual intervention," which I read as a call for ceaseless imaginative leaps. Only through putting on an unending series of imagined cloaks can we hope to shift identification to idealization and learn to love the culturally unlovable. Love is no longer a strident force powering an aesthetic intervention in politics—as we saw in Haraway—but is here a gift caught in culture's potent but often nonconscious exchanges over the constitution of commonsense (hegemony). In other words, Silverman's appeal to love does not itself escape the logic of alienation and exchange constitutive of capitalism, even as her primary example (the homeless) articulates the very contradiction of capitalism.

Silverman's next chapters turn to a closer look at film and filmmakers. In the end, she invests the filmmaker with the ability to convey and manipulate "network[s] of images" (100) and is careful to note that this ability is not necessarily a consciously willed act. But if it is not consciously manipulated, then how does it function within a conscious political program? In a culture already saturated with images and other semiotic systems, how can we not see Silverman's oppositional images as yet one more commodity seeking our purchase? As other commodities try to win our support by tapping into our nonconscious desires, so too does Silverman attempt to hook our desires, though in ways that refuse the cultural norms.

I have tried to visualize what a Silvermanian feminist politics would look like, but I cannot get beyond a dark auditorium filled with people watching nonhegemonic movies, hoping to love otherness; or a dark cutting room with filmmakers bent over their work, hoping to enable the idealization of the other. Love drops out of *Threshold of the Visible World* after Silverman's third chapter. Perhaps her turn to the concepts of the look, the gaze, and the screen are attempts to understand why her utopian project is impossible. In the end she concludes, "All that is available to us is the possibility of effecting a 'good enough' approximation [of the ideal], and—through it—of shaking a little stardust onto the otherwise quotidian expanse of human existence" (225). We travel in her text from love to acceptance, from passion to a pat on the shoulder, from resistance to resignation in the face of the symbolic.

Irigaray will extract political purchase precisely from the impossibility that seems to defeat Silverman. To me Silverman's insights seem to be structured as disavowal: *I know very well that homelessness represents the form of abjection most threatening to my life as a well-to-do intellectual, nonetheless . . . I insist on a politics that works through an imaginative process devoid of all social critique except the acknowledgement of the reality of particular devalued bodies.* Silverman's resort to the gap between the world of the spectator and the world of the film is critical, but she does not stand in that gap, as Haraway wishes to stand in the open window of life.

Luce Irigaray

Luce Irigaray's text, *I Love to You,* forcefully asserts the necessity of love within a Marxist political strategy. Also, her writings are sprinkled liberally with references to G/god, the divine, salvation, and redemption. It is not obvious how the reader should conjoin these two strains. She does not deploy a methodologically vague application of love (as do Haraway and Silverman), but rather a vague use of religiously connotative language that ties her overt political platform to her indirect philosophy of love. She asserts that love can be our salvation and that the future society for which we hope will come to pass, if only we think through sexual difference. Irigaray thus employs love's religious valences to further her political program.[12]

Like Silverman, Irigaray prefaces her work with a confession, a personal drama that she unveils behind or before the theory. Why? Her book reads as a manifesto for the fundamentality of sexual difference and, at times, for the male/female couple. What are the agendas and investments that clarify these claims? I shall argue that the answer to both questions lies in the salvific, religious function of an indirect love.

The parameters of Irigaray's project enter into her prologue, the site of her confessional. In these pages Irigaray tells of meeting the man to whom she dedicates *I Love to You,* Renzo Imbeni. In a cadence similar to Silverman's proclamation of love, she begins: "We met in Bologna, on May 30th, 1989, in San Donato, the reddest quarter of a very red city."[13] Although she does not call San Donato the city of love, Irigaray speaks of Imbeni in words that belie a "passion" (16) for him (15):

> So alive, faces light up around him. Alive, he saves a city from pollution and makes it a habitable place once again. . . . Alive, he is daring and unsubmissive, but he does have respect both for nature and for others. . . . He only makes promises he can keep. It is possible to have faith in him. One can take from him without renouncing one's self.

This is no ordinary love story, however, no personal history that justifies and explains her political (albeit academic) excursus. The importance of this love or passion lies not in the relationship it engenders—as the love of Farocki fuels Silverman's study of the visible world—but in its unexpected foreshadowing of a society that is currently impossible to imagine. Imbeni, we learn, is the mayor of this town, and his party invited Irigaray to debate him on the occasion of his election to the European Parliament. The invitation cited the topic of debate as "New Rights in Europe," a topic that calls up Irigaray's long-standing conviction that fighting for equal rights is futile since enacting any just, legal rights for women (and men) will require working through the reality of sexual difference.[14] Irigaray notifies the women leaders of the town's party, who have some concerns about her visit; but instead of mollifying their concerns, the communication ignites it (2–6). Where she expects solidarity, she finds only alienation. When the debate begins, Irigaray's first action again unsettles everyone. She calls for an immediate change in protocol to ensure a balance of questions and responses from men and women. Imbeni's reaction to her request is the start of what Irigaray calls the "miracle" (7). Where she expects resistance and lack of understanding, she finds solidarity. From this point in the text, she describes Imbeni as supportive, trustworthy, a careful listener, intelligent in his responses, and respectful (8–9), terms that connote both intervention and pause, both a reaching out toward and a holding back from.

To me, her language of miracle and praise suggests that Irigaray's encounter with Imbeni symbolizes a love that is possible but still not fully actual between men and women. This is not a personal love that, like Silverman's, raises the specter of the power of love in all areas of life. Nor is it a love, as in Haraway, that spirals into sticky networks of gender, race, nationality, and power. Rather, the material complications of Irigaray's brief encounter tease a thread of real love from the realm of the possible and justify her hope for structural change in the social (and therefore personal) relations between the sexes. The encounter truly is a miracle, a fleeting but tangible intervention of the divine, the experience of which legitimizes new thoughts and new hopes. Except for the fact that the event occurs between this woman, Luce Irigaray, and this man, Renzo Imbeni, it is not at all personal. It is political and spiritual; it is redemptive.[15]

Irigaray turns the "love story" into a four-part template for her argument in *I Love to You*. First, she argues that the dynamics of sexual difference are fundamental to the dynamics of social interaction generally. Second, she reworks Hegel's concepts of recognition and negativity as facets of a redemptive love that reflect her focus on sexual difference. Third, she plots lines of connection between redemptive love and felicity. And, fourth, she visualizes and advocates for social change as the (nonutopic) impossible.

The first facet—the fundamentality of sexual difference—is evident in the prologue's rhetorical opposition between the women who "should" have supported her but did not and the man who, surprisingly, did. We grasp this opposition better in the book's first essay, "Introducing: Love between Us." She there observes that Marx pinpointed the origin of man's exploitation of man in man's exploitation of women, by which Marx meant both the sexual division of labor and the economic exchange of women that constitutes familial and kin structure (19). Irigaray contends that civil law should acknowledge the differences between women and men, who do encounter different obligations with respect to the social. Reading the prologue through this Marxian lens, the lack of solidarity Irigaray received from the women in San Donato directly parallels the lack of solidarity she expected from Imbeni. The two co-constitute one another, for the possibility of mutual relations between women hinges on who women are or can be in this world of men, this world of *one*, as she calls it.[16] Relations between women do not *depend* on relations between men and women, but, more subtly, Irigaray denies that women actually exist, except as posited in relation to men. In Marxian terms, women are simply (and still) the tools and commodities of men. In Lacanian terms, the logic of the phallus rules the symbolic order, and whatever women are, they are so only within the constraints of that rule. Irigaray thus implies that women have yet to come into being. Until the world is "at least two" (35), relations between women are infected by the monologic of phallocentrism. Irigaray implies that although the reality of sexual difference underlies other differences as surely as the exigencies of the market underlie all our interpersonal exchanges, still the difference is not yet actual. Still we have a world that operates under the logic of the one (the male, the phallus), a world that refuses to acknowledge actual difference.[17] Irigaray writes, "Sexual difference is probably the issue in our time which could be our 'salvation' if we thought it through."[18] In fact, at the end of a discussion critiquing Hegel's denial of sexual difference, she ties the urgency of theorizing sexual difference directly to (Christian?) love: "We still know nothing of the salvation love can bring" (29).

Because of the fundamentality of sexual difference, Irigaray structures the prologue as an encounter between a man and a woman; because she thinks humans do not yet think through sexual difference, she describes the encounter as "miraculous." Breaking through the reign of the symbolic forms the only hope for social change. The ability to enact such a breakthrough, however, requires nothing less than a divine vision of a currently impossible future. She writes of her debate with Imbeni: "There were the elements for a future whose horizon so often seems grim. There were decisive contributions concerning what lies beyond the fallen Marxist regimes. There was hope in a rationality, civility, culture and love that remain to be built between women and women" (10).

The future to which she gestures promises a society that takes seriously the reality of sexual difference instead of trying to ignore or deny it. Love between women will be possible only when (after?) love between men and women becomes possible, when full (interpersonal, social, legal) recognition of sexual difference is actualized and enables the creation of that new society. Irigaray's focus on the couple indicates less a fall into heterosexism than a subtle means of suggesting how a rereading of love might usher in a different mode of being in the world. Irigaray evokes this different mode through the trope of Buddha gazing at a flower. The gaze and the flower serve, she argues, as "spiritual" models for how "we can train ourselves to be both contemplative regard and the beauty appropriate to our matter, the spiritual and carnal fulfillment of the forms of our body" (25). In meditating upon that which is other than him, Buddha demonstrates respect for materiality and difference (he does not "uproot" the flower [24]), as well as the ability to attain spiritual enlightenment. To use Hegelian terms, Buddha exemplifies the means of achieving the universal without sacrificing the particular. Toward the end of her treatise Irigaray inserts this religious notion into her philosophy of love: "Buddha becomes spirit while remaining sensible, awakened flesh. Surely this is a fine lesson in love?" (140).

The self-limitation that constitutes the religious experience arises out of Irigaray's reinterpretation of Hegelian negativity as that which opens a gap into which a saving love can flow. This reinterpretation of negativity forms the second facet of the argument of *I Love to You*, and she bases it on a rethinking of Hegel's concept of recognition. In *Phenomenology* Hegel theorizes recognition[19] as what the self gains from the other by mastering the other in the process of becoming in and for oneself. Irigaray rejects this theorization, arguing that the self truly acknowledges the other only as one "who will never be mine."[20] The ability to grant this acknowledgment of a wonderful difference that remains apart from myself[21] requires a self-imposed moment of negativity, a sense of the negative that Irigaray calls both "the limit of one gender in relation to the other" and "possibility of love and of creation" (11).

Irigaray's work of love differs from Haraway's and Silverman's in three important respects: (1) it is conscious and intentioned;[22] (2) because it is intentioned, love does not work *through* any particular medium (like film or storytelling); and (3) she justifies her use of love not through personal love or theory but through a material and political encounter. Irigaray guides us to contemplate the possibilities of love through narrating an actual, conscious, and intentioned encounter with it. She *testifies* to the power of love by telling us how it conjured a filament of the impossible future that shone momentarily in her (our) universe of being. The testimony symbolizes the possibility of a currently impossible future and steers our energies not toward love itself but toward creating the conditions under which love would be transforming, namely, the work of thinking sexual difference. Though conscious and intentioned, this work of love also is indirect. "And so," she writes, "I love to you, rather than: I love you" (102).

At the opening to a chapter titled "Practical Teachings: Love—Between Passion and Civility," Irigaray writes: "At this time—of the globalization and universalization of culture—but when this globality and universality are now ungovernable and beyond our control, making us divided and torn between differing certainties, opinions, dreams or experiences, it seems appropriate to return to what is governable by us here and now: love" (129). Irigaray's debate with Imbeni gifts her with a feeling of recognition, a feeling that inspires her to reflect on Hegel's theorization of recognition. The latter inspires her to rework her understanding of the labor of the negative, which asserts the reality of freedom and the necessity of political rights, but only as these are exerted in and through the limitation of one's own being that opens a space for the being of the other. This necessary moment of negativity between men and women brings us Irigaray's connection between a redemptive love and felicity. Negativity enables an apt and productive happiness by "giv[ing] positive access—neither instinctual nor drive-related—to the other" (13). Denying the instinctual or drive-related character of negativity raises its status as *work*, something we attain by pausing, something we reach for by letting go. Characterizing the path to felicity in this manner does not presume its success, though it is the actual glimpse of felicity she gained in the debate with Imbeni that leads her to her conclusions. Felicity entwines with love, as the force between those who are sexually different, men and women, a force that will call forth a new society. For this reason she calls the work toward this apt and productive happiness "our primary cultural obligation" (15). Attaining felicity depends on liberating ourselves from "ignorance, oppression and the lack of culture that weighs so heavily upon this essential dimension of existence: sexual difference" (15). "Love, even carnal love, is therefore cultivated and made divine. The act of love becomes the transubstantiation of the self and his or her lover into a spiritual body. . . . Love is redemption of the flesh through the transfiguration of desire *for* the other (as an object?) into desire *with* the other" (139). This love is our "salvation"; it redeems us and it redeems the world.

Love works through an aesthetics of indirection, which Irigaray foregrounds through advocating the impossible: "I am, therefore, a political militant for the impossible," she writes (10). Writing of the felicity brought about by an indirect love, a love borne of the work of the negative, is in no way spinning tales of utopia or envisioning a program we cannot imagine or sense. Her politics of love—a return to what is governable by us today—evolves directly out of her philosophy of love—I love to you—which itself arises from reflections mandated by an actual, political encounter. Her methodological indirection construes both the form and content of her project (as it does Haraway's project), but only as a means of explicating a political encounter that grounds and frames the very writing of her text, an encounter that symbolizes the "miraculous" that is possible in every encounter. It is the miracle of pausing, of letting go, of withdrawing, *in order that* one can resume, reach out, connect.

Irigaray draws her text to a close with a rereading of the annunciation. God comes to a girl named Mary and speaks to her. God praises her and then asks her, will you be my lover? "It is only thanks to your *yes* that my love and my son may be redemptive. Without your word, we may not be carnally redeemed or saved" (140). And God waits.

God waits.

With this startling image of God's pausing for a woman's response, I draw to a close my own reflections on feminist theory's turn to love. To me Irigaray's text poses an assertion and question: "*This* happened to me. What would the world look like if this happened every day, in every exchange?"

Conclusion

In a decade in which the futility of identity politics has been thoroughly chewed by feminist (and other) academics and yet still lies undigested in our stomachs, a decade in which any achieved political alliance has been met with scorn, criticism, nostalgia, or—as in Eastern Europe, the Middle East, and Afghanistan—death, what tools are given us (academics, theologians) for building the worlds we can still, but barely, imagine? Unless we give up all hope of being able to act in this world for the sake of a better one, it seems we have only the tools that appear impotent in both academic and popular culture alike. Love certainly fits that mold. It is a concept academically scorned and found skimming every surface of mass culture despite the prevailing cynicism of postmodernity. Though not many would take seriously the old Coke commercial of diverse peoples holding hands in a circle and singing about their compassion for the world, love still saturates the movies, the 'zines, the sitcoms, and the Billboard charts. To me, however, it is precisely its rejection by the academic establishment and its sappy omnipresence in pop culture that works to love's benefit as a tool for incarnating leftist political dreams. Deploying love sidesteps questions of how to forge a commonality based on identity and presumes a vague but potent commonality based on affect. Irigaray makes explicit this project that remains implicit in the works of Haraway and Silverman, namely, the yearning for a bonding that can yield an effective politics without necessitating a *kenosis* of the self. In enjoining us to consider love as politically effective, Irigaray, Haraway, and Silverman demonstrate a turn to the religious that is vital, material, and political, precisely because it is quiet, indirect, and vague.

NOTES

1. Donna Haraway, *Primate Visions: Gender, Race, and Nature in the World of Modern Science* (New York: Routledge, 1989), 1.

2. Rembert Hüser, "Crossing the *Threshold*: Interview with Kaja Silverman," *Discourse* 19.3 (1997): 3–4.

3. Luce Irigaray, *I Love to You: Sketch of a Possible Felicity within History*, trans. Alison Martin (New York: Routledge, 1996), 32.

4. For corroboration of this argument from a nonfeminist perspective see Slavoj

Zizek, *The Fragile Absolute; or, Why Is the Christian Legacy Worth Fighting For?* (New York: Verso, 2000). The notion of the unthought is Foucault's.

5. See, e.g., Kevin Bales's haunting account of the world's poor in *Disposable People: New Slavery in the Global Economy* (Berkeley: University of California Press, 1999).

6. Haraway, *Primate Visions*, 1. Subsequent page references to *Primate Visions* are embedded in the text.

7. Haraway's use of Teresa de Lauretis suggests that she draws this epigraph from her. De Lauretis provides the full quotation from Mulvey in *Alice Doesn't: Feminism, Semiotics, Cinema* (Bloomington: Indiana University Press, 1984), 103: "Sadism demands a story, depends on making something happen, forcing a change in another person, a battle of will and strength, victory/defeat, all occurring in a linear time with a beginning and an end."

8. See Patrick Buchanan, *The Death of the West: How Dying Populations and Immigrant Invasions Imperil Our Country and Civilization* (New York: St. Martins, 2001), quoted in Philip A. Klinkner, "The Base Camp of Christendom," *The Nation*, March 11, 2002, 25: "Only the mass reconversion of Western women to an idea that they seem to have given up—that the good life lies in bearing and raising children and sending them out into the world to continue the family and nation—can prevent the Death of the West."

9. See also Haraway's essay, "Situated Knowledges," in her *Simians, Cyborgs, and Women: The Reinvention of Nature* (New York: Routledge, 1991), 192–93.

10. Ibid., 224.

11. Kaja Silverman, *Threshold of the Visible World* (New York: Routledge, 1996), x. Subsequent page references to *Threshold of the Visible World* are embedded in the text.

12. Irigaray directly attacks institutional religion's sense of God ("God is nothing more than the keystone of the order that still leaves us silent"; *I Love to You*, 44). And yet just as Heidegger rejected Christianity while still employing its words and motifs, so Irigaray swims in a sea of Christian language and ritual, all the while attempting to redirect its currents.

13. Ibid., 1. Subsequent page references to *I Love to You* are embedded in the text.

14. According to Irigaray, rights currently are framed around a purportedly neutral, unsexed subject. Irigaray thus exposes the illusions of this framing, joining other feminists in seeing the subject before the law as always already male. But she also qualifies that exposure by claiming that the subject before the law is always already phallic; in other words, actual male subjects and female subjects do not exist because sexual difference itself has no image or voice in current legal settings.

15. The first sentence corroborates the political frame, for instead of settling on the man or on love (as does Silverman's preface), her notice of the rendezvous ("We met . . .") moves immediately to its political context ("the reddest quarter of a very red city"). Toward the end of the prologue, Irigaray evidences the entwining of politics and religion or spirituality in her project: "Happiness must be built by us here and now on earth, where we live, a happiness comprising a carnal, sensible and spiritual dimension in the love between women and men, woman and man, which cannot be

subordinated to reproduction, to the acquisition or accumulation of property, to a hypothetical human or divine authority" (*I Love to You*, 15).

16. See her chapter "Human Nature Is Two" (ibid., 35–42 passim).

17. She writes, "The changes to be made in mother-daughter relationships are connected to this transformation of relations between the two genders of the human species, requiring the transition to a culture which is not reducible to a single gender, nor reducible to a sexed dimension that is simply genealogical, and thus to patriarchy or matriarchy" (ibid., 26).

18. Luce Irigaray, *An Ethics of Sexual Difference*, trans. Carolyn Burke and Gillian C. Gill (Ithaca: Cornell University Press, 1984), 5.

19. Alison Martin translates *reconnaissance* as "recognition," but Gail Schwab suggests that "acknowledgment" is a better rendition "because it includes some of both 'gratitude' and 'recognition.' " See Gail Schwab, "Sexual Difference as Mode: An Ethics for the Global Future," *Diacritics* 28.1 (1998): 77.

20. See Irigaray's chapter "You Who Will Never Be Mine" (*I Love to You*, 103–8).

21. My use of "wonderful" here draws on Irigaray's reading of Descartes. See her chapter "Wonder: A Reading of Descartes' *The Passions of the Soul*" (*Ethics of Sexual Difference*, 72ff.).

22. I do not have the space here to discuss her words about intentionality, but they merit close attention.

9

Theology and the Power of the Margins in a Postmodern World

Joerg Rieger

Modern theology has broadened the horizons of theological reflection. It has opened its doors wider and admitted a larger group of people, thus making the task of theology more democratic in many ways. Rather than leaving matters of reflection about God to the clergy and a small number of authorized specialists, modern theologians found that everybody shares in an awareness of God. But modern theologians also felt that people share in this awareness of God to varying degrees. The ones who were seen as closest to God—and thus most competent in thinking about God—were the members of the middle class: particularly intellectuals and others at the peaks of modern civilization, usually male and always of white skin color, Europeans and Euro-Americans like myself. These people are, interestingly enough, still the main target for most of our mainline churches in the United States even today and make up the majority of the leadership.[1]

In recent times, the horizons of theology have been broadened once again. Many of the principles of modern theology are challenged, for instance, by the broad cultural and economic shifts associated with what we now call postmodernity. One of the basic elements of postmodernity is a growing awareness of the limits of the self—not the human self in general, but the modern, middle-class self. This self, as the postmoderns claim, is no longer master in its own house. At least, it is no longer the sole master and has to share its power to a certain degree with others. There is a basic sense now that we do not exist in isolation. The modern self can no longer simply colonize, missionize, or exclude others without second thoughts.

The postmodern and postcolonialist self now finds it necessary to realize the existence of other people and (at least) to signal its benevolence where it reaches out to others. This new awareness of other people often includes a rudimentary appreciation for their difference and otherness. Here theological reflection broadens once again: the value of other people is beginning to rise, including the value of women and people of other cultures and races that often were not even on the map before. Pluralism and multiculturalism are now seen as positive values by many theologians. Others, among them evangelicals and post-liberals, make use of the broadening moves of the postmodern by reclaiming various parts of the Christian tradition. The voices of Christianity throughout the ages, many of them pushed aside by modern theology, tend to add different flavors as well to the theological enterprise.[2]

But there is another perspective whose distinctiveness is often overlooked at the end of modernity. The horizons are broadened not just from a post-modern perspective, but also from the experience of people on the margins of the postmodern world. Liberation theologians, for instance, have challenged modern thought not primarily because there is no room for ideals like multi-cultural difference and other forms of diversity, but because it neglects the lives of people at the margins and on the underside. The liberation perspective goes beyond the pluralism of postmodern thought, claiming not merely respect for people who are different but a special concern for those who are margin-alized and oppressed. In the words of Latin American liberation theologians— words that are mirrored also in some official documents of the church—there needs to be a preferential option for the poor.[3] This preferential option has been understood as rooted in God's own option for people on the margins, recorded in both the Old and the New Testaments. God's justice introduces new images of justice that go beyond our commonsense notions of justice. God's justice is based on the covenant relationship established by God which does not let go of the "least of these," those who are usually overlooked by universal notions of justice.[4]

Here theological reflection is broadened once again: people from the margins are entering the field and—this is the new insight that goes beyond plu-ralism and multiculturalism—*all* of theology needs to take their perspectives seriously. Liberation theologies are not the special interest theologies of people on the margins. In the words of the Apostle Paul (1 Corinthians 12:26), "If one member suffers, all suffer together." This has implications even for those of us who belong to the mainline, and it broadens our horizons. As a middle-class person I need to learn to think about God in relation to the lower classes; as a man I need to learn to think about God in relation to women; as a Euro-American I need to learn to think about God in relation to African Americans, Hispanic Americans, Asian Americans, and Native Americans; as a North American I need to learn to think about God in relation to people in South

America and other continents. This broadening move is crucial. We may never understand God without the perspective of those who are different, including in a special way the perspectives of those on the margins. The point of view from the position of the repressed throws new light on reality as a whole.[5]

What all this means is that we have now at least two critiques of modernity which help broaden our horizons. They raise different yet at times related questions. In this essay I will investigate what happens when these two critiques of modernity meet in situations of pressure that push toward liberation. What can postmodernity learn from the preferential option for the poor and from liberation theologies? And, what elements of postmodern thought might become an ally in the struggle for liberation?

Critique of Identity

One of the major insights of postmodern thought in its various forms is that the modern self's sense of identity is an illusion. We are not who we think we are. That is a scary thought—especially for those of us who tend to think that our success in life is self-made. Those of us in positions of power and authority tend to assume that our identity is secure because we have produced it ourselves: who we are is due to our own personal effort and merit. Postmodern thinkers destroy precisely this illusion when they remind us that our identity is never self-made. Who we are is always a product of various other factors. Poststructuralism, for instance, one of the most well-known forms of postmodern thought, emphasizes language: our language is never self-made; rather, it is inherited from others. Moreover, poststructuralists have argued that no one can control language, since language itself is a free-floating phenomenon that does not immediately provide access to hard-and-fast reality. Others emphasize culture: we are born into certain cultural settings which shape us to a large extent. Both language and culture are, of course, tied to issues of power.[6] Yet others emphasize political and economic factors: we must not forget that political and economic forces also shape who we are, reaching all the way into our deepest desires and feelings. After all, is it not the declared goal of the advertising industry to shape desire?

The point is the same: who we are is to a considerable degree shaped by outside factors. If this is true, our middle-class North American belief in individualism needs to be seen for what it really is: an illusion. There has never been a "self-made man." It is common sense, of course, that our identity is the product of many different factors, including our families, education, and nationality. But postmodern thinkers have made us aware of a broader range of factors—many of them more hidden—that shape who we are. This critique of identity offers a major challenge to those in power. We are not the self-made people that we think we are. We are not masters in our own house but are driven by various other forces that control us. Our success is produced on the basis of many factors.

People on the margins add a decisive point to this postmodern awareness, especially where they remind us that our success is often built on the back of others—on their labor and efforts and, at times, even on their misfortune and suffering. The amazing success of Europe and the United States, for instance, cannot truly be understood without the histories of conquest, colonialism, and slavery that provided both inexpensive raw materials and the labor forces necessary to build empires. In this context, even the North American stories of the Western frontier are not simply stories about people who knew how to take things into their own hands; despite the amazing achievements of individuals, these stories are also about people who built their identity on the back of others whose land they expropriated. The same is true, of course, for modern-day business executives; here success is tied to "lean production" and the creation of the largest short-term profit margins possible on the backs of workers both at home and abroad.

But how does the postmodern critique of identity relate to those without power, to nonpersons? Isn't it ironic that the notion of identity is called into question precisely at a time when people at the margins, like ethnic minorities, the poor, and women, are finally gaining some degree of self-worth and self-identity? African American writer bell hooks reminds us that the critique of identity can be problematic for those who are still fighting for their own identity. But, she adds, this critique can also be useful if it leads to a better understanding of the multifaceted nature of the identity of people at the margins. The critique of identity goes against the old racist myths of essential blackness, for instance, a myth that claims that African American people can be understood in terms of one factor only.[7] The critique of identity reminds us that African American people cannot be understood simply in terms of the factor of "blackness" and helps us understand the problem: such universal categories are invariably determined by those in power. In this case, repression operates on the basis of universalizations and generalizations which do not necessarily have to take a negative form. Positive stereotypes of identity can serve a similar repressive purpose.

French psychoanalyst Jacques Lacan has made a similar point about the situation of women in patriarchal systems—the powers that be tend to control others not just by sheer force but also by defining their identity. Women—and the same is true of ethnic minorities, poor people, and others at the margins—are often either romanticized or demonized: the two sides of the same coin. Men, for instance, tend to draw up idealistic images of women, a process that looks like a rather harmless thing at first sight. Isn't it a nice gesture to put others on a pedestal, especially those who are frequently overlooked by the powers that be? But in idealizing and romanticizing women, men reassert control: they are the ones who determine what women are to be like. They are the ones who know what women in general are all about. Women, in turn, liberate themselves not by buying into the romantic illusions and enjoying them, but by breaking out. They begin to liberate themselves when they understand with Lacan that "*the* woman does not exist"—the woman as an ideal created by the male fantasy. The same is true for other oppressed groups: "*The poor do not exist*," as one of the first epigraphs of my book *Remember the Poor* states, means that the universal category is false. That is not to say that women and poor people are not real—just the opposite: they are so real that they cannot and must not be defined in terms of the fantasies of those in power, whether they are men or the wealthy.

In this way, the postmodern critique of identity can help theology as a whole connect with the everyday lives of marginalized people and the important contributions that they can make. When we interrupt the processes not only of demonizing others but also of idealizing and romanticizing them, the "power of the poor in history"—the title of an important book by Gustavo Gutiérrez—appears in new light. The critique of identity becomes an important tool in deconstructing the stereotypes of the powerful who seek to define people on the margins in terms of a unified identity and a common essence in order to pull them back into the system. The challenge is geared to the process of universalization in which such identities are misused by those in charge—and which covers up the fact that the dominant system needs the margins.[8] Only in a second step will we need to examine this in terms of the struggle for identity of people at the margins.

Part of the power of the margins lies in a flexible identity that can never be quite grasped in terms of the status quo. Marcella Althaus-Reid, an Argentinean theologian teaching in Scotland, points out that indigenous women know a few things about postmodernism and the end of the grand narratives of the Western world since they are themselves subjects of fragmentation, and due to the fact that they have long lost their own narratives. These lessons do not derive from any awareness of the technicalities of postmodern discourse but from their life experiences.[9] Nelly Richard, one of the most prominent theorists of the postmodern in Latin America, also acknowledges a certain space that is produced for "cultural peripheries" once the Eurocentric models of modernity are challenged.[10] Here, a fundamental distrust of Western ways of thinking manifests itself, and the monopoly of the universal categories of those in power can no longer be maintained, whether they manifest themselves in theological, historical, sociological, anthropological, or other discourses. In this context indigenous traditions and other cultural manifestations affected by repressions can play liberating roles where they expose the overarching system in power, be it modernist or postmodernist. At this point, there is no longer any need to construct yet another universalizing and totalizing system.

The so-called subaltern study groups have explored similar issues. These groups study phenomena of subordination and oppression along different lines, including class, age, gender, caste, and social position.[11] In its founding statement, the Latin American Subaltern Studies Group argues that analysis must go beyond the study of a "unitary, class-based subject and its concomitant assumption of the identity of theoretical-literary texts produced by elite intellectuals."[12] Here, the postmodern critique of identity is deepened by a closer look at the actual situation of the people. The group points out that "the subaltern is not one thing"; in other words, it is not an easily defined reality such as *the* poor or *the* people. The subaltern is rather a "mutating, migrating subject."[13] In the words of John Beverley, "Subalternity is a relational rather than an ontological identity—that is, a contingent, and overdetermined identity (or identities)."[14] Feminist theorists have made a similar point: once we realize that identities on the margins are complex, we need to go beyond universal categories such as "woman" and "feminine gender identity."[15] This notion of the subaltern adds a whole new dimension to the ambiguous postmodern concerns for otherness and difference that are often not much more than adaptations to the postmodern market, as I will argue below. Here, new and stronger forms of otherness emerge that deal with the broadest possible range of those who might be considered the "least of these": the plight of the workers, as well as of the unemployed, the homeless, the peasants, and even children who endure various forms of oppression. Thus the preferential option for the poor becomes much broader than before, a move which requires not only greater awareness of who is sucked into the position of the other in today's world, but also a whole new set of encounters with people beyond one's own horizon of class, gender, race, and social location.[16] Here, the theological world broadens, not only through a wider horizon but also through the challenges posed by a whole new group of theologians emerging out of nowhere, as it were—from the margins.

The postmodern critique of identity is aimed at the definitions of identity that move from the top down and that pretend to be universal.[17] There is no identity that exists apart from relationships and structures of power and that can be determined once and for all. The search for identity by those who are only now developing a sense of their own worth is not the problem, since subalternate identities are acutely aware of relationships and structures of power which crush them and include an awareness of their fragile natures. The problem has to do with the process of universalization in which such identities become oppressive once more.

The strategies of what has been called "identity politics" become less important at this point. Resisting the powers that be by affirming the identity of one's own group can even be counterproductive. Not only can this lead to a minority group unconsciously adopting the dominant images and prejudices, for instance, of femininity or blackness. Such hard-and-fast identities also often lead to a fragmentation of interests among people on the margins and thus to the dissolution of resistance in postmodern pluralism where each group seems to be fighting only for itself. Legendary writer and activist Angela Davis talks about the position of black women not in terms of hard-and-fast identities but as a "provisional identity that allows the move beyond identity politics."[18] In this way, new coalitions between interests of race, class, and gender might emerge. While all of us need to begin with our provisional identity—with who we are at first sight—we must not stop there. As an African-American woman, Davis finds those projects most interesting "that consider 'women of color' a point of departure rather than a level of organizing."[19] She argues for the formation of coalitions that are "unpredictable or unlikely." Those coalitions are grounded not in identity but in political projects where people resist domination and oppression and tie together not only the usual groups that might be seen as resisting, such as prisoners, immigrant workers, and labor unions, but also others such as prisoners and students.[20] This makes sense also for theological reflection from the margins: moving beyond narrowly conceived identity politics, broad new collaborative projects become possible.

Resisting Oppression

Liberation theologies have been rooted not first of all in the minds of theologians but in actual resistance to specific forms of oppression. This is why there has never been a generic type of liberation theology—a fact that has often escaped the theological establishment. Latin American liberation theology, for instance, understood that the poverty of millions of people was not self-caused and, therefore, not due to a lack of personal effort or to being at a somehow less "developed" stage in history. Poverty is closely related to oppressive economic systems. At the same time in the North, African American liberation theologians realized that even though slavery had been abolished and racism had been challenged in the civil rights movement, their people were still not free. Feminist theologians became increasingly aware of the fact that, despite some gains for women such as the right to vote, half of humanity was still not taken seriously in both society and the church. Those are only a few examples. Today others have joined the resistance; in the United States women of African American, Hispanic, and Asian descent have contributed their own visions.

But how is oppression to be resisted? There is always the danger that certain forms of resistance lead to a mere reversal of power structures. Revolutions that do not move from the bottom up appear to be particularly problematic in this sense. The modern middle-class revolutions of the eighteenth century in France and North America, for instance, might need to be rethought in this light. The driving forces in those revolutions were not necessarily those who suffered the most—the impoverished masses. While power did shift hands and the power base broadened, it was soon pulled into another cycle of self-centeredness. Power was now funneled into the hands of another strata of society which, while having a somewhat broader basis, still did not include those who suffered the most. In the newly founded United States, for instance, democracy meant that only men with a certain amount of property and social standing were allowed to vote. While the end of rule by the British monarchy led to power being shared by a larger group, most people, including women, men without property, and slaves, remained at the margins. Their marginalization was not a mere accident but was in many ways necessary for the development of the new nation: the economy of the antebellum South was heavily based on slave labor, and the overall economic and geographic expansion of the United States is linked with the various pressures imposed on other marginalized groups (e.g., Native Americans, Mexican Americans, and Asian Americans). Ultimately, one master was exchanged for another, and the middle class took over more or less where the monarchy had been forced to leave off. Without trying to give overly simplistic explanations of complex processes, the peculiar nature of this situation needs to be recognized. There is a latent danger that resistance ends in reversals of power if the deeper repressions of a system are not taken into account.

In sum, it seems that in these middle-class revolutions the problems are merely pushed around. The recent phenomenon of the so-called culture wars is only the latest example of a situation where problems are pushed around with little real change. The culture wars resemble earlier middle-class struggles in that the reality of people on the margins does not play a role and is of no interest to the participants, except in a top-down way. The existence of the margins surfaces in the culture wars, for instance, in the debates about what constitutes the literary canon (should one admit "nontraditional" texts?) or about welfare. But the margins are addressed in terms of the center. Nowhere is this clearer than in the welfare debates, where the disagreement is about method (do we need welfare programs or character training?) while the basic assumptions are the same in both camps: both assume that the task is to find ways in which we can integrate the marginalized back into the system. In short, the margins are objectified in the center's struggle to define itself.

The fact that resistance has at times led to such reversals of power is often used to discourage resistance in general. Does resistance necessarily have to lead to the kinds of reversals where the self-centeredness of one group in power is simply replaced by the self-centeredness of another, even though perhaps more broad-based, group? Some of the major themes of modernity may—despite their liberating intent—have taken the topic of self-centeredness one step further. The winner takes all—this attitude is justified frequently on ground of the doctrines of social Darwinism. And humanistic and democratic ideals have been fueled by images of humanity that were not universal—as modernity claimed—but rooted in certain images of humanity that were defined by the white, male, intellectual, and entrepreneurial members of the middle class. It is not surprising, for instance, that the Declaration of Human Rights, developed during the French Revolution and at the basis of our modern understanding of freedom and liberation, does not include the right of equal access to property. But there are other forms of resistance.

The postmodern critiques of identity and of the modern middle-class self, as well as a sustained concern for otherness and difference, may be useful in developing new and more effective strategies of resistance. Replacing the modern self in its imagined self-sufficiency and power with yet another self with a similar configuration will not make much of a difference. We need a different model. Those of us who resist oppression need to understand first of all that we are not God—a basic theological insight that has at times been repressed in modernity. We are not in positions of absolute control. Furthermore, we are not the individualistic monads or the self-made people of the American dream—another basic theological insight. We need to realize that our identity is built in relation to others (our parents, teachers, friends) and often also on the back of others (low-wage laborers across the globe and at home, women, minorities). This insight is especially important for those of us who stand in solidarity with the oppressed, yet who do not suffer much direct oppression ourselves. While it seems to me that oppressed people themselves are usually quite aware of their limits, of their webs of relationships and dependencies, and of the fact that they are not God, these are lessons that those of us who join in their struggles need to learn time and again. When people thus stop playing God, there is a good chance that we might become aware more clearly of God's own role in resisting and transforming the powers that be! Here the problem is perhaps not first of all the oft-lamented dualisms of the modern scientific worldview (even though the mentality of control is embodied in these theories as well), but the more organic and relational vision of a social Darwinism according to which only the fittest survive and natural selection weeds out the weak.

In this context, the mushrooming critiques of individualism and the exhortations to establish community are no longer helpful in resisting the powers that be. Not only do they tend to cover up the parasitic nature of our identity, they also help reproduce this attitude of control in a form of group egoism. If efforts to build community do not take into account that what distorts community is not individualism but oppressive relationships, they will end up perpetuating the status quo (exemplified, for instance, by the so-called gated communities and the segregation found in the large majority of our church communities). When this is clear, a simple reversal of power might be avoided. We need to shape new ways of living together and new ways of building community. From a Native American perspective, Robert Allen Warrior has argued that even the oppressed must learn to participate in the struggle for liberation "without making their story the whole story. Otherwise the sins of the past will be visited upon us again."[21] Warrior exemplifies this in terms of the Exodus story and the conquest of the Promised Land: Do the Israelites engage in simple reversals of power? What happens to those who are not on the side of the people of Israel? The biblical accounts themselves present different undercurrents, according to which Israel either took over the Promised Land or developed in processes of assimilation with the inhabitants of the land.[22]

In sum, we can now clarify a few common misunderstandings. First, liberation theology and the option for the poor has nothing to do with a type of revolution that simply turns things upside down and puts absolute control in the hands of yet another group. This misunderstanding is rooted in our own middle-class history, coming out of the modern revolutions in the West. Simple reversals of power are not inevitable.

Second—and this misunderstanding represents the ever more popular opposite extreme—liberation theology is not about helping the poor or about trying to solve the problems of people under pressure and in need. This misunderstanding is related to contemporary attitudes toward social change and reinforces both the role of those in power and those who are repressed. Whether the models are based on images of development, economic and social progress, or so-called compassionate conservatism, nothing will ever change when those in power try to take things into their own hands. This will simply turn other people into our own image.

A third misunderstanding poses itself in relation to a postmodern mindset. Here liberation seems to be accomplished through pluralism, multiculturalism, and what is now called "diversity management." But does this postmodern revolution ever reach the margins?[23] Or is it pulled into the logic of the market that—in its diverse manifestations that reach even into the church—realizes that in order to stay in business we need to increase the reach of our products?[24] Such approaches to diversity broaden the horizons somewhat, but do not lead to a fundamental challenge of the powers that be.

Liberation theologies will be able to put up any significant resistance to oppression only where they maintain sufficiently strong forms of solidarity with the oppressed. Solidarity transforms both oppressor and oppressed, leading to new and constructive avenues of resistance and new ways of living. The only thing that will keep our resistance honest, therefore, is a renewed option for the poor—an ever closer connection with the margins.

Challenging Postmodernity from the Margins

The perspectives from the margins invite a critique of modernity broader than that advanced by postmodernism, thus expanding and challenging the postmodern perspective itself. Standard definitions of both modernity and postmodernity usually forget their confinement to a First World perspective. Yet modernity has deeper roots than the European Enlightenment and the Industrial Revolution. As Latin American philosopher and theologian Enrique Dussel has argued, modernity needs to be seen in relation to Columbus's arrival in the New World in 1492.[25] Modernity does not begin with René Descartes, Immanuel Kant, and the ideas of other famous philosophers, but with Christopher Columbus, Hernando Cortés, and—we might add from a North American perspective—continues with the founding fathers of the United States of America. Columbus's "I conquer" precedes the Cartesian "I think therefore I am" by almost one hundred years—and both attitudes reverberate in the affirmation of the United States's Manifest Destiny in the new continent. In all of these models, other people are subordinated to the expanding powers of the modern self. The ability of the modern European and North American self to define itself as self-in-control is fueled by oppressive relations to the natives in both Americas, as well as by oppressive relations to the slaves taken from Africa and all those others who labored in the mines, in the manufactures, in the fields, and in the homes. We can understand neither modernity nor postmodernity from within, without a look at its margins, without an encounter with those who are repressed.[26] The postmodern critique of modernity makes sense only if it manages to give more thought to what these encounters with repression mean for us today.

For this reason, postmodernist discourses need to be broadened in relation to what is now called postcolonial discourse.[27] Modernity is the time when both Europeans and North Americans are deeply involved in colonial enterprises. This throws new light on my own identity as a Euro-American as well. To a large degree the modern self has established itself in the subjugation of those who are other. More than 85% of the world have been colonized by Europe at one point or another, and "only parts of Arabia, Persia, Afghanistan, Mongolia, Tibet, China, Siam and Japan have never been under formal European government."[28] While the modern colonial histories have by and large drawn to a close, this history of subjugation continues in different ways. The U.S. response to the terrorist attacks of September 11, 2001, for instance, has targeted the modern heirs of the first three of these uncolonized parts of the world (Arabia, Iran/Iraq, and Afghanistan), and the global-market economy has its own ways of putting pressure on places like China.

Postcolonial discourse reminds us, further, that both the modern and the postmodern realities are tied into economic issues in a complex sense. Postcolonial theorist Ania Loomba reminds us that "modern colonialism did more than extract tribute, goods, and wealth from the countries that it conquered"— these facts are common knowledge. What is less well known is the fact that colonizing nations also "restructrured the economies of the latter, drawing them into a complex relationship with their own, so that there was a flow of human and natural resources between colonised and colonial countries."[29] The genesis of modernity, capitalism, and colonialism is, therefore, related in much deeper ways than is often recognized; not only did the colonized countries contribute the raw materials for capitalist production, they also provided the context for capitalism. Once we realize how modernity, capitalism, and colonialism have grown hand in hand, postmodernity appears in new light as well: we need to pay closer attention to its relation to contemporary forms of global and transnational capitalism, including new forms of economic "colonialism." Postcolonial discourse itself and the whole idea of a postcolonial world need to be seen in this light, too.

Given this expanded understanding of modernity and postmodernity, postmodern critiques of the modern need to be reevaluated in light of the encounter with the subjugated other. This leads us to a rereading of several key concepts of contemporary postmodernist discourse. From the perspective of the other, the postmodern critique of identity and the postmodern concerns for pluralism, difference, and otherness appear in a new light. Multiculturalism, while it gives more room to others, often feeds right back into the market. Multiculturalism is marketed as fun by diverse business enterprises such as media outlets like MTV, fashion designers, the restaurant industry, and many others. Such commodified forms of multiculturalism are no longer threatening, and it should not come as a surprise that the suburbs—still the safe havens of the middle class—have become the most racially diverse places in the country.[30] Postmodern pluralism thus tends to create a safety net that keeps people from plunging into the awareness of social conflict, the tensions between rich and poor and between those in power and those without power. Gutiérrez has observed that despite the postmodern appreciation for otherness, difference, and even a renewed interest in the stories of the people, there seems to be a certain amnesia when it comes to the plight of the poor.[31] Postmodern minds are entertained by differences to such a degree that the challenges tend to fade from view: the fragmentation of our lives increases the fun-factor. We love the colorful traditions and artifacts of other cultures for instance—we even plan our vacations around them—as long as they don't challenge us. Mission trips to other parts of the world—sponsored by more and more churches in the United States—are easily sucked up into this mentality as well: the differences end up in slide shows and presentations that celebrate the generosity of the sending body rather than the challenge posed by the other.

It may seem paradoxical, but the so-called postmodern turn to the other is in danger of covering up the challenge of the other. Forms of this cover-up appear also in different reactions of contemporary theology as it engages the postmodern. The tensions of postmodernity (created precisely where the other is subdued) can be interpreted away as nothing more than a series of accidents that call for a calming response. Theologian Terrence Tilley suggests that one's terror in a postmodern world can be calmed by gathering and telling the stories of various communities.[32] Postmodern tensions can also be interpreted as part of human existence in general, as in Mark C. Taylor's postmodern theological and philosophical adventures. Since the center is no longer as clearly visible as in the days of high modernity, we all appear to be on the margins now.[33] Along those lines, difference and otherness are once more integrated as part of the status quo, the way things are. If the actual burden of those pressured by postmodernity to live in inhumane conditions is not considered, even popular traditions and cultures can be used to reconstruct safe havens for power and privilege once modernity's safe havens have been defeated. Obviously, such an approach does not challenge the powers that be.

Postmodern sensitivities are ambiguous. Postmodern theorists (whether they are aware of it or not) are not presenting us with abstract ideas, invented in the ivory towers, but with the logic of our age with all its distortions and problems. For this reason we cannot stop at the most common level of postmodern critique—merely unveiling the internal idiosyncrasies of modernity and of the modern self. We need to go one step further and take into account the deeper tensions of the present which are part of the postmodern condition and which may have indeed worsened in the transition from modernity, such as the concentration of wealth in the hands of a few, the power of the global market, and the harsh character of life at its margins. Many numbers indicate that the gap between rich and poor is growing larger—even within the United States and even during the tremendous economic boom of the 1990s. Worldwide over thirty thousand children are dying every day from preventable causes.

Facile endorsements of postmodernity are shattered precisely when we get in touch with the reality of the other person, the marginalized.[34] Here a new challenge emerges—revealing the asymmetries of a pluralistic society in which the powerful are still powerful and the powerless are still powerless. Well-meaning references to difference, to otherness, and to relations to the other person reach their deepest moments of crisis when having to deal with the question of who and what put (and is holding) the other in its place.

The reality of the other, of people at the margins, is not a mere accident—a colorful addition to a "tossed salad" (a popular image among pluralists) and something that just happens to be there—but one of the creations of modernity in collaboration with the free market that has not disappeared in postmodernity. Difference and otherness are, therefore, not primarily philosophical principles but structures deeply ingrained in our societies. Postmodern theory can no longer afford to neglect this part of modern history.

In North American theology, feminist thinkers have been among the first to perceive the problem. Over a decade ago Sharon Welch, for instance, called attention to the fact that the marginalized are not recognized as part of the postmodern voice.[35] Welch points out that even the work of Jean-Francois Lyotard, one of the postmodern founders, ends up coopting the world's different peoples and cultures "as the components of an ephemeral personal style" due to his failure to listen to the margins.[36] Yet Lyotard's critique of the grand narratives of modernity—the stories that the powerful tell about themselves—does not have to end up in the pluralism of micronarratives where everyone can pick and choose at whim. Here the postcolonial perspective is helpful: the critique of the grand narratives of the colonialists is based on their oppressive and exclusive character rather than on some general claims that grand narratives are always a bad idea. The goal is, therefore, not to celebrate micronarratives in general and to increase the number of narratives, but to pay attention precisely to those micronarratives that have been excluded and repressed.[37]

In order to develop a deeper understanding of the interaction of postmodernity and the margins, the notion of the symptom as developed by Jacques Lacan may be helpful. Lacan shows that that symptoms of suffering and conflict are not merely accidental and essentially insignificant deviations from an otherwise normal state, deviations that can, therefore, be cured away. This is usually the way the status quo, whether modern or postmodern, tends to interpret symptoms. Most of our welfare policies, for instance, whether the social programs of modern liberalism or the various proposals of postmodernity (from compassionate conservatism to more progressive strategies of urban renewal), are based on the idea that people on the margins need to be integrated into an otherwise well-functioning system. In these perspectives the lives of people on the margins are indeed seen as accidental and essentially insignificant deviations from an otherwise normal state (people who are down on their luck, people who for some reason lack the resources that "normal" people have). People on the margins, therefore, are classified as objects of welfare or charity; they are seen as a "job to be done"; in short, they are in need of being reintegrated into the system.

Lacan suggests a radically different point of view. He argues that symptoms are in fact the products of the prevailing system itself. Symptoms are the result of repressions produced by the system. They are the things that are pushed below the surface and that guarantee the smooth functioning of the system. Symptoms, created in repressions, are thus indicators of the true nature of the system. In simply trying to cure away the symptom without looking deeper, the truth of the system is constantly covered up.[38] The symptom is, thus, not just the product of a curious accident that can be cured away. For Lacan, it is in listening to the symptom in a process of analysis that one finds the key to an understanding of the mechanism of the powers of the dominant system of which one is a part.[39] Moreover the symptom, thus understood, is also at the source of new energy for resisting the powers that be. Here, Lacan reminds us, is where desire is shaped and reshaped. One might also argue that the pressures built up in the symptom create counterpressures.[40]

This adds a crucial new element to the postmodern concern for difference. Difference is no longer just the free and accidental flow of difference where nobody gets hurt (one of the favorite notions of postmodern theorists is the linguistic concept of "metonymy," the free flow of difference on the level of the signifier). Fresh encounters with the margins remind us that difference now needs to be seen in light of mechanisms of repression, where the identity of one person or group is established on the back of others (Lacan describes these mechanisms with the linguistic concept of "metaphor," calling attention to those signifiers which have been repressed from the happy flow of difference at the surface level).[41] In this way, the postmodern turn to the other can no longer bypass the question "who put the other in its place?" The concern for the margins reminds us that people usually do not marginalize themselves and, ultimately, points to the truth about the system itself. In this sense, post-modern theology, even where it is interested in liberation theology, popular culture, difference, and the other, makes sense only where it begins to take a deeper look below the surface.

It is clearer now why the encounter with the margins is more crucial in postmodernity than ever before, especially in light of the postmodern concerns for difference and otherness. Current notions of otherness and difference— celebrating an end to the rigid identities of modernity and the free flow of difference—end up being smoke screens if they do not take into account those deeper ruptures of global society and the harsh character of its margins. The reality of the other, the marginalized, is not a given or a mere accident. The realities of life on the margins are in many ways the creation of modern market economy, industrialization, colonization, and efforts at civilization—processes which have changed form but have not necessarily ended in postmodern times. In this context, references to the other are not only politically and socially but also theologically useless if they do not at the same time raise the question who and what put (and is holding) this other in its place of repression even in the postmodern world.

If theology is serious about the turn to the other, it needs to pay more attention to people pushed to the margins in all walks of life, in order to learn what is holding them in place. Theologies that have often been designated "special-interest theologies," such as feminist theology, African American the-ology, Hispanic theology, *mujerista* theology, and womanist theology, now be-come common-interest theologies, since they hold an important key to understanding the truth about all of us.[42]

Conclusion

From my perspective as a Euro-American male theologian it seems that even in postmodernity few things are more important than developing respect for the other person, especially for those whom we have pushed and continue to push to the margins and the underside of society. This includes a variety of people, including children, women, ethnic minorities, low-income workers and those who cannot be employed due to cutbacks and "lean production," people in other parts of the world whose resources we use, and those who challenge our lifestyles through different sexual, political, and other orientations. We need to realize that in isolation we cannot be fully human—we never could, as the dehumanizing tendencies in both modernity and postmodernity have shown in their own ways. In isolation, we will never find out the truth about ourselves, who we really are, nor will we have the energy to change anything of substance. Ultimately, in isolation we cannot survive. In this situation, the postmodern concerns for the deconstruction of the modern self's autonomy, for difference and otherness, for popular culture, and for the margins point in the right direction and might yet help to create an opening for listening more closely to what we have repressed and to become acquainted with the plight of the other.

Top-down approaches will no longer work. Handouts or charity—understood as taking care of the needy—may make things worse if they only make people on the top feel better about themselves. Neither will things change through broad-based welfare programs that assume that all we need to do is integrate more people into the system. In either case, everything stays as it is. Top-down approaches in theology will no longer work, either. Telling people at the margins what and how to think about God always ends in creating them in our mirror image. We can no longer afford to think about God from the narrowness of one perspective alone—and the perspectives from the top seem to be the most narrow. At the same time, however, romanticizing people at the margins will no longer work either. In romanticizing others we simply reaffirm our own control—and the theological horizon will remain as narrow as before.[43] In all of these cases we miss what liberation theologians have called the "power of the poor."

One of the things that might be learned from the initial responses to the terrorist attacks on the World Trade Center in New York City and the Pentagon on September 11, 2001, is that situations of high pressure and innocent suffering bring people together. In this tragedy, pressure and suffering became matters of common interest that cut to the core of our identity and split open the illusionary identities of control and security that we had constructed for ourselves. In this situation, not only a new sense of solidarity emerged but new questions were raised—if only for a short time. Before it could be suppressed, the incredulous question "why is this happening to us?" led to some deeper suspicions, perhaps best captured in the term *blowback*—a new word created by none other than the CIA in reference to the unintended consequences of the pressure tactics of U.S. foreign policy.[44] Unfortunately, critical sentiments were quickly filtered out. Structures for such filtering processes created prior to these events kicked in: not long before September 11, for instance, the FBI had provided U.S. teachers with lists that would help them identify students that were likely to commit acts of lethal violence. One characteristic that required screening, according to these lists, is students' "resentment over real or perceived injustices."[45]

How can this attitude be changed? We need to recognize and develop more respect for the contributions of those in situations of pressure. This can happen, of course, only by daring to look outside of the ivory towers and gated communities, and it will include—this is the hardest part—the risk of being challenged by others. There is another aspect of learning to respect others that I want to mention in closing. This aspect undergirds my argument as a whole and grounds its theological impulse. I have seen many signs that in learning to respect other people, particularly those whom we often overlook, we can also learn again how to respect God, whom we likewise often overlook. Learning to respect people at the margins teaches us an important lesson about theology—and here the circle closes: In our time, no talk about respect for God— the genuine subject of theology—will make any difference whatsoever if it is not closely related to learning new respect for other people.[46] Where we fail to recognize the actual difference of others, the difference of the divine Other (the divine resistance to the way things are) cannot be fully appreciated either. If we miss the transforming power of others, we also miss the transforming power of God as Other.

NOTES

1. For the background of this argument see Joerg Rieger, *God and the Excluded: Visions and Blindspots in Contemporary Theology* (Minneapolis: Fortress, 2001), chap. 1.

2. In postmodern thought, there is a basic appreciation of otherness and difference. Meaning is produced no longer by establishing identity but by dealing with difference and different perspectives.

3. Pope John Paul II, Encyclical Letter "Sollicitudo rei socialis" (On social concern; December 30, 1987), 42, talks about "the option or love of preference for the poor" as "an option, or a special form of primacy in the exercise of Christian charity, to which the whole tradition of the Church bears witness." The pope encourages the "embrace [of] the immense multitudes of the hungry, the needy, the homeless, those without medical care and, above all, those without hope of a better future" (76–77), concluding that our daily lives and our decisions in the political and economic fields must be marked by these realities.

4. This is the point that has been most often misunderstood in interpretations of the various liberation theologies. There is a fundamental difference between the biblical notions of justice which allow for God's election and special care within specific relationships and commonsense notions of justice based on distributive concepts according to which everybody ought to be treated exactly the same and which thus often overlook the fact that there are enormous differences between human beings and that some of the gaps continue to grow.

5. This is one of the basic points of my book *Remember the Poor: The Challenge to Theology in the Twenty-First Century* (Harrisburg, Pa.: Trinity Press International, 1998).

6. See, for instance, the work of Michel Foucault, who in his own ways re-

minded us of the various levels of meaning of the fact that knowledge is power; *Power/ Knowledge: Selected Interviews and Other Writings, 1972–1977*, ed. Colin Gordon (New York: Pantheon, 1980).

7. bell hooks, "Postmodern Blackness," *Postmodern Culture* 1.1 (Sept. 1990): 9–11.

8. Gayatri Chakravorty Spivak, *A Critique of Postcolonial Reason: Towards a History of the Vanishing Present* (Cambridge: Harvard University Press, 1999), 6ff., has shown how even the highly philosophical Enlightenment systems of Kant and Hegel need the "native informant."

9. Marcella Althaus-Reid, *Indecent Theology: Theological Perversions in Sex, Gender, and Politics* (New York: Routledge, 2001), 3. She goes on to explain that "probably these women and children sitting in the streets with their merchandise do not remember that they are miraculous survivors of one of the greatest destructions of the Grand Narratives the world has ever seen" (4). The allusion is of course to Jean-François Lyotard's interpretation of postmodernity as the critique of metanarratives. See Jean-François Lyotard, *The Postmodern Condition: A Report on Knowledge*, Theory and History of Literature 10, trans. Geoff Bennington and Brian Massumi, foreword by Fredric Jameson (Minneapolis: University of Minnesota Press, 1984).

10. Nelly Richard, "Cultural Peripheries: Latin America and Postmodernist Decentering," in *The Postmodern Debate in Latin America*, ed. John Beverley, José Oviedo, and Michael Aronna (Durham: Duke University Press, 1995), 221. Richard suspects, however, that this is not going far enough and that even in postmodernity the periphery is not allowed to really speak for itself.

11. The subaltern, according to Ranajit Guha (cofounder of the South Asian Subaltern Studies Group), is "a name for the general attribute of subordination . . . whether this is expressed in terms of class, caste, age, gender and office or in any other way." Quoted in John Beverley, *Subalternity and Representation: Arguments in Cultural Theory* (Durham: Duke University Press, 1999), 26.

12. Latin American Subaltern Studies Group, "Founding Statement," *boundary 2* 20.3 (Fall 1993): 114. The document points out that identity was the theme of the sixties and seventies.

13. Ibid., 121.

14. Beverley, *Subalternity and Representation*, 30.

15. Postmodern feminist pioneers Nancy Fraser and Linda J. Nicholson, *Feminism/Postmodernism* (New York: Routledge, 1990), 391, point out that "postmodern-feminist theory would dispense with the idea of a subject of history. It would replace unitary notions of 'woman' and 'feminine gender identity' with plural and complexly constructed conceptions of social identity, treating gender as one relevant strand among others, attending also to class, race, ethnicity, age and sexual orientation." More recently, efforts to relate issues of gender, colonialism, and religious discourse have carried this argument to the next step. See *Postcolonialism, Feminism, and Religious Discourse*, ed. Laura E. Donaldson and Kwok Pui-lan (New York: Routledge, 2002).

16. Spivak has questioned whether the subaltern can speak for itself. But this issue cannot be resolved in general terms. Spivak's example is widow immolation in colonial India. The widow who is to be burnt together with her deceased husband has

indeed little room to express herself. See the discussion in Ania Loomba, *Colonialism/Postcolonialism* (New York: Routledge, 1998), 233ff. But there are other places where the subaltern does speak in various ways (in my book *Remember the Poor*, I argue that these forms of speaking are often produced in the very places of repression). The notion of the subaltern reminds us that even within the ranks of the colonized there are different groups. Loomba puts it like this: "In fact if we really believe that human subjects are constituted by several different discourses then we are obliged to consider these articulations. Thus, in order to listen for subaltern voices we need to uncover the multiplicity of narratives that were hidden by the grand narratives, but we still need to think about how the former are woven together" (241).

17. Regarding the reconstruction of the identity of the oppressed, Sharon Welch makes a helpful suggestion when, in response to Foucault's critique of authorship, she comments that "what is dead is not the author per se but the author who can assume the mantle of universality." Sharon Welch, *A Feminist Ethic of Risk* (Minneapolis: Fortress, 1990), 150.

18. Angela Davis, "Reflections on Race, Class, and Gender in the USA," *The Angela Davis Reader*, ed. Joy James (Oxford: Blackwell, 1998), 313.

19. Ibid., 320. She reminds us to avoid the "pitfalls of essentialism."

20. Ibid., 324. The essays in a recent book on the question of class identity and postmodernity (*Re/presenting Class: Essays in Postmodern Marxism*, ed. J. K. Gibson-Graham, Stephen Resnick, and Richard Wolff [Durham: Duke University Press, 2001]) argue along similar lines: fluid and uncentered understandings of class identity counter an imagined capitalist totality and provide new and creative means of resistance. See, e.g., the introduction, 16–21.

21. Robert Allen Warrior, "A Native American Perspective: Canaanites, Cowboys, and Indians," in *Voices from the Margin: Interpreting the Bible in the "Third World,"* ed. R. S. Sugirtharajah (Maryknoll, N.Y.: Orbis, 1991), 294.

22. See, for instance, the differences between Joshua and Judges.

23. At present, the problematic character of the postmodern concern for otherness and difference is perhaps realized most clearly by those who are closest to actual oppression and marginalization. From a Latin American perspective, Neil Larsen talks about the naïveté of postmodernism, tied to the belief that once difference is allowed to take over, the imperialistic power of modern universalisms is overcome. Neil Larsen, "Postmodernism and Imperialism: Theory and Politics in Latin America," in *The Postmodern Debate in Latin America*, ed. John Beverley, José Oviedo, and Michael Aronna (Durham: Duke University Press, 1995), 110–34. Larsen's article has played an important role in the Latin American debate of postmodernism. For other critiques of the postmodern from the periphery cf. the essays in *South Atlantic Quarterly* 92.3 (Summer 1993) and in *Postmodernism Debate in Latin America*.

24. Michael Hardt and Antonio Negri, *Empire* (Cambridge: Harvard University Press, 2000), 138, point out the parallels between the postmodern and the global market economy: "When we begin to consider the ideologies of corporate capital and the world market, it certainly appears that the postmodernist and postcolonialist theorists who advocate a politics of difference, fluidity, and hybridity have been outflanked by the strategies of power." The postmodern strategy of introducing difference and otherness is effective primarily where power is based on identity and binaries. But

where the power of the status quo itself appropriates otherness and difference, new ways of resistance need to be explored.

25. Enrique Dussel, *Von der Erfindung Amerikas zur Entdeckung des Anderen: Ein Projekt der Transmoderne*, Theologie Interkulturell 6 (Düsseldorf: Patmos, 1993), 10.

26. Cf. also Enrique Dussel, *The Underside of Modernity: Apel Ricoeur, Rorty, Taylor, and the Philosophy of Liberation*, ed. and trans. Eduardo Mendieta (Atlantic Highlands, N.J.: Humanities Press, 1996).

27. Bill Ashcroft, Gareth Griffiths, and Helen Tiffin, eds., *The Postcolonial Studies Reader* (New York: Routledge, 1995), 117, point out that the critique of the "the deconstruction of the centralised, logocentric master narratives of European culture, is very similar to the post-colonial project of dismantling the Centre/Margin binarism of imperial discourse." Some postcolonial texts, of course, precede the postmodern icons Derrida and Foucault: "The rejection of the Cartesian individual, the instability of signification, the location of the subject in language or discourse, the dynamic operation of power: all these familiar poststructuralist concepts emerge in post-colonial thought in different guises which nevertheless confirm the political agency of the colonised subject."

28. Loomba, *Colonialism/Postcolonialism*, xiii.

29. Ibid., 3.

30. "Suburbia, the New Melting Pot," *Dallas Morning News*, December 12, 2001, pp. 1A, 12A. In a well-to-do suburb of Dallas, Plano, shoppers for homes "do not seem interested in finding neighborhoods with a particular racial makeup. . . . They just look at whatever they can afford."

31. Gustavo Gutiérrez, "Liberation Theology and the Future of the Poor," in *Liberating the Future: God, Mammon, and Theology*, ed. Joerg Rieger (Minneapolis: Fortress, 1998).

32. In a postmodern world of difference, the turn to localized communal practices and stories seem to provide a safe haven. Tilley thus ends by inviting theology to "gather together and tell stories of God to calm our terror and hold our hope on high." Terrence Tilley, *Postmodern Theologies: The Challenge of Religious Diversity* (Maryknoll, N.Y.: Orbis, 1995), 150.

33. Taylor is concerned about those "marginal people" who are "suspended between the loss of old certainties and the discovery of new beliefs." Mark C. Taylor, *Erring: A Postmodern A/theology* (Chicago: University of Chicago Press, 1984), 5.

34. Latin American thinkers continue to remind us of this. See Gutiérrez, "Liberation Theology and the Future of the Poor," and the work of Nelly Richard and George Yúdice.

35. Welch, *Feminist Ethic of Risk*, 145ff. Teresa L. Ebert, "The 'Difference' of Postmodern Feminism," *College English* 53.8 (December 1991): 899, has pointed out that "difference in postmodern thought displaces social contradictions." A feminist perspective, on the other hand, knows that differences are not free floating but are related to social contradictions. For this reason, the other inscribed within the system needs to be taken more seriously.

36. Welch, *Feminist Ethic of Risk*, 148.

37. Loomba, *Colonialism/Postcolonialism*, 249: "We need to move away from global narratives not because they necessarily always swallow up complexity, but be-

cause they historically have done so, and once we have focused on these submerged stories and perspectives, the entire structure appears transformed."

38. Cf. Jacques Lacan, "Seminar 22 R.S.I." (1974–75) in *Ornicar?* 4 (1975): 106. For an interpretation and further reference, cf. Slavoj Zizek, *The Sublime Object of Ideology* (New York: Verso, 1989), 23ff.

39. Zizek, *Sublime Object*, 128, interprets this process in light of the situation of Jewish people in Nazi Germany.

40. See Rieger, *God and the Excluded*, chap. 5.

41. See Jacques Lacan, "The Agency of the Letter in the Unconscious or Reason since Freud," in *écrits: A Selection*, trans. Alan Sheridan (New York: Norton, 1977), 164. Metonymy stands for the notion of structural difference. Lacan defines it as the word-to-word connection. Metaphor is the substitution of one word by another.

42. Cf. Joerg Rieger, "Developing a Common Interest Theology from the Underside," in *Liberating the Future: God, Mammon, and Theology*, ed. Joerg Rieger (Minneapolis: Fortress, 1998).

43. The point of my book *Remember the Poor* is to find new ways beyond this dichotomy.

44. See Chalmers Johnson, *Blowback: The Costs and Consequences of American Empire* (New York: Holt, 2000).

45. Henry A. Giroux, "Mis/Education and Zero Tolerance: Disposable Youth and the Politics of Domestic Militarization," *boundary 2* 28.3 (2001): 87 n. 76.

46. See my book *God and the Excluded*.

Index